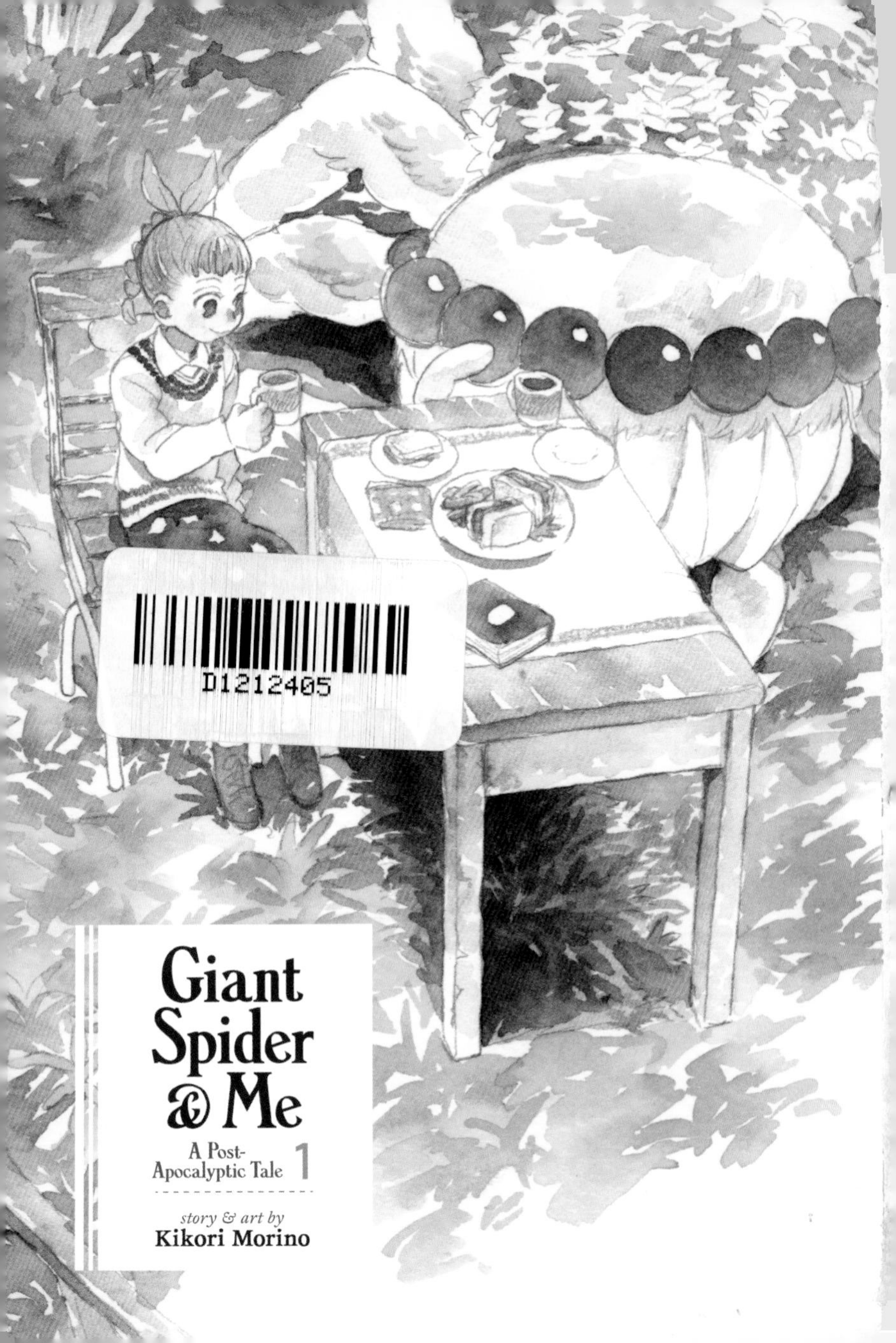

Giant Spider & Me

A Post-Apocalyptic Tale 1

story & art by
Kikori Morino

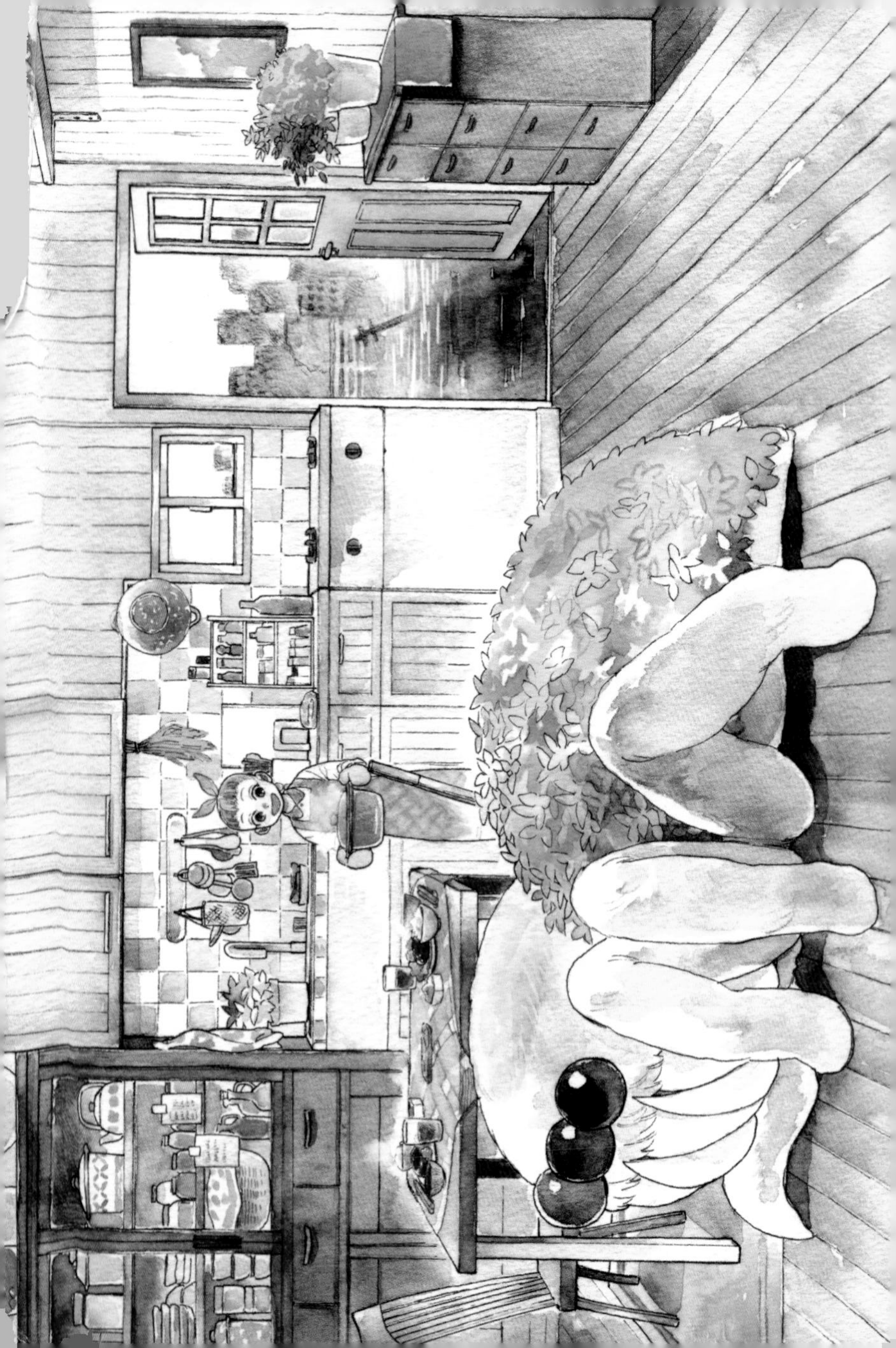

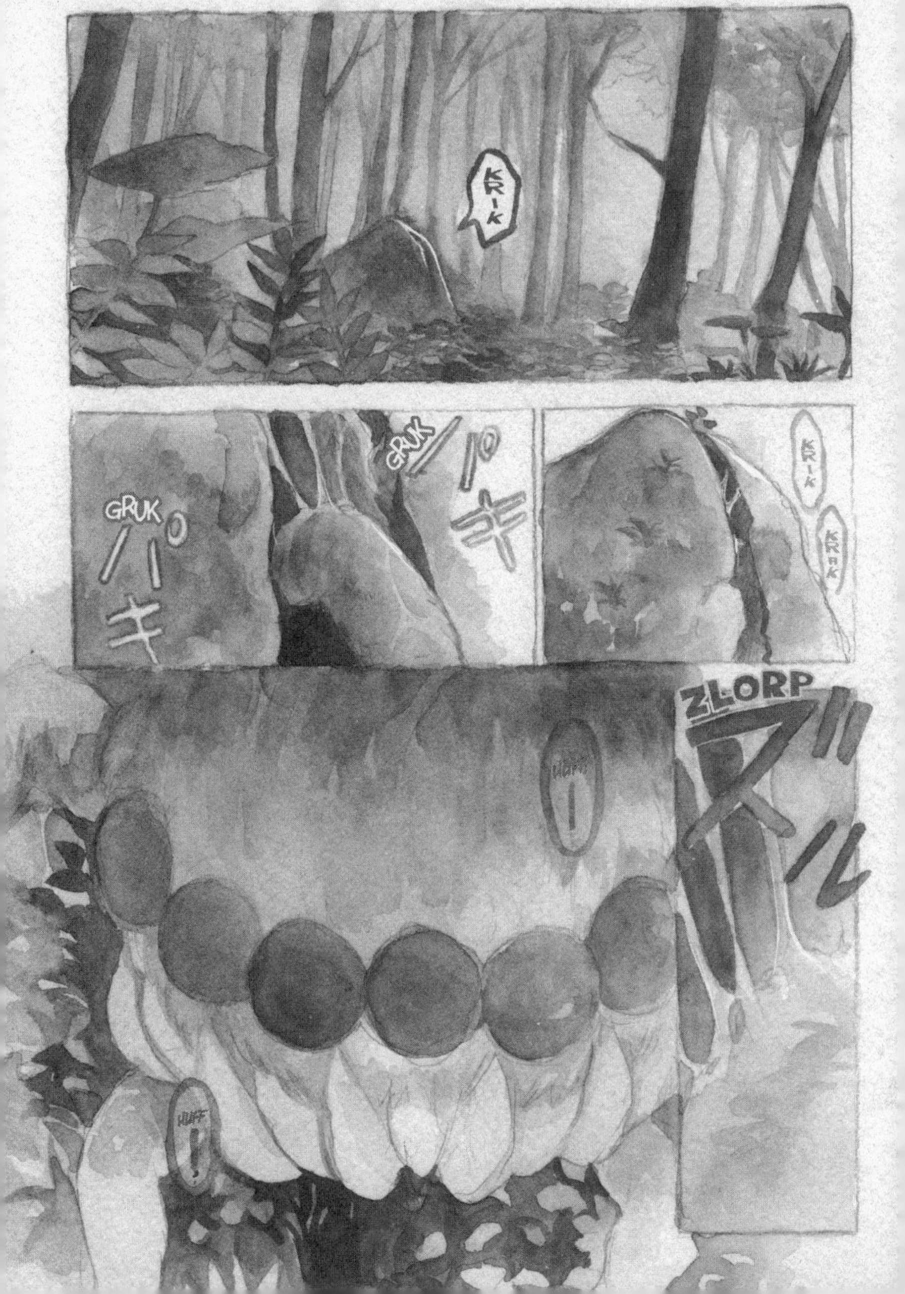
KRIK
KRIK
KRIK
GRUK
パキ
GRUK
パキ
ZLORP
ズル

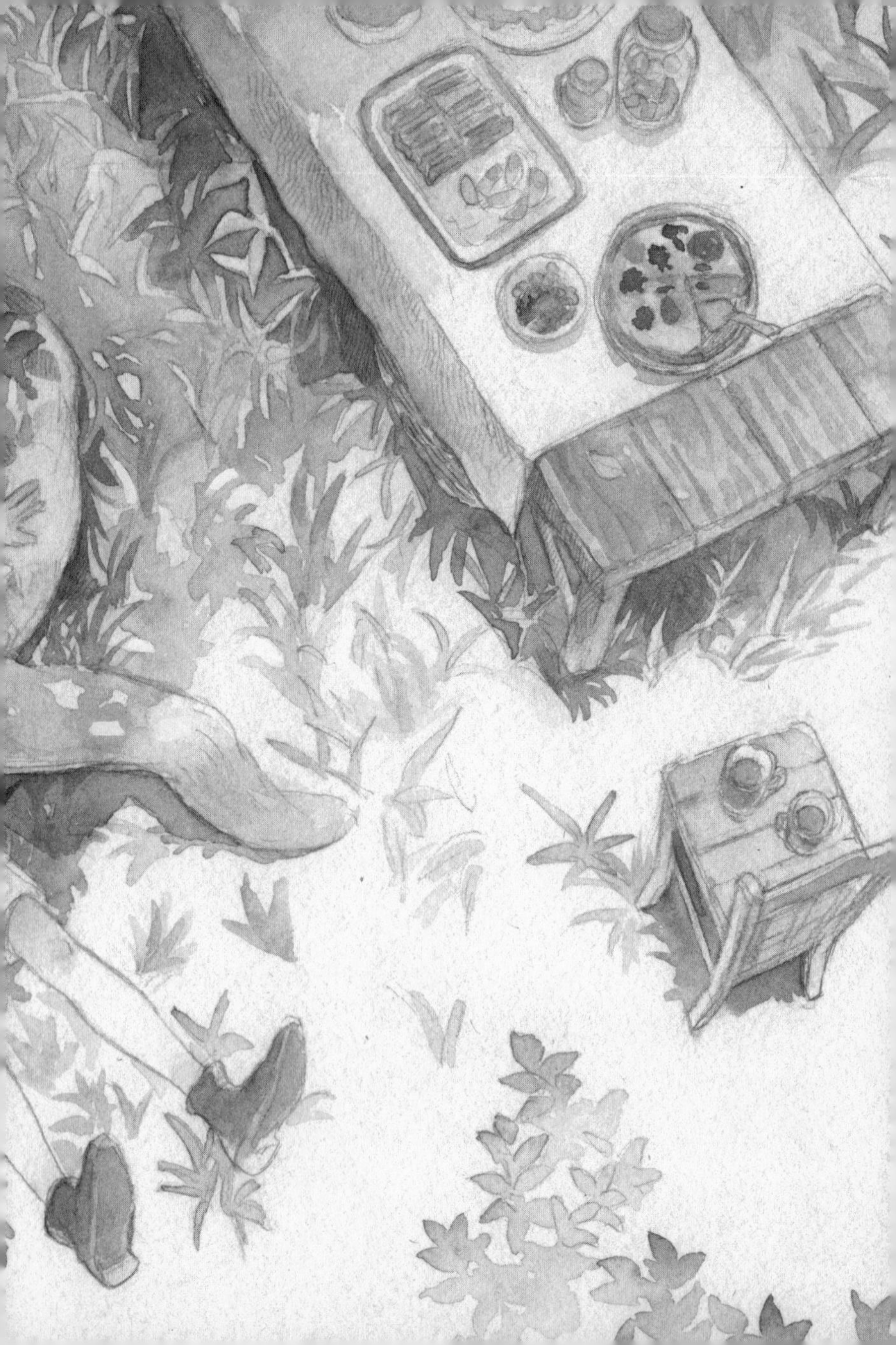

Chapter 1: Unexpected Encounters & Chewy Pumpkin Dumplings

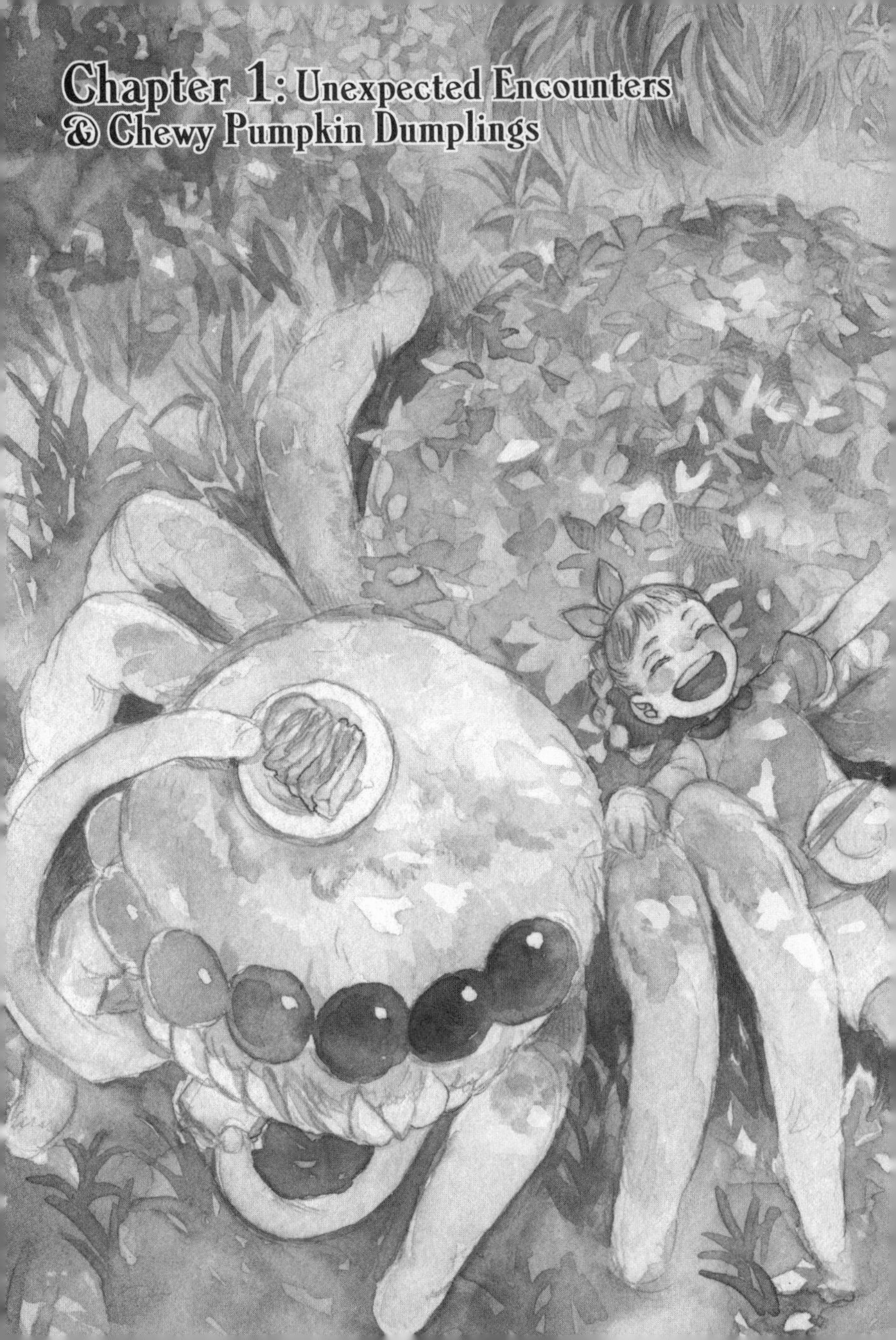

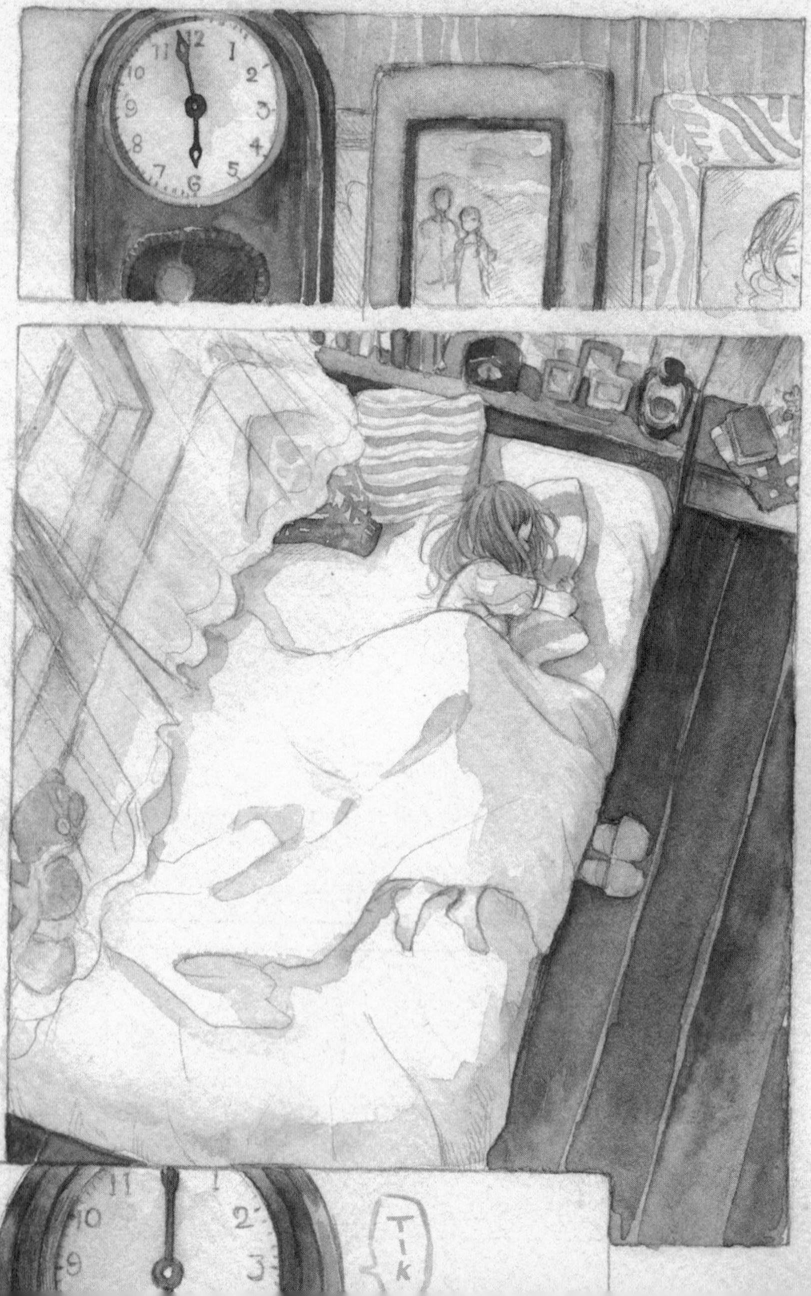
TIK

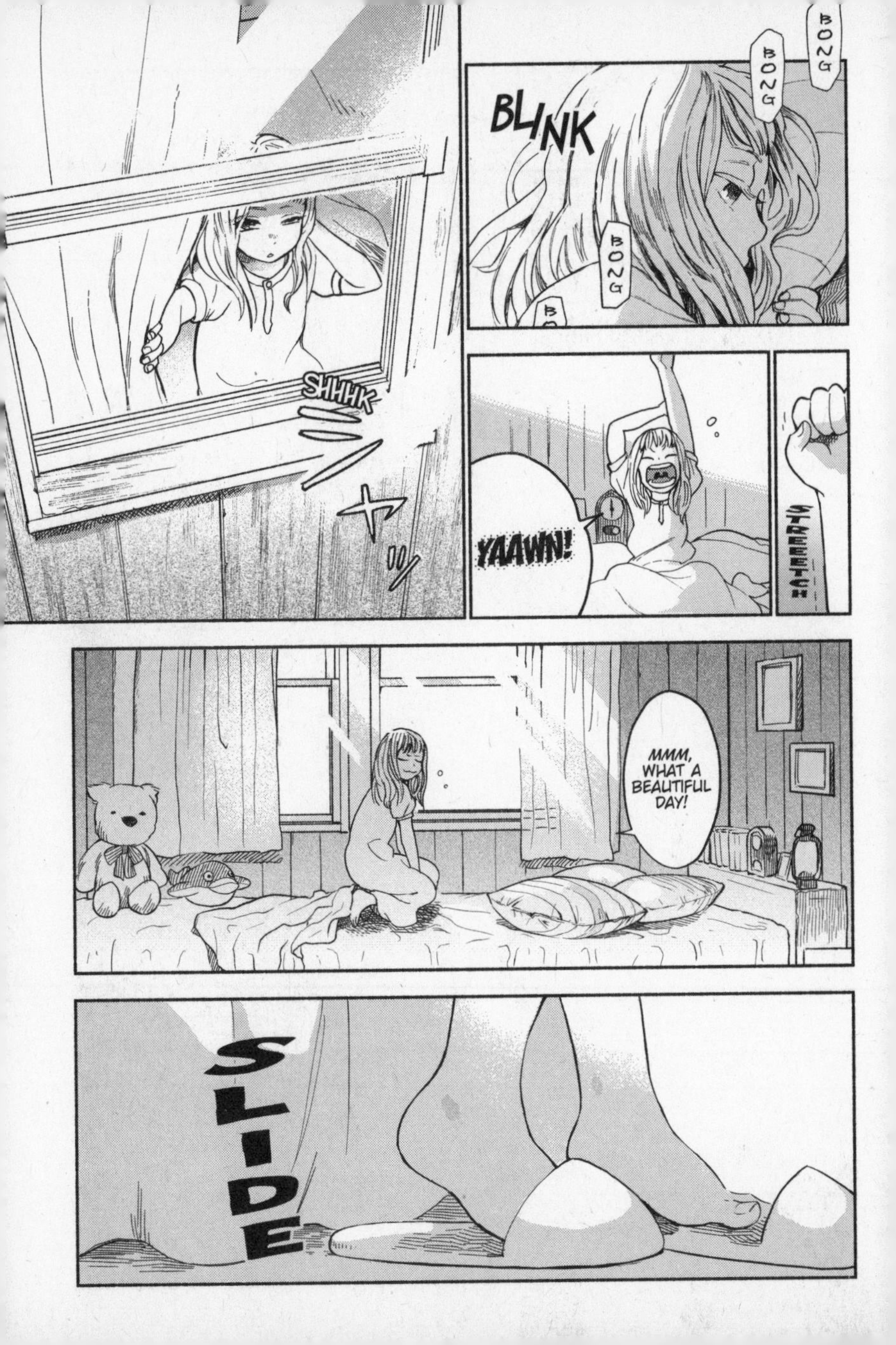
BONG
BONG
BLINK
BONG
STREEETCH
YAAWN!
SHHHK
MMM, WHAT A BEAUTIFUL DAY!
SLIDE

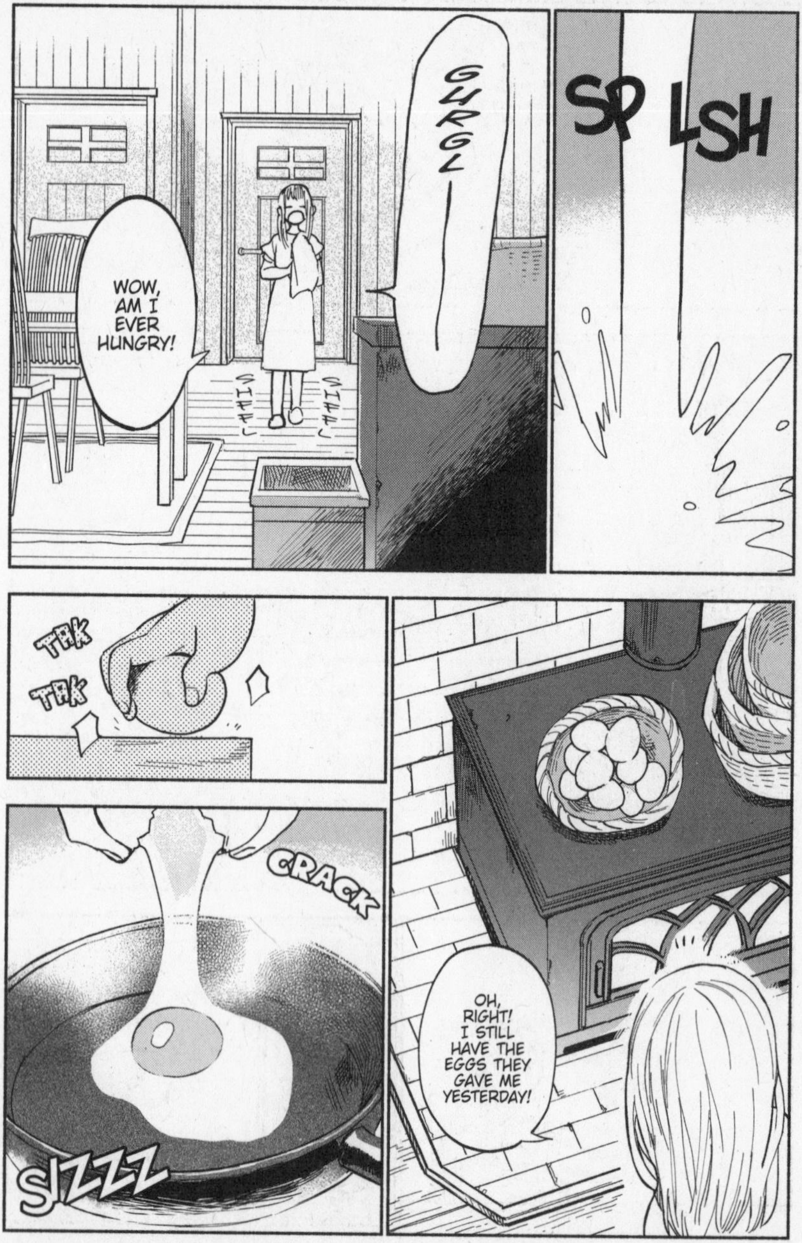
SPLSH
GURGL
WOW, AM I EVER HUNGRY!
SHFFL
SHFFL
OH, RIGHT! I STILL HAVE THE EGGS THEY GAVE ME YESTERDAY!
TAK
TAK
CRACK
SIZZZ

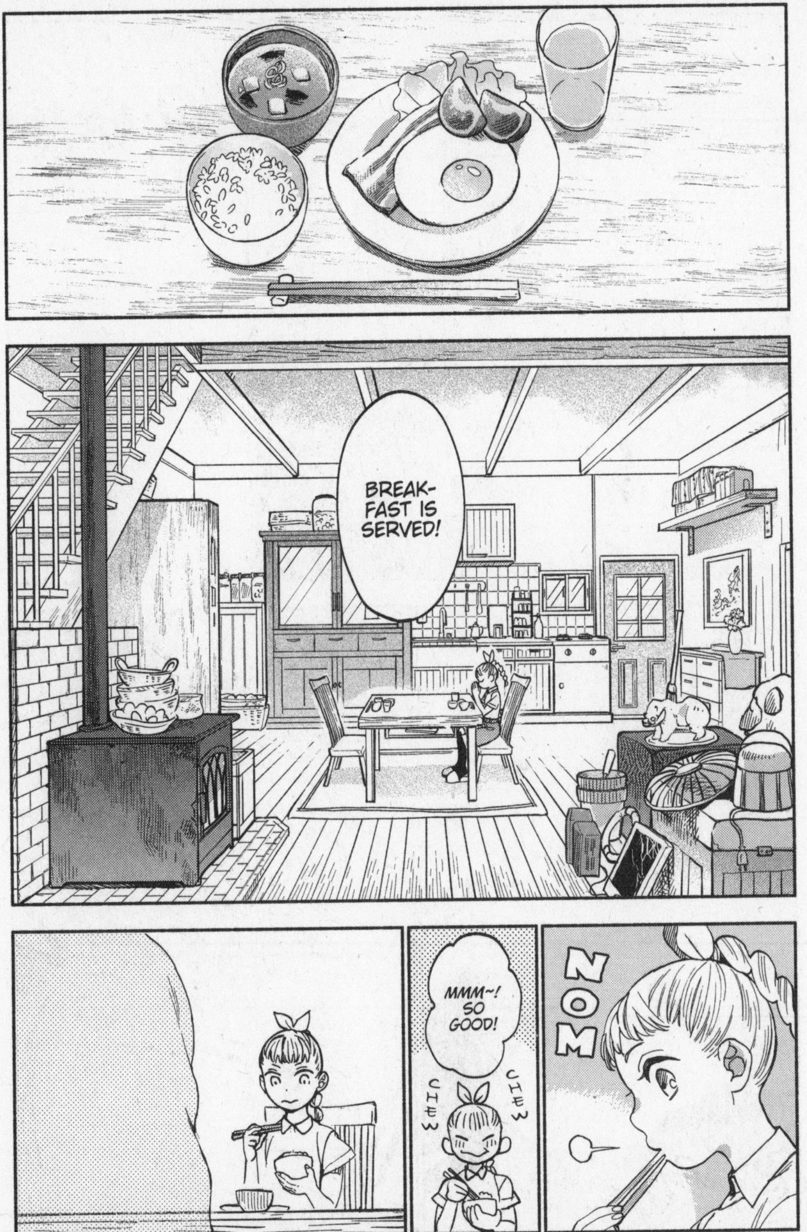
BREAK-FAST IS SERVED!
NOM
MMM~! SO GOOD!
CHEW
CHEW

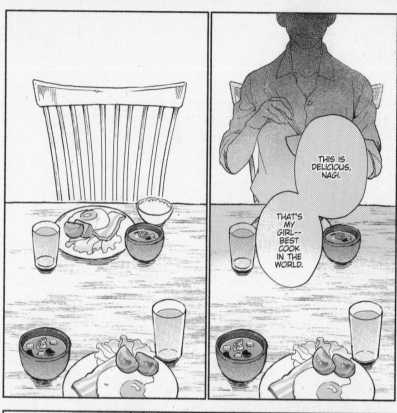

THIS IS DELICIOUS, NAGI.

THAT'S MY GIRL-- BEST COOK IN THE WORLD.

CHEW...

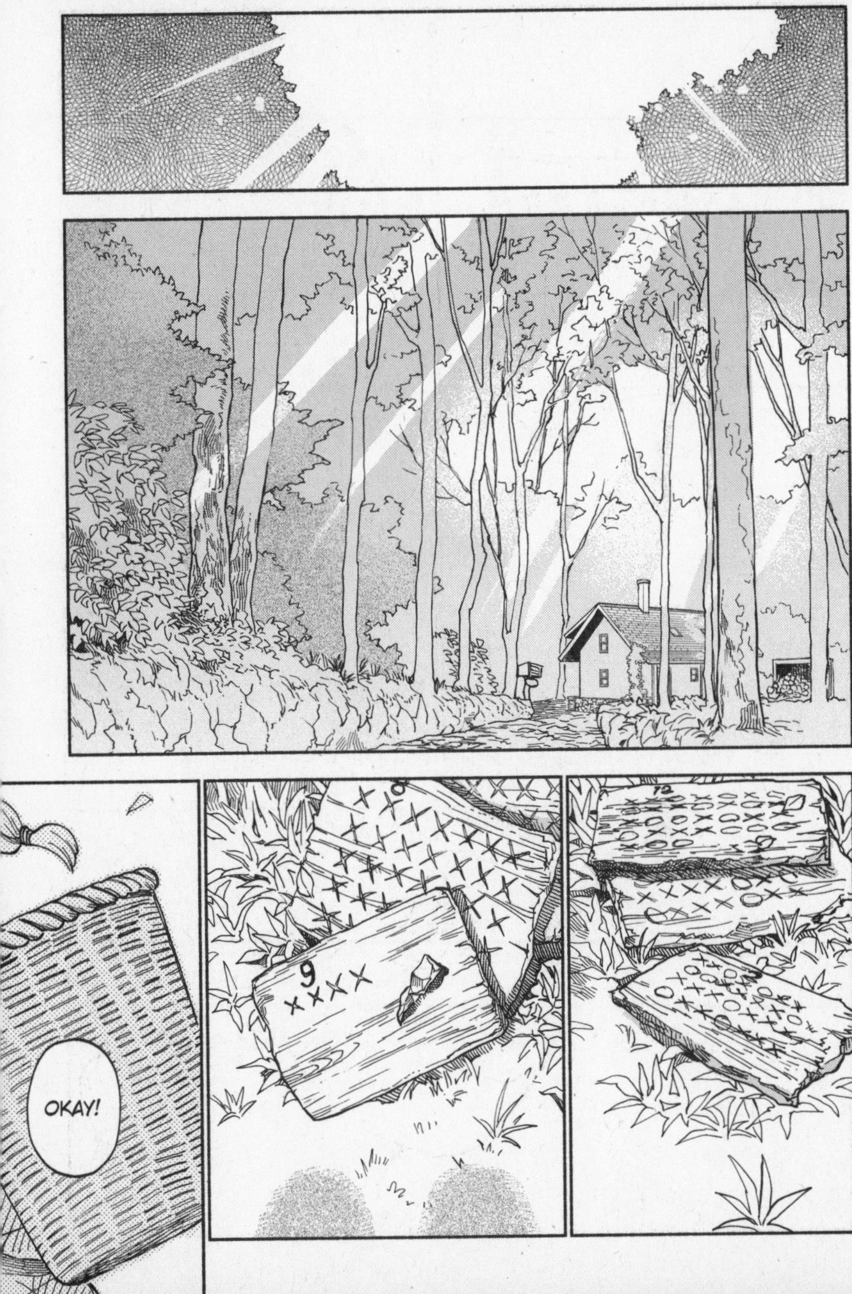
OKAY!

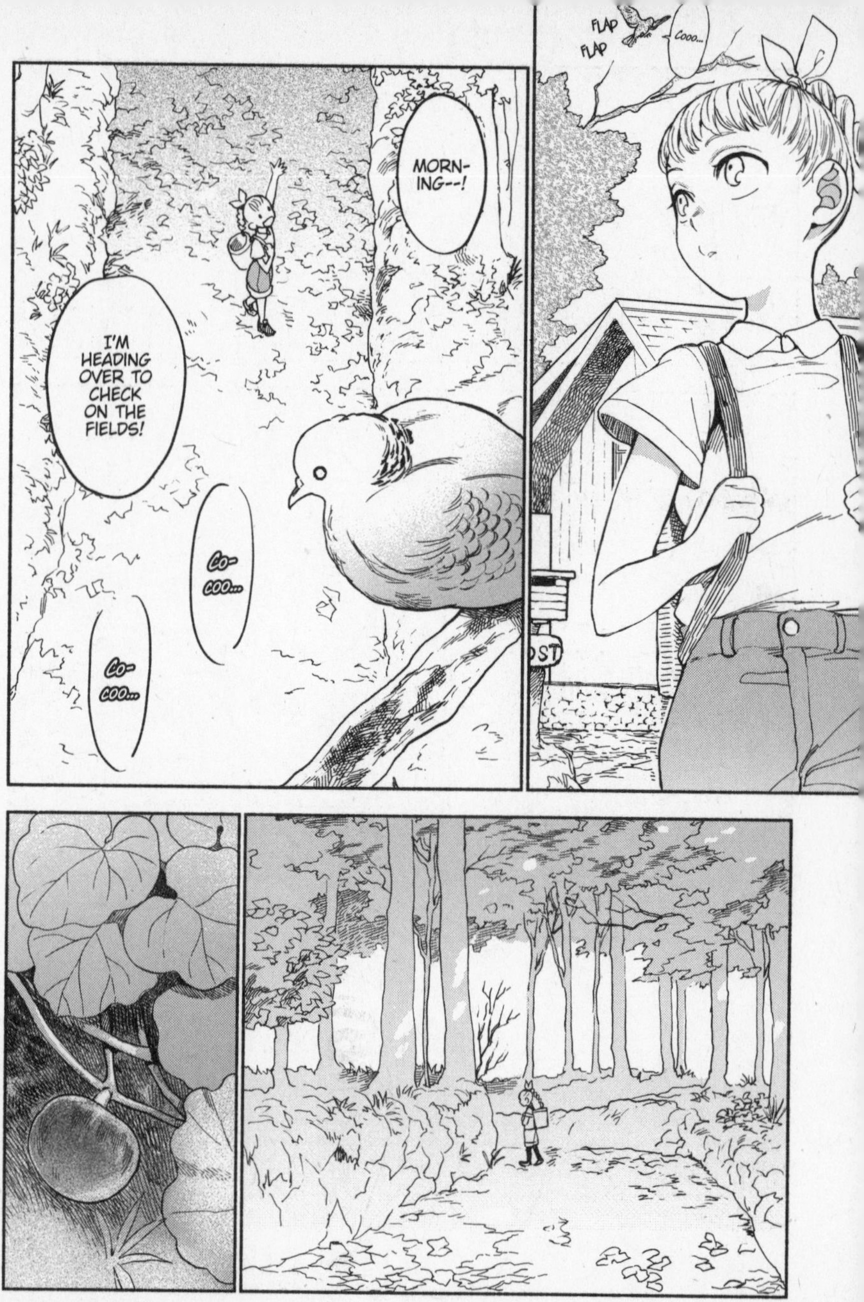
FLAP
FLAP
Cooo...
MORNING--!
I'M HEADING OVER TO CHECK ON THE FIELDS!
Co-coo...
Co-coo...

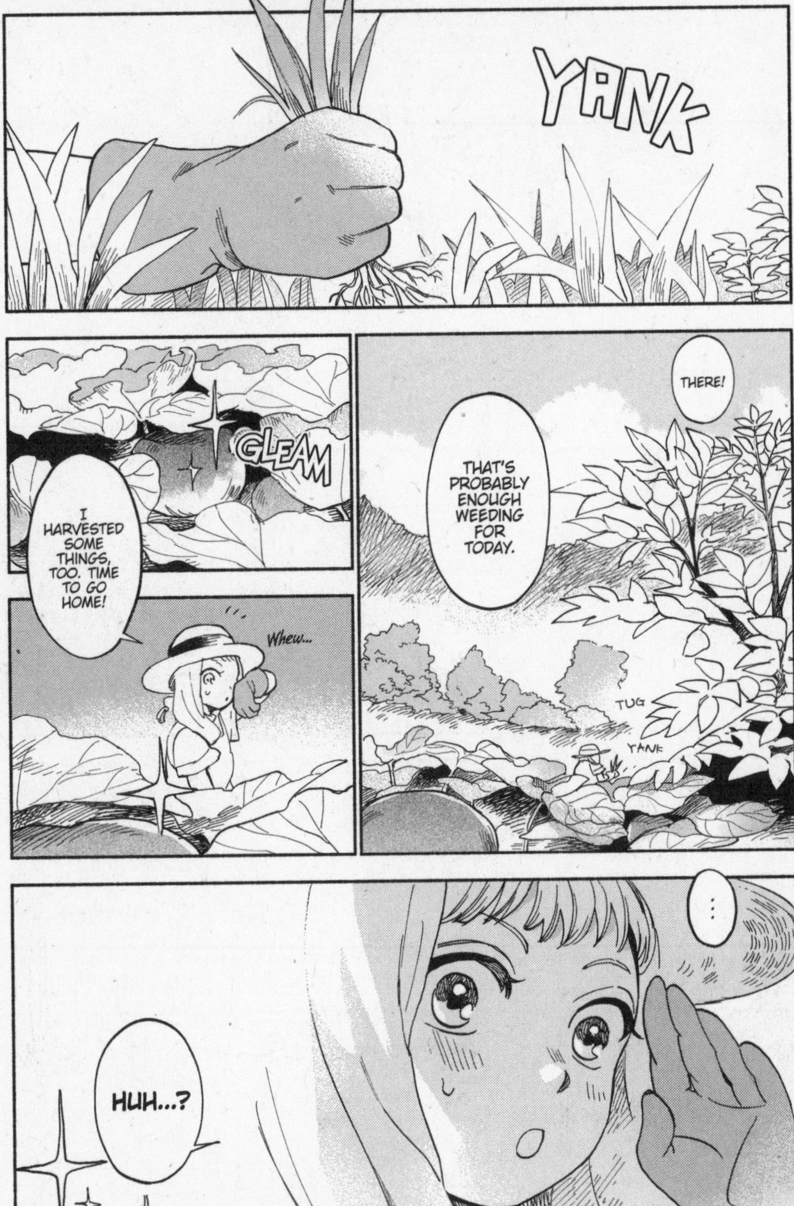
YANK
THERE!
THAT'S PROBABLY ENOUGH WEEDING FOR TODAY.
TUG
YANK
GLEAM
I HARVESTED SOME THINGS, TOO. TIME TO GO HOME!
Whew...
...
HUH...?

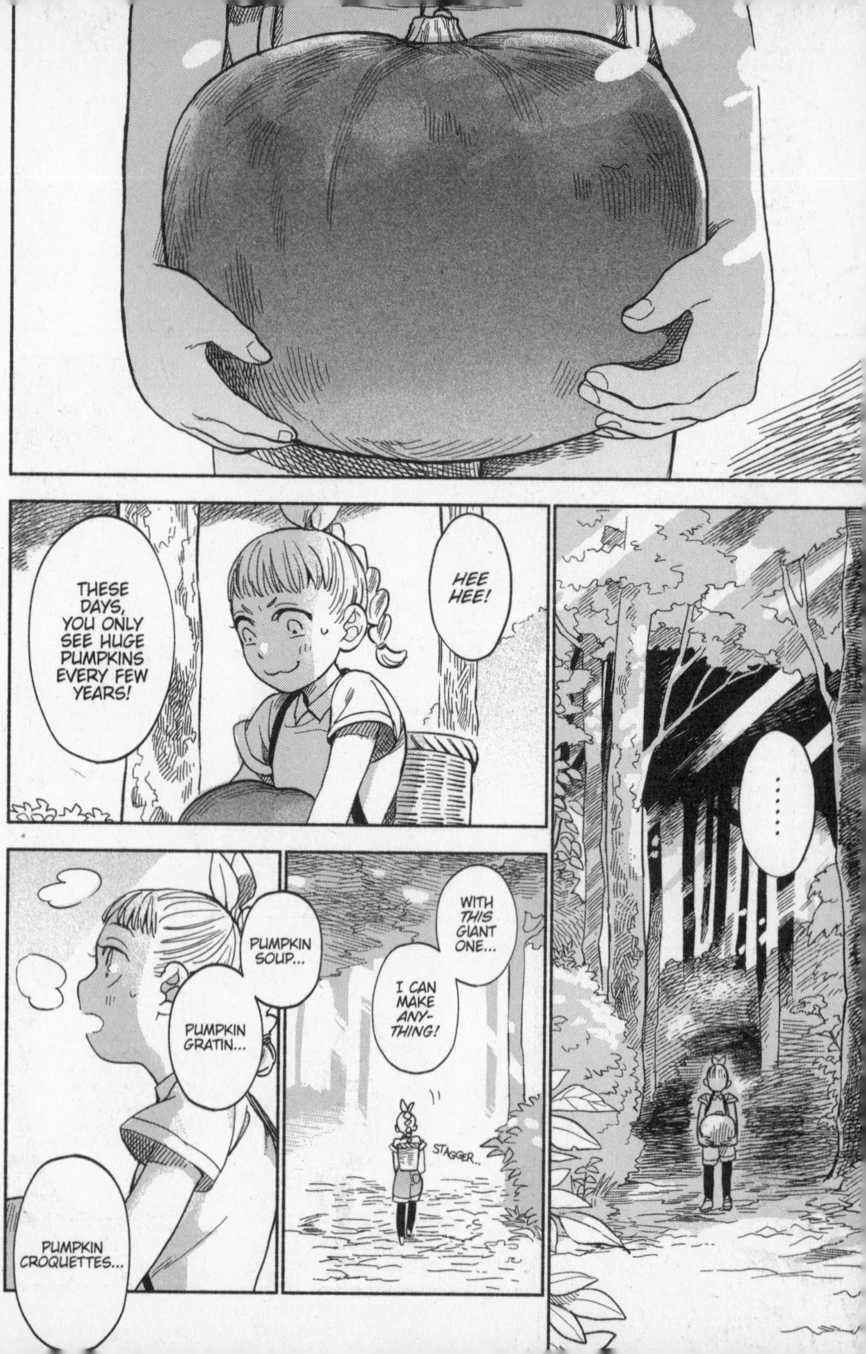
HEE HEE!
THESE DAYS, YOU ONLY SEE HUGE PUMPKINS EVERY FEW YEARS!
WITH THIS GIANT ONE...
I CAN MAKE ANY-THING!
STAGGER...
PUMPKIN SOUP...
PUMPKIN GRATIN...
PUMPKIN CROQUETTES...
......

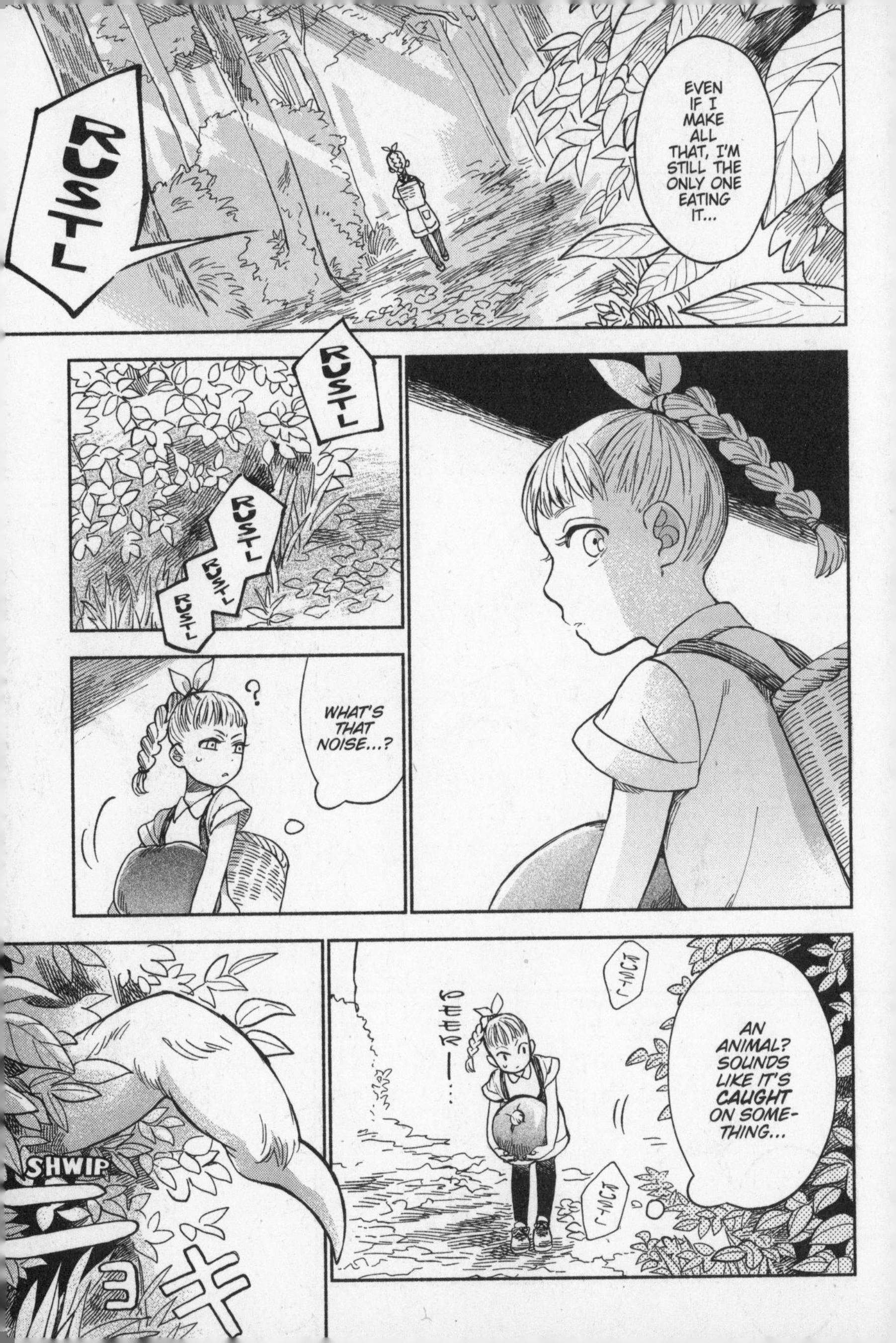
EVEN IF I MAKE ALL THAT, I'M STILL THE ONLY ONE EATING IT...
RUSTL
RUSTL
RUSTL
RUSTL
RUSTL
?
WHAT'S THAT NOISE...?
AN ANIMAL? SOUNDS LIKE IT'S CAUGHT ON SOME-THING...
PEER—...
SHWIP

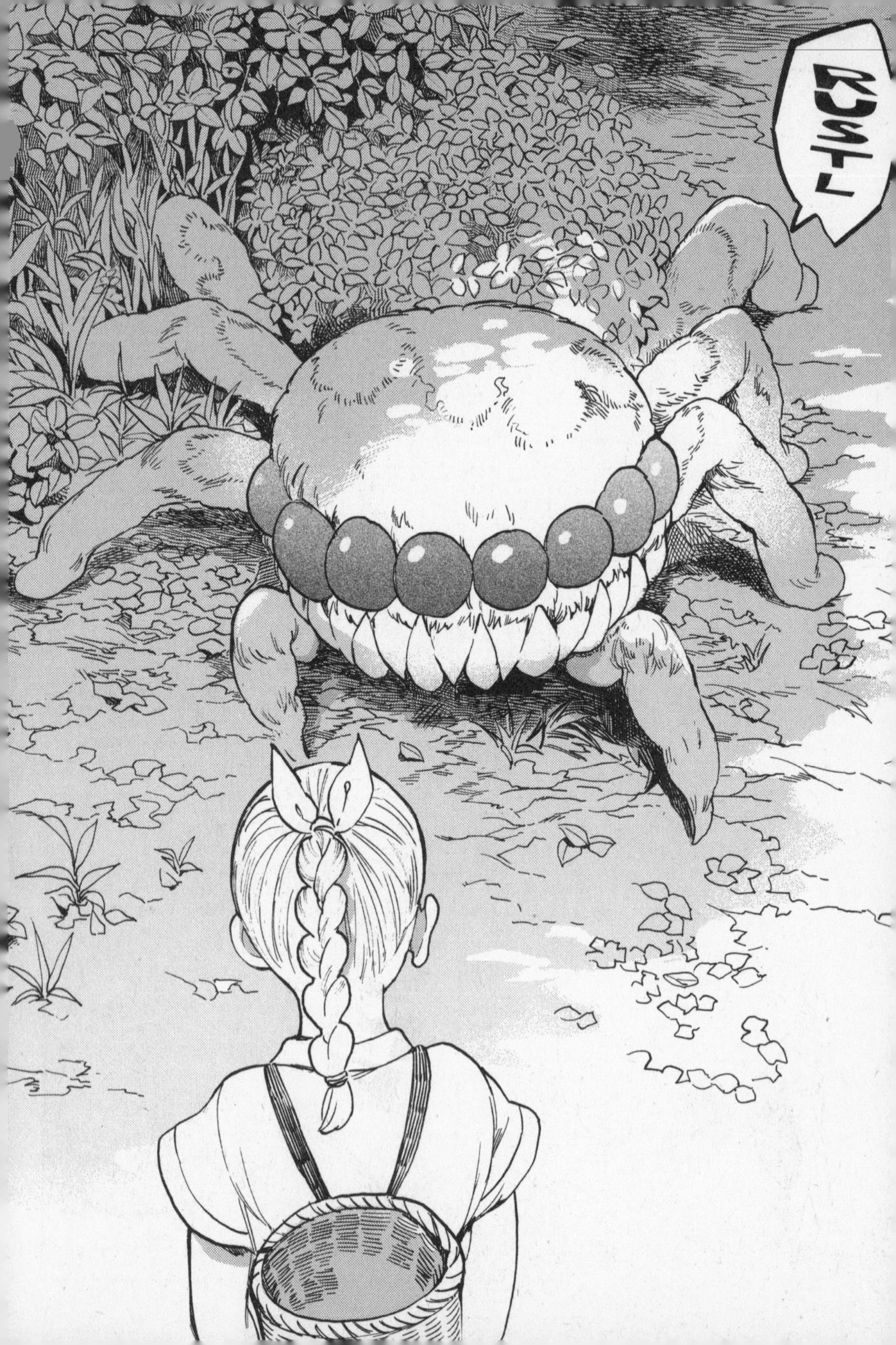
RUSTL

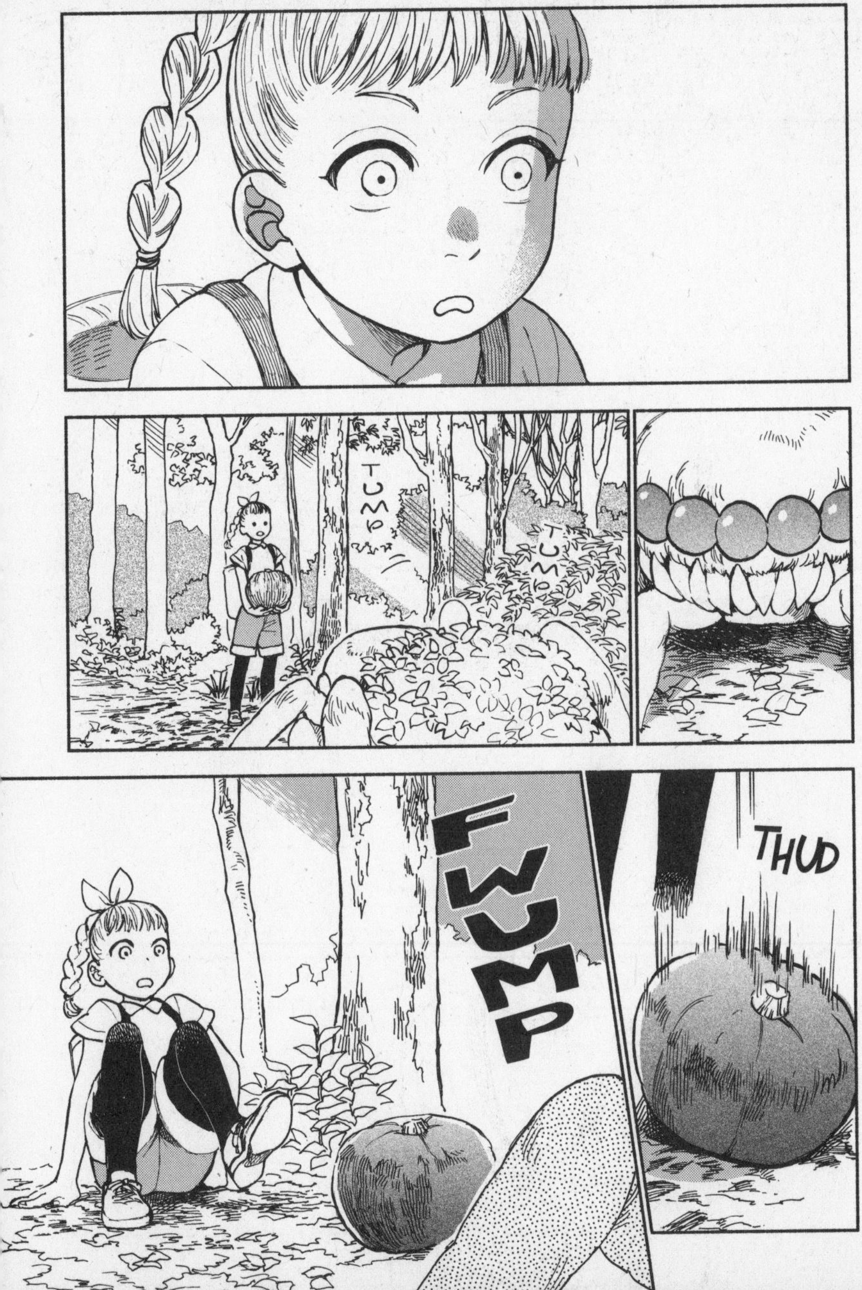
TUMP
TUMP
THUD
FWUMP

WH- WHA...?
A...A GIANT... SPIDER...?!
NYOOOP
EEEK!
ST- STAY AWAY --!
FREEZE

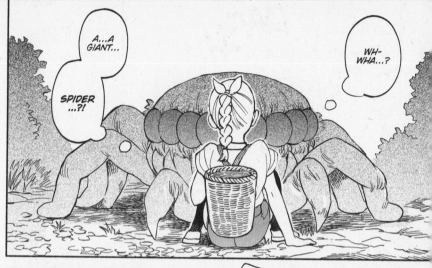

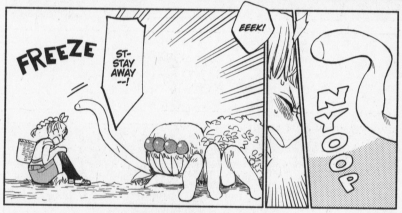

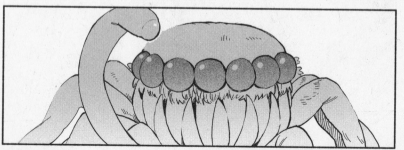

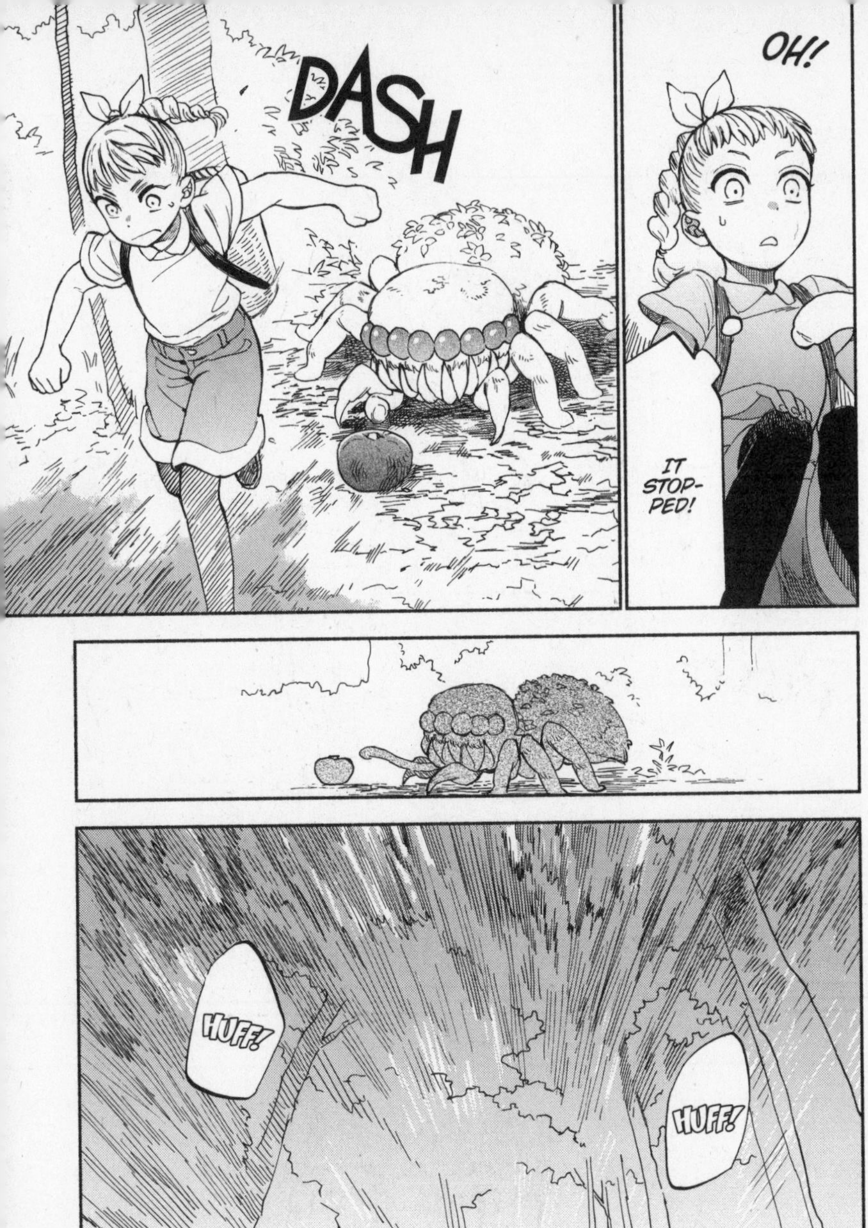
OH!
IT STOP-PED!
DASH
HUFF!
HUFF!

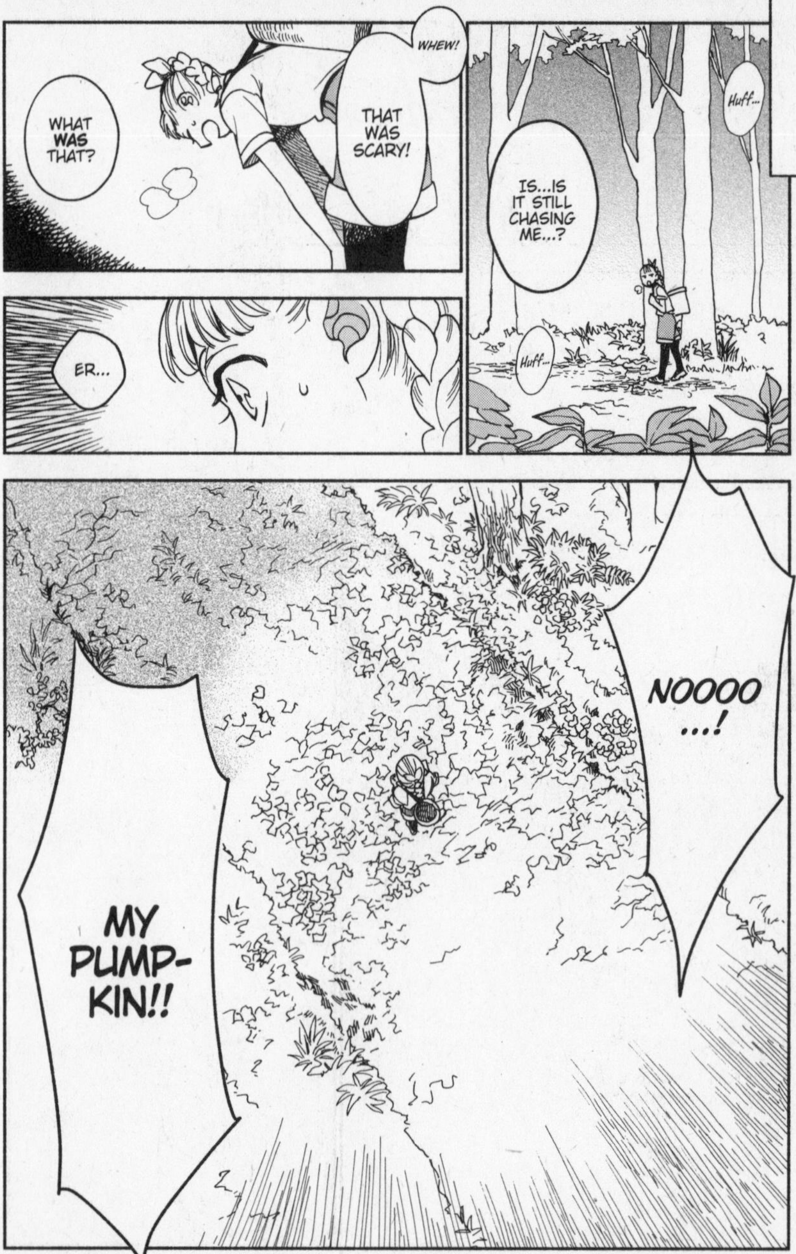
Huff...
IS...IS IT STILL CHASING ME...?
Huff...
WHEW!
THAT WAS SCARY!
WHAT WAS THAT?
ER...
NOOOO ...!
MY PUMP-KIN!!

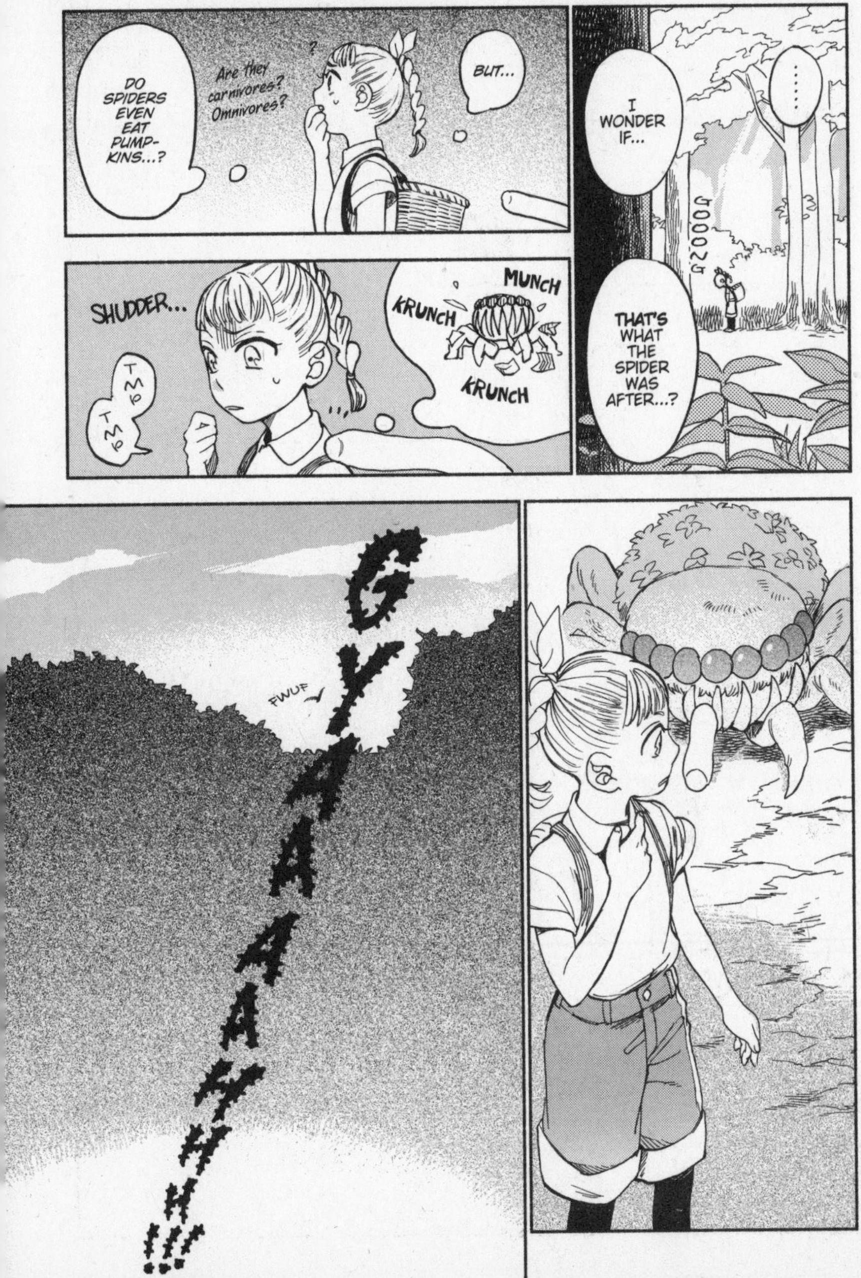
......
I WONDER IF...
GOOONG
THAT'S WHAT THE SPIDER WAS AFTER...?
BUT...
?
Are they carnivores? Omnivores?
DO SPIDERS EVEN EAT PUMPKINS...?
MUNCH
KRUNCH
KRUNCH
SHUDDER...
TMP TMP
GYAAAAHHH!!!
FWUF

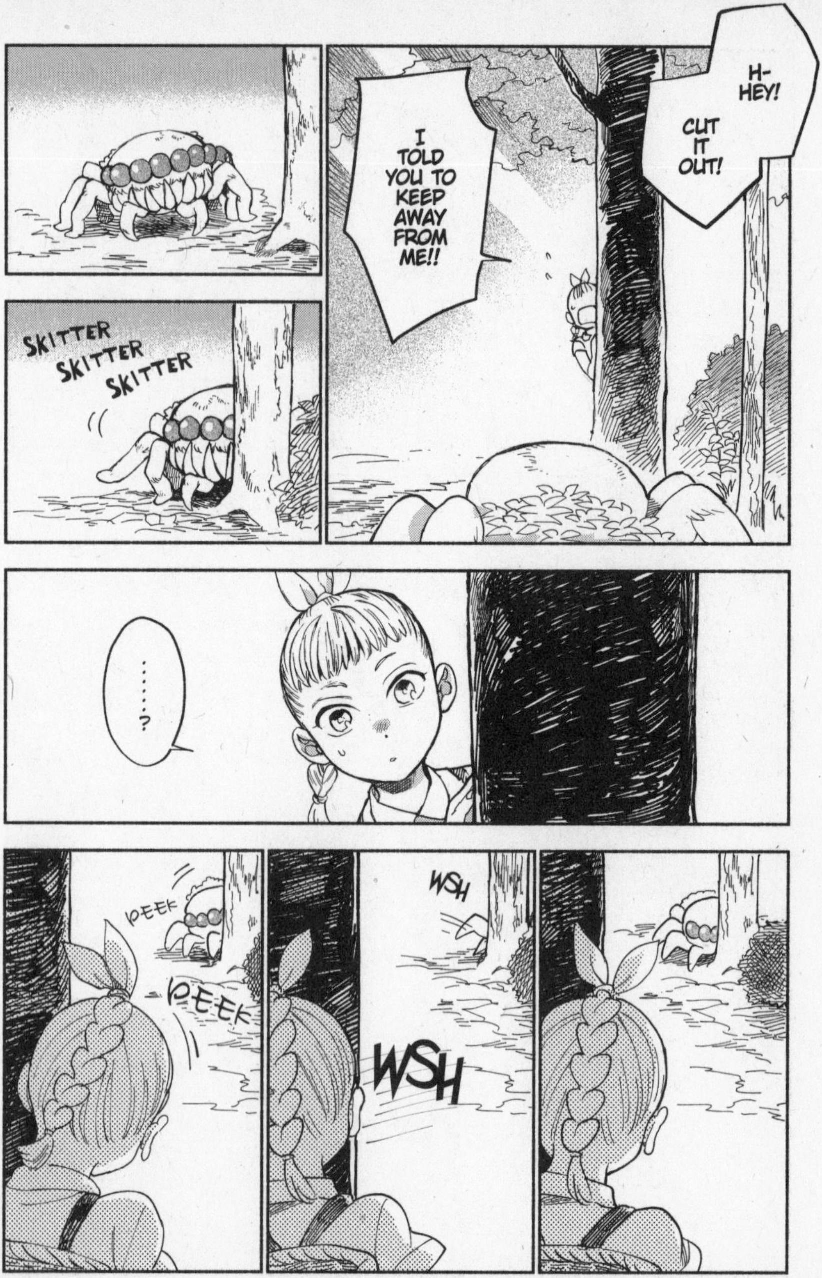
H-HEY! CUT IT OUT!
I TOLD YOU TO KEEP AWAY FROM ME!!
SKITTER SKITTER SKITTER
......?
WSH
WSH
PEEK
PEEK

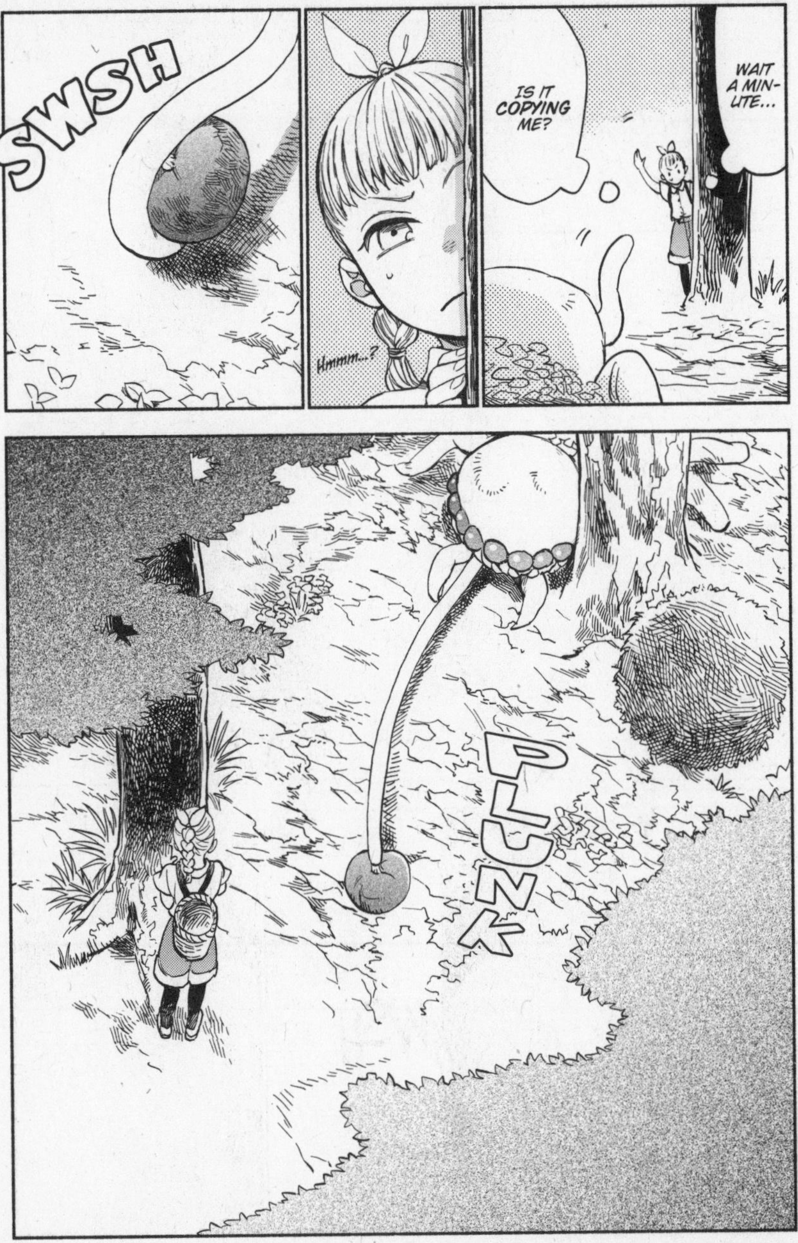
WAIT A MIN-UTE...
IS IT COPYING ME?
Hmmm...?
SWSH
PLUNK

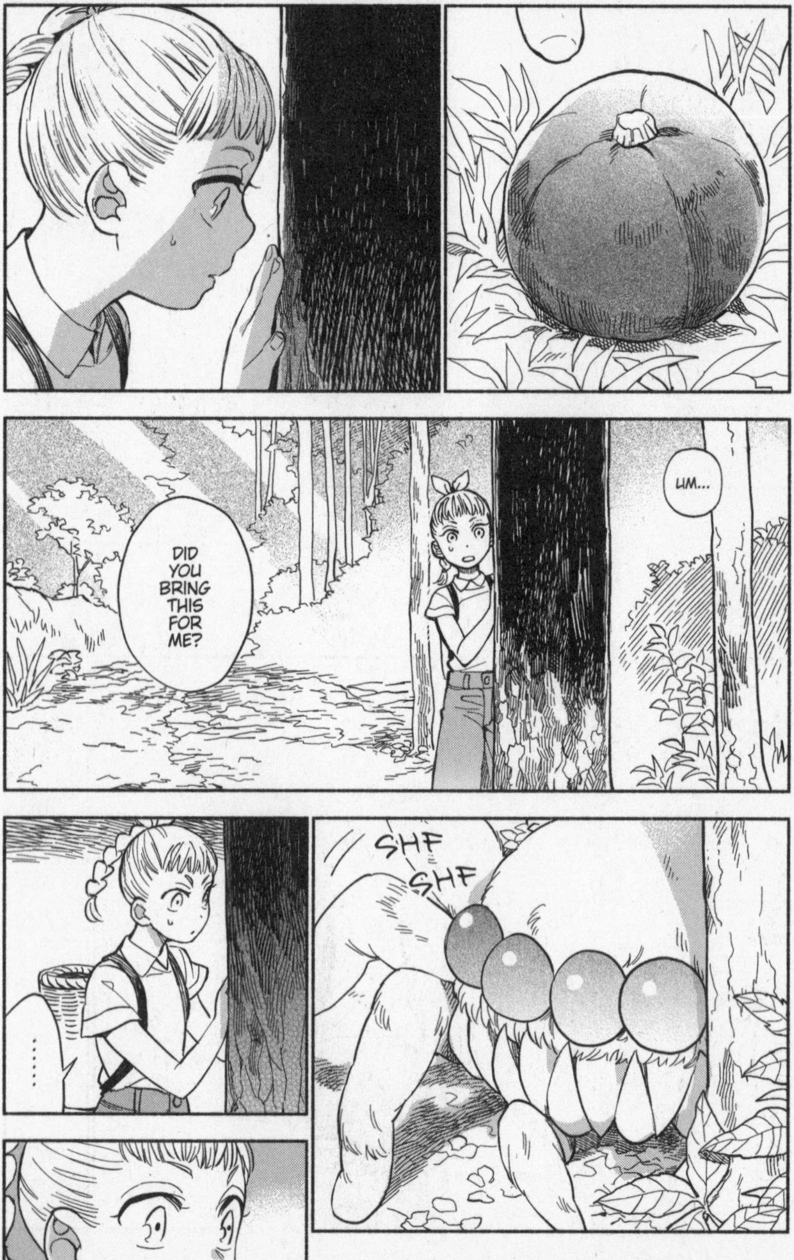
UM...
DID YOU BRING THIS FOR ME?
SHF SHF
......

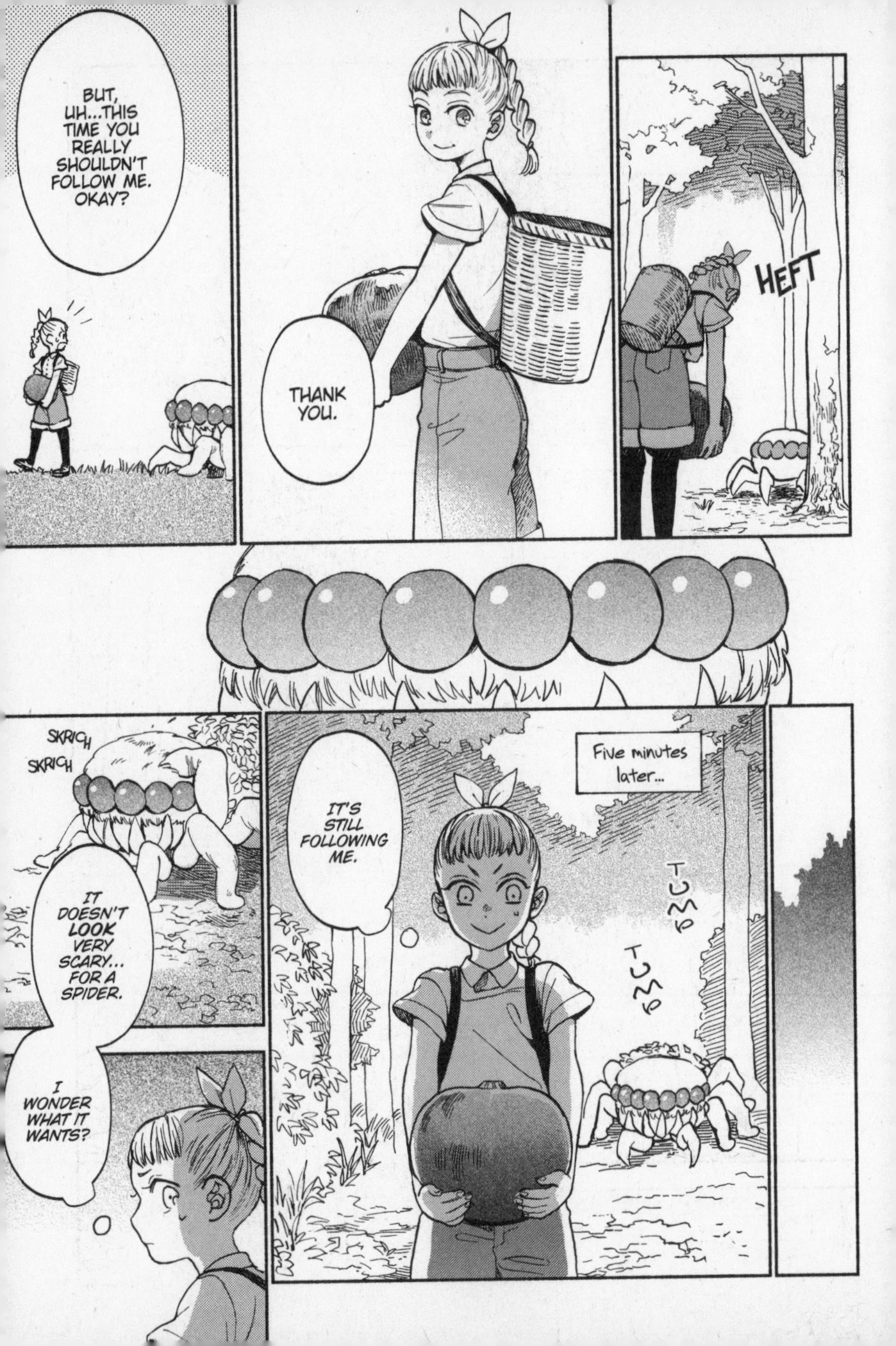
HEFT
THANK YOU.
BUT, UH...THIS TIME YOU REALLY SHOULDN'T FOLLOW ME. OKAY?
Five minutes later...
IT'S STILL FOLLOWING ME.
TUMP
TUMP
SKRICH
SKRICH
IT DOESN'T LOOK VERY SCARY... FOR A SPIDER.
I WONDER WHAT IT WANTS?

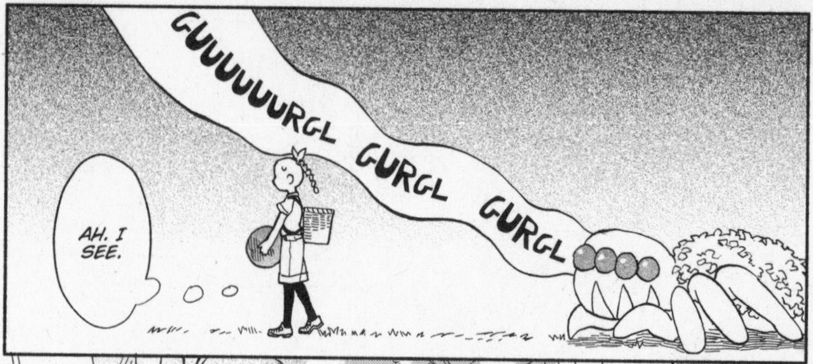
GUUUUUURGL GURGL GURGL
AH. I SEE.
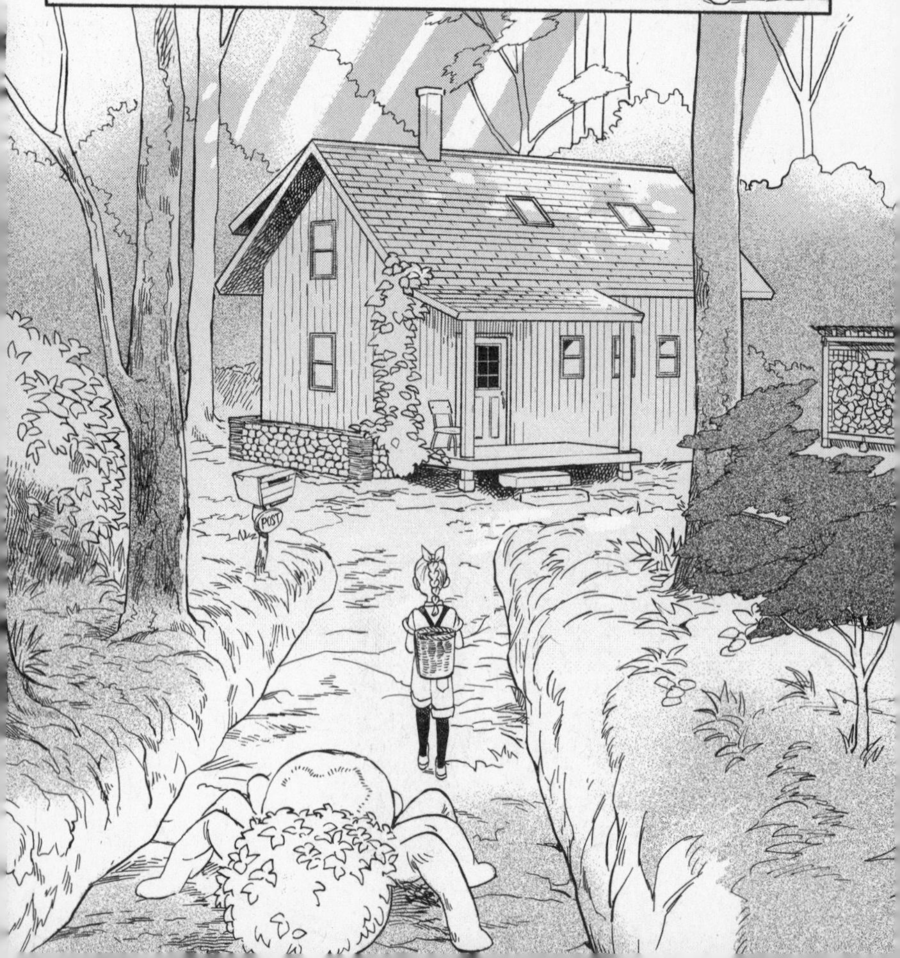
POST

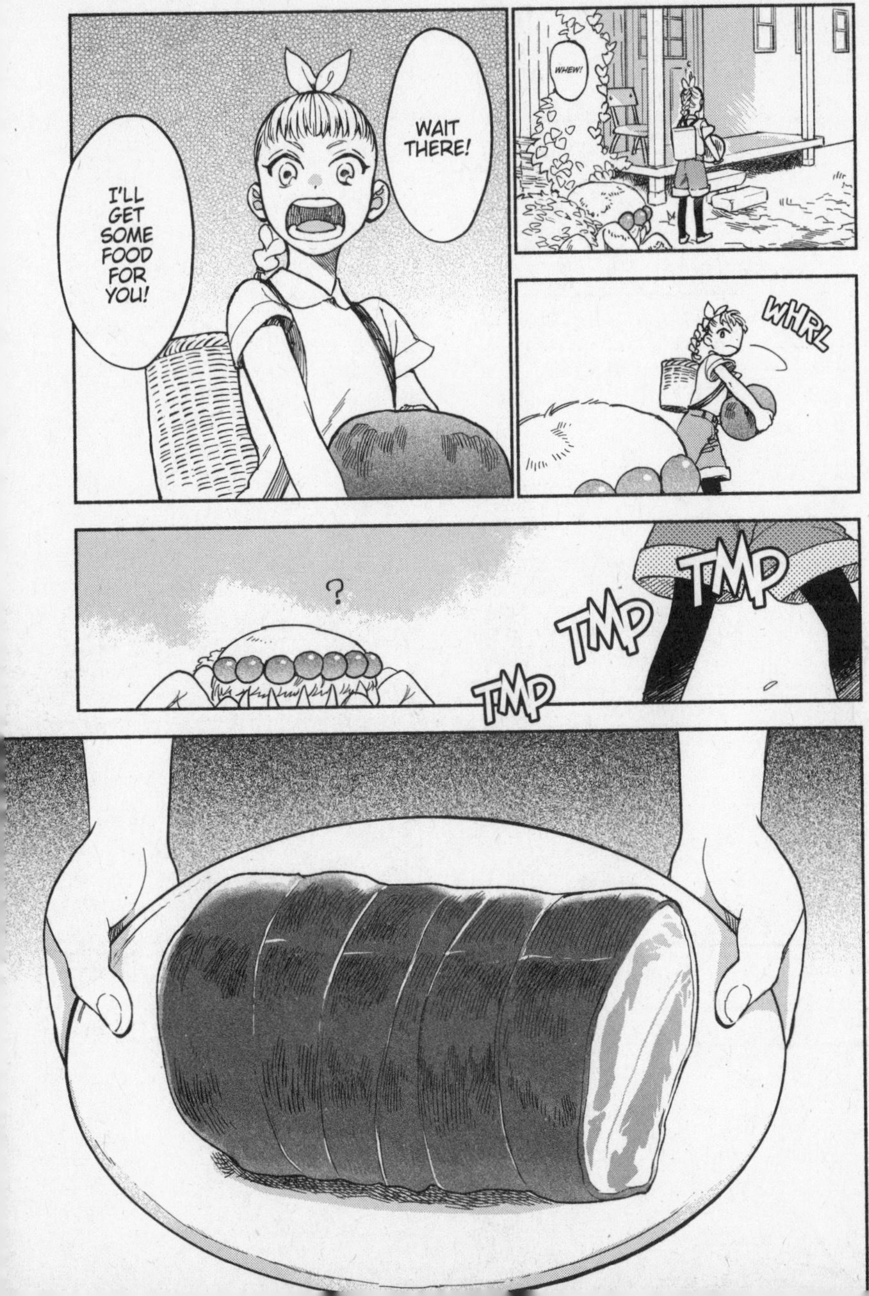
WHEW!
WHRL
WAIT THERE!
I'LL GET SOME FOOD FOR YOU!
TMP
TMP
TMP
?

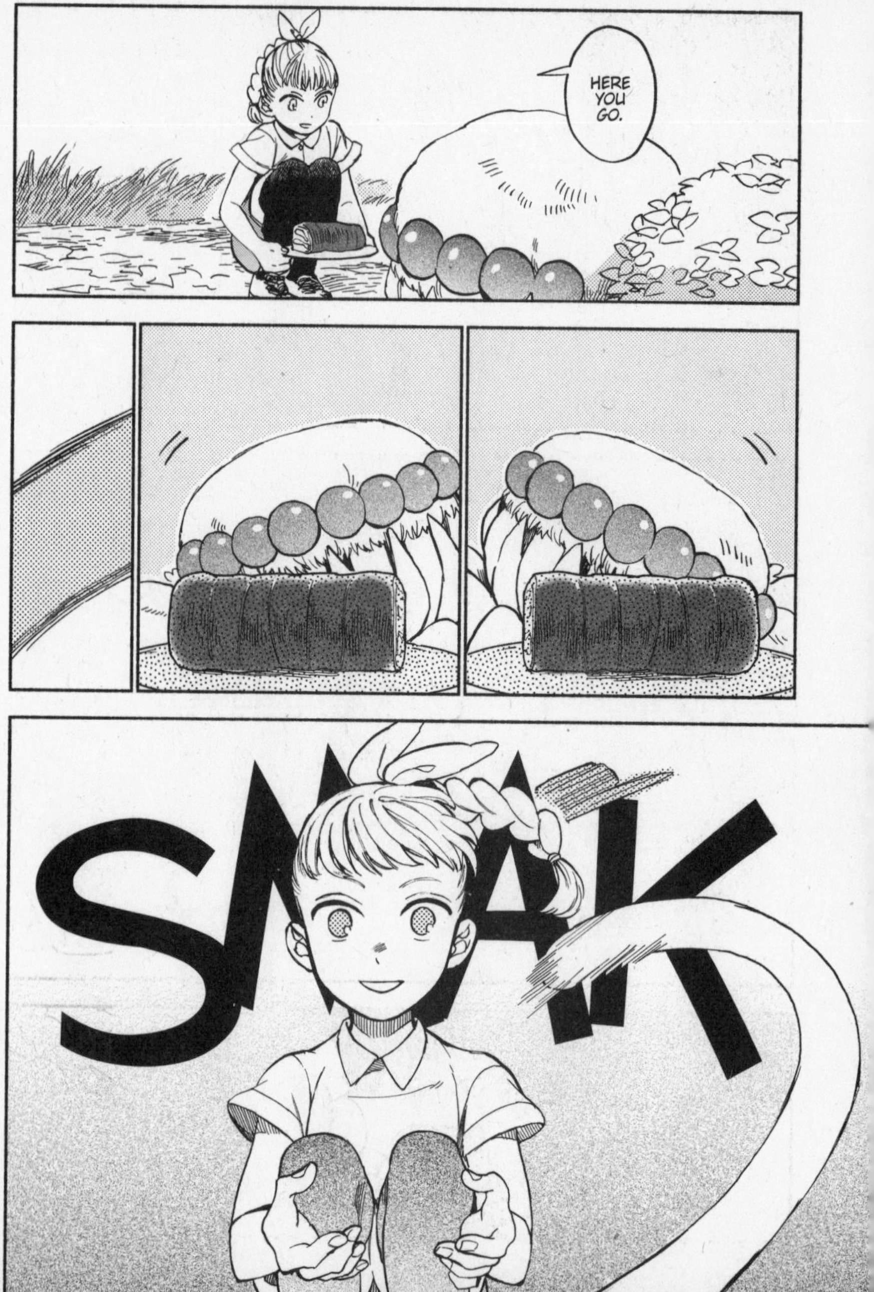
HERE YOU GO.
SNAK

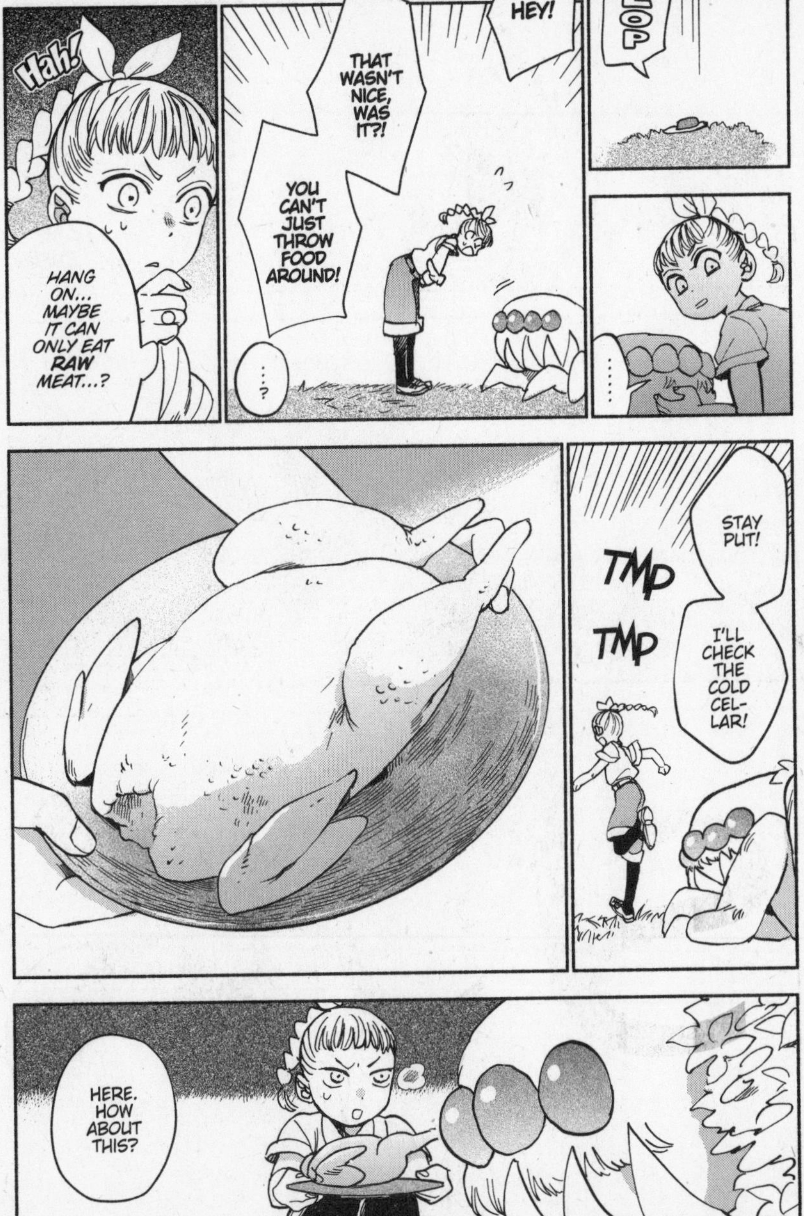
PLOP
HEY!
THAT WASN'T NICE, WAS IT?!
YOU CAN'T JUST THROW FOOD AROUND!
...?
Hah!
HANG ON... MAYBE IT CAN ONLY EAT RAW MEAT...?
STAY PUT!
I'LL CHECK THE COLD CEL-LAR!
TMP
TMP
HERE. HOW ABOUT THIS?

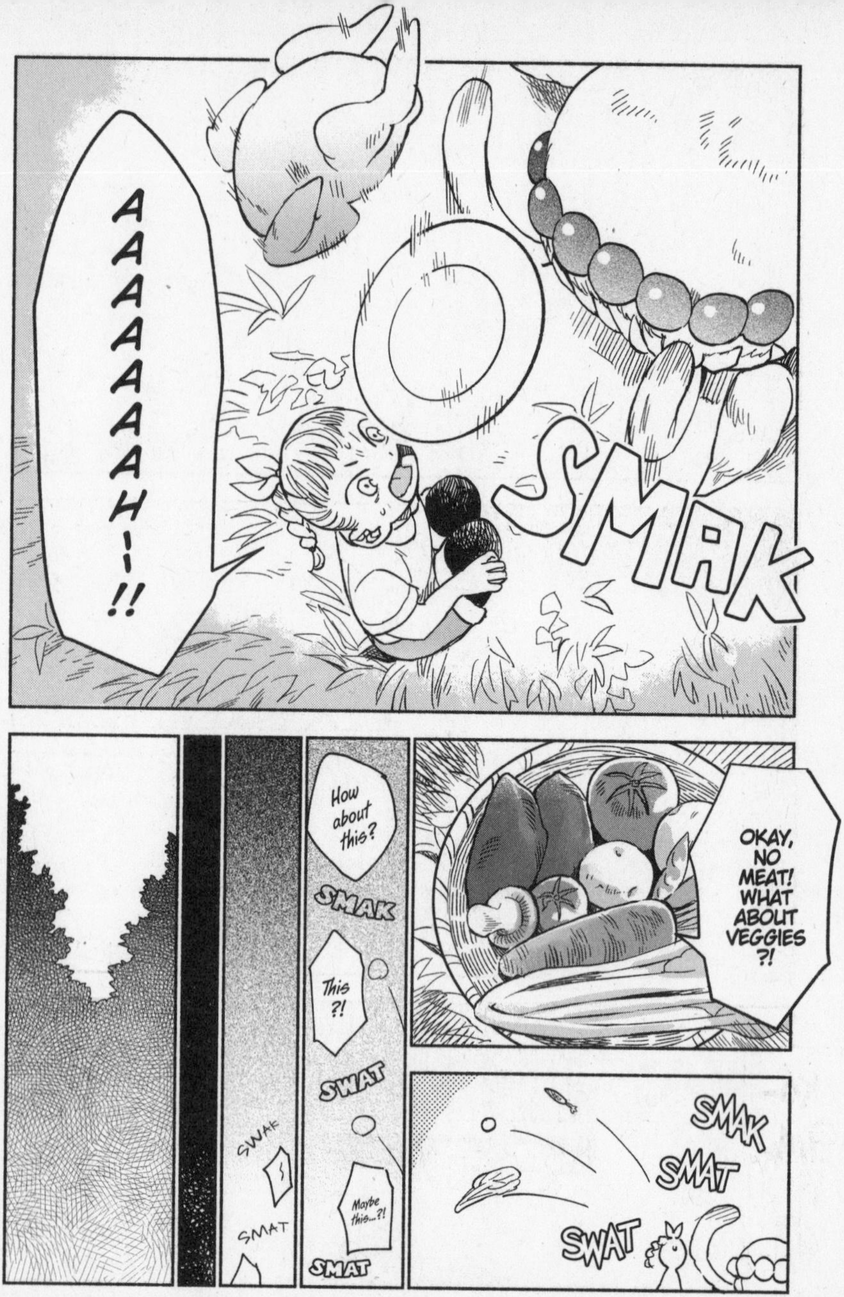
SMAK
AAAAAAAAH!!
OKAY, NO MEAT! WHAT ABOUT VEGGIES?!
SMAK
SMAT
SWAT
How about this?
SMAK
This?!
SWAT
Maybe this...?!
SMAT
SWAK
SMAT

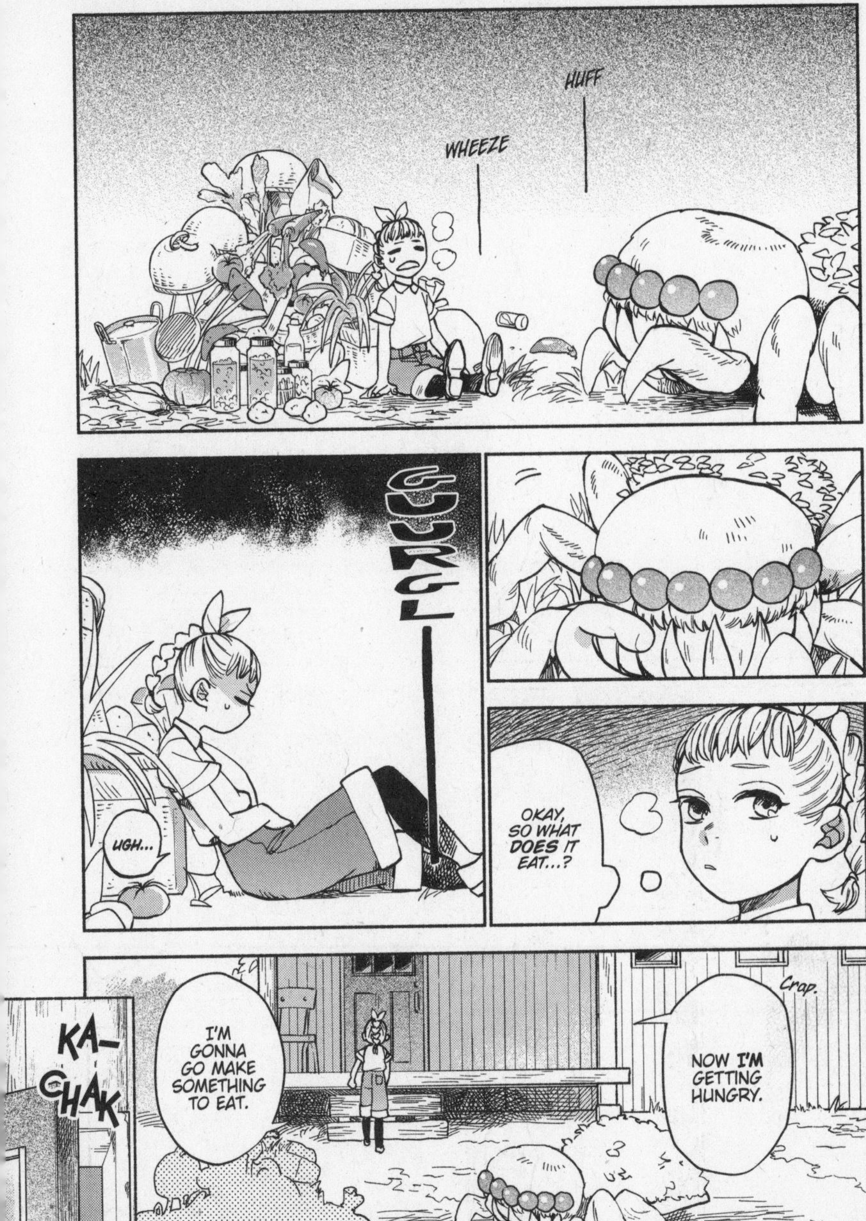
HUFF
WHEEZE
OKAY, SO WHAT DOES IT EAT...?
GUURGL
UGH...
Crap.
NOW I'M GETTING HUNGRY.
I'M GONNA GO MAKE SOMETHING TO EAT.
KA-CHAK

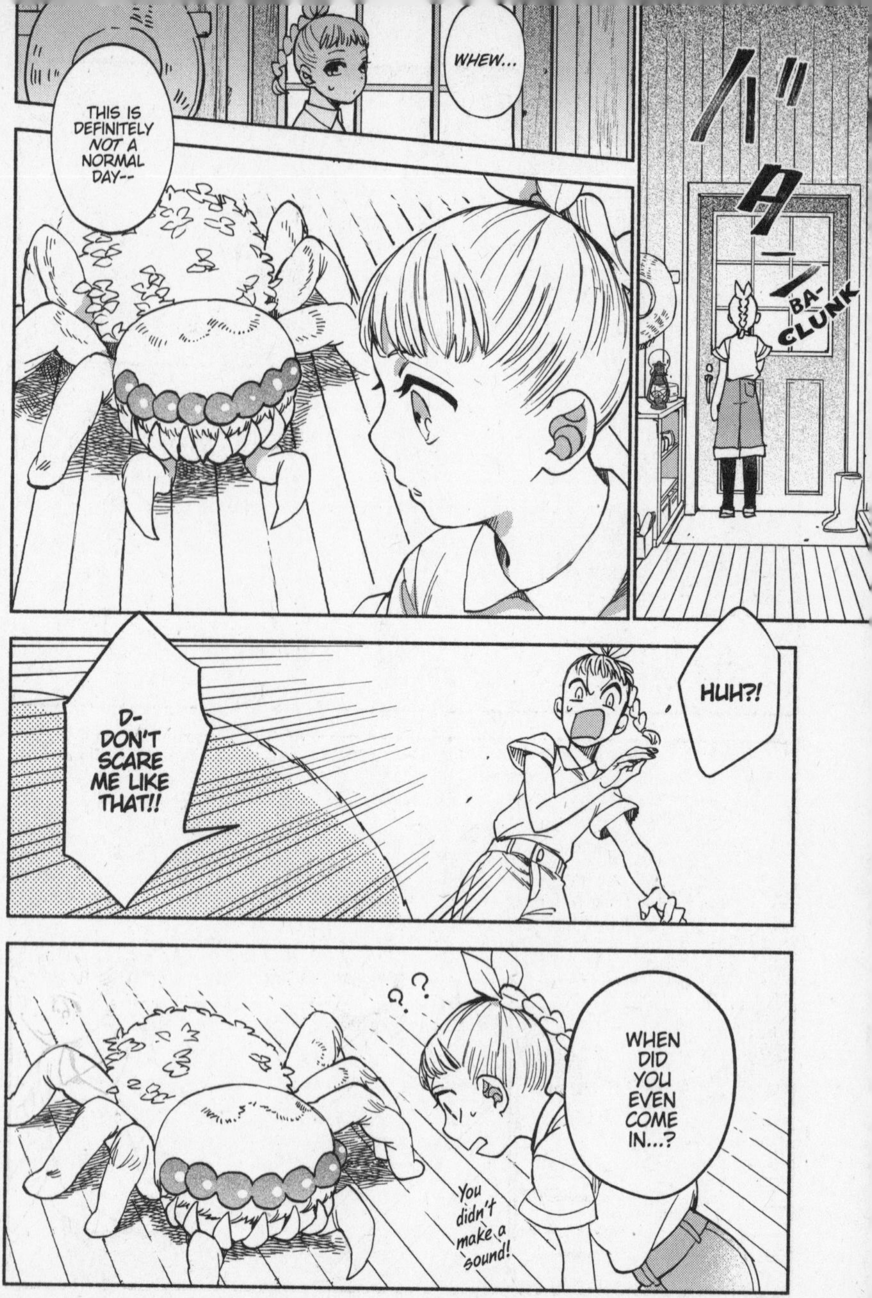
バタン
BA-CLUNK
WHEW...
THIS IS DEFINITELY NOT A NORMAL DAY--
HUH?!
D-DON'T SCARE ME LIKE THAT!!
? ?
WHEN DID YOU EVEN COME IN...?
You didn't make a sound!

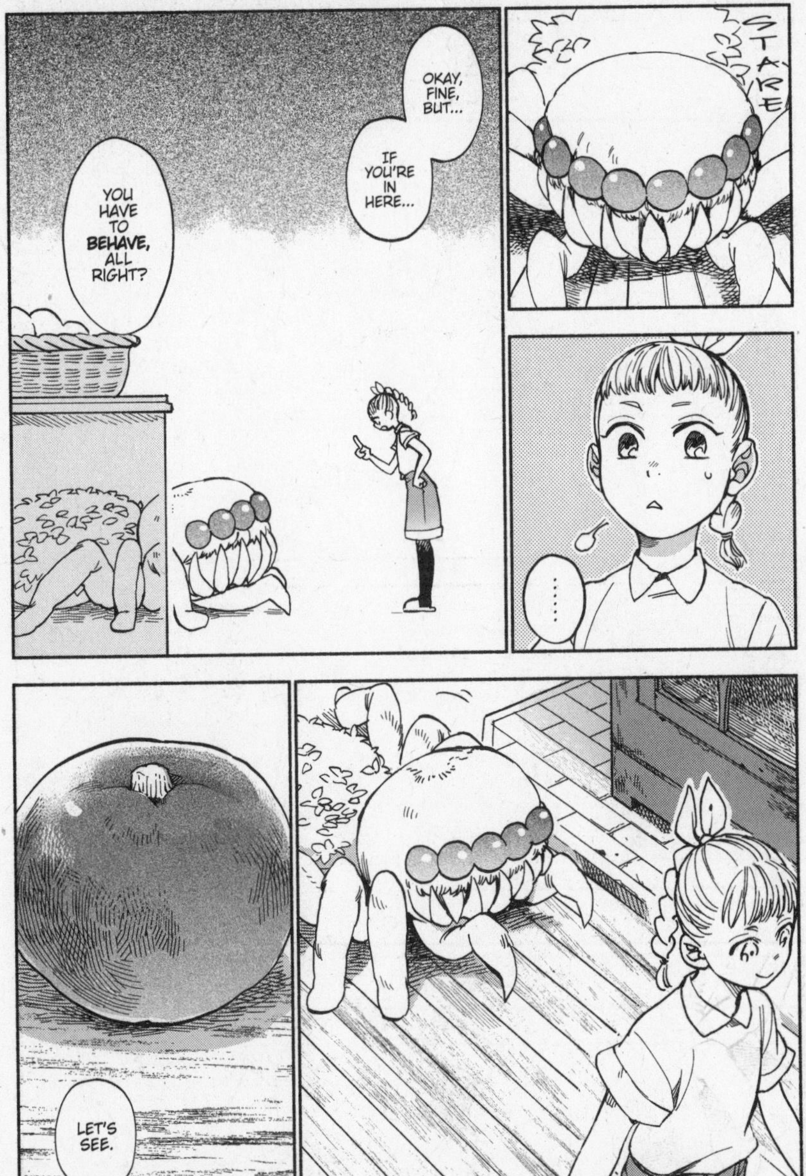
STARE
......
OKAY, FINE, BUT...
IF YOU'RE IN HERE...
YOU HAVE TO **BEHAVE**, ALL RIGHT?
LET'S SEE.

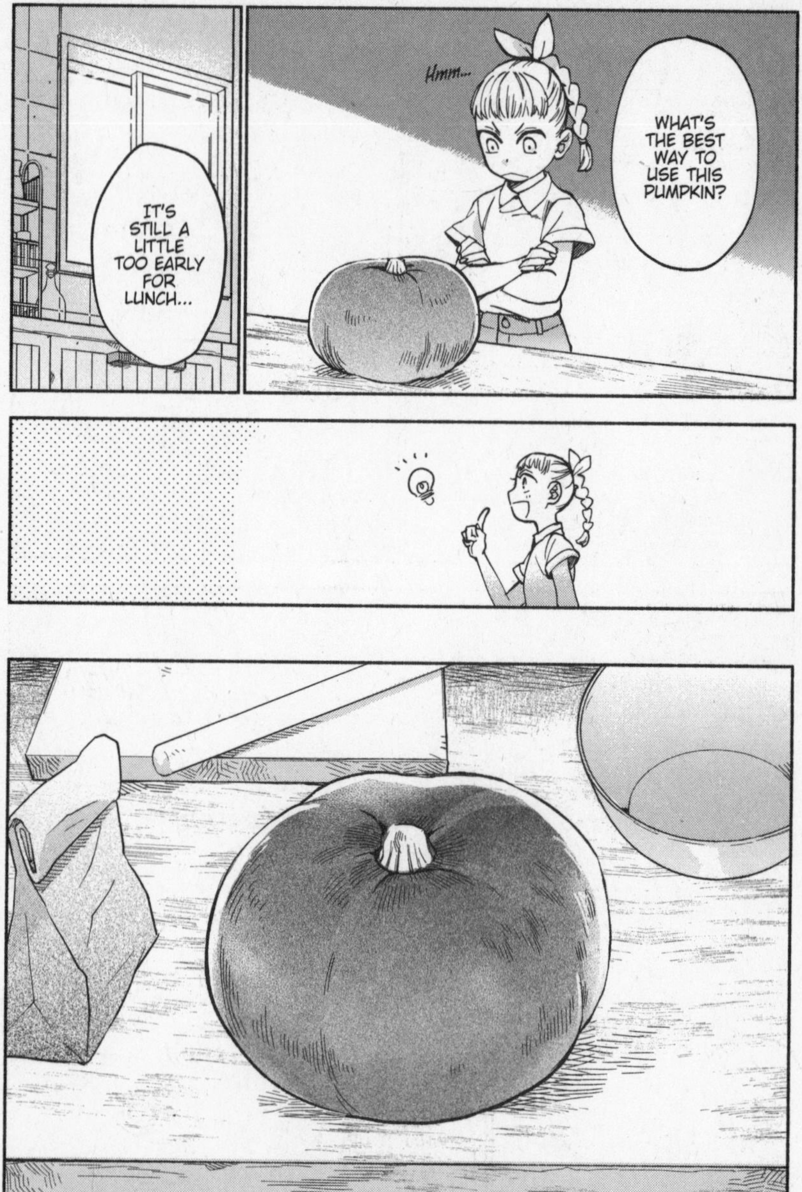
WHAT'S THE BEST WAY TO USE THIS PUMPKIN?
Hmm...
IT'S STILL A LITTLE TOO EARLY FOR LUNCH...

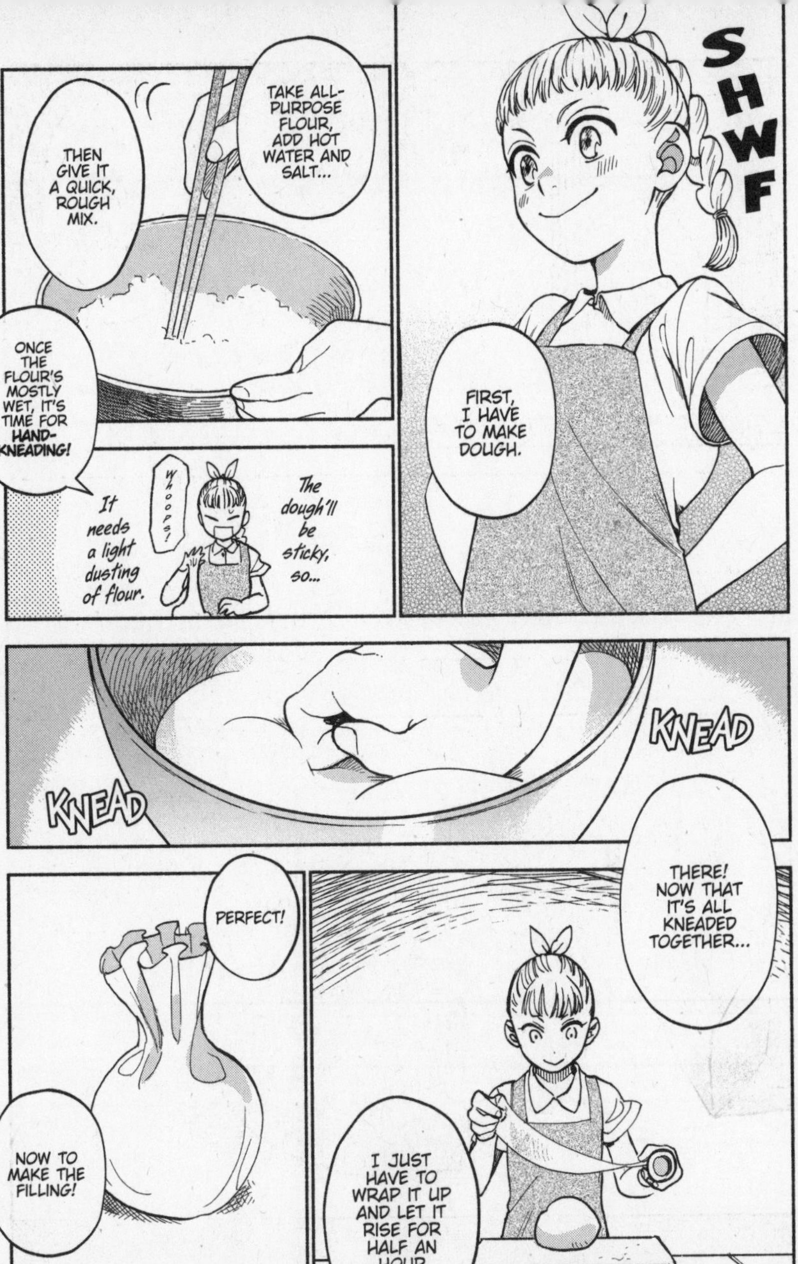
SHWF
FIRST, I HAVE TO MAKE DOUGH.
TAKE ALL-PURPOSE FLOUR, ADD HOT WATER AND SALT...
THEN GIVE IT A QUICK, ROUGH MIX.
ONCE THE FLOUR'S MOSTLY WET, IT'S TIME FOR **HAND-KNEADING!**
The dough'll be sticky, so...
Whoops!
It needs a light dusting of flour.
KNEAD
KNEAD
THERE! NOW THAT IT'S ALL KNEADED TOGETHER...
I JUST HAVE TO WRAP IT UP AND LET IT RISE FOR HALF AN HOUR OR SO.
PERFECT!
NOW TO MAKE THE FILLING!

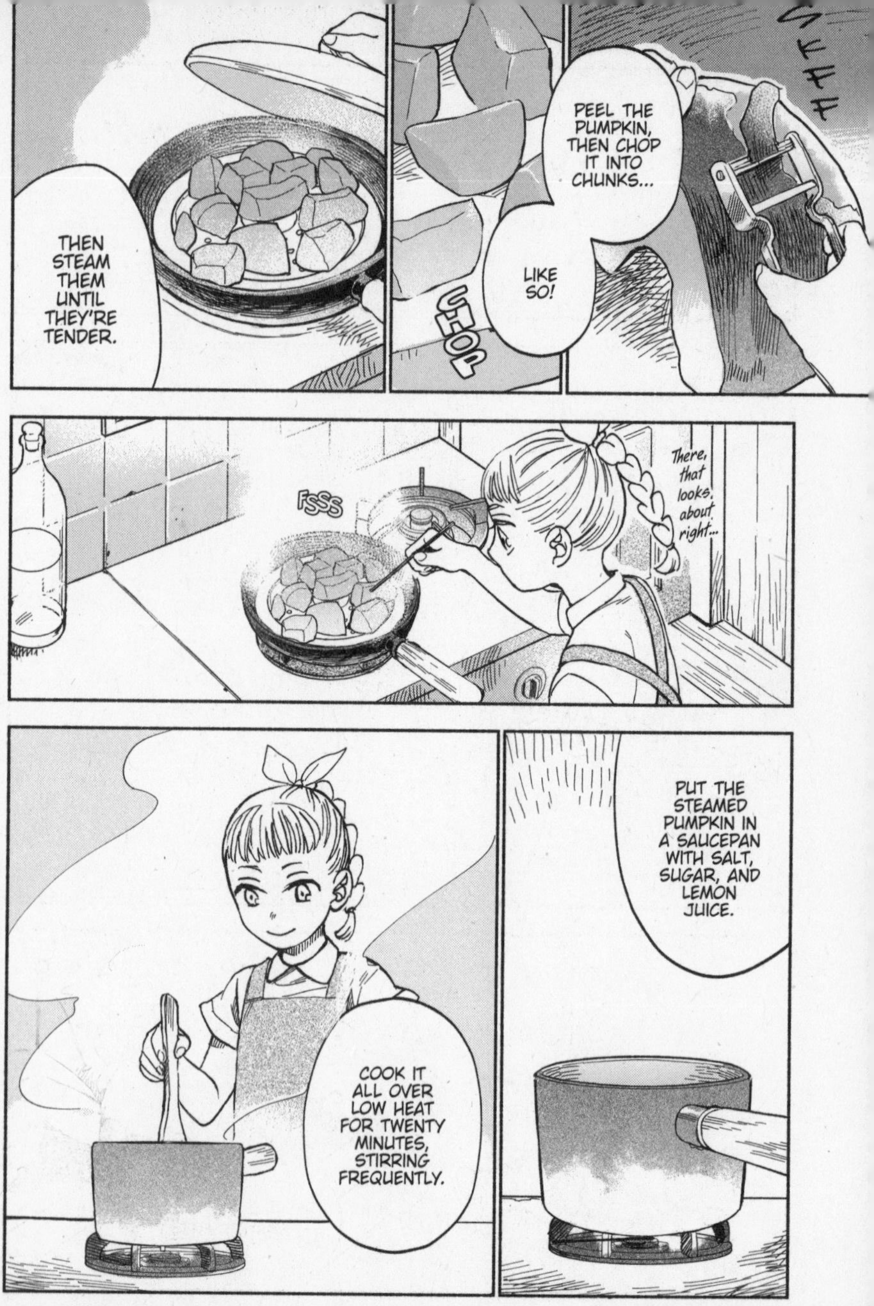
PEEL THE PUMPKIN, THEN CHOP IT INTO CHUNKS...
LIKE SO!
CHOP
THEN STEAM THEM UNTIL THEY'RE TENDER.
There, that looks about right...
FSSS
PUT THE STEAMED PUMPKIN IN A SAUCEPAN WITH SALT, SUGAR, AND LEMON JUICE.
COOK IT ALL OVER LOW HEAT FOR TWENTY MINUTES, STIRRING FREQUENTLY.

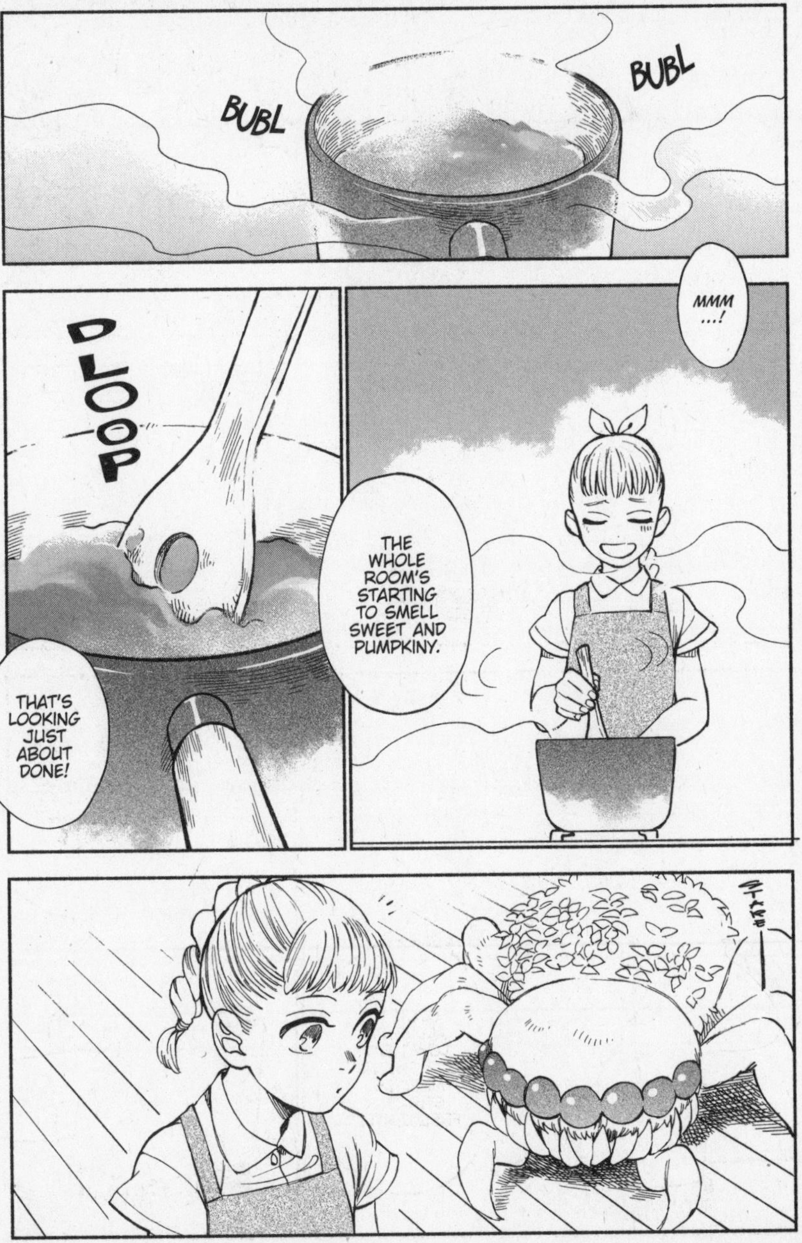
BUBL
BUBL
MMM ...!
THE WHOLE ROOM'S STARTING TO SMELL SWEET AND PUMPKINY.
DLOOP
THAT'S LOOKING JUST ABOUT DONE!
STARE

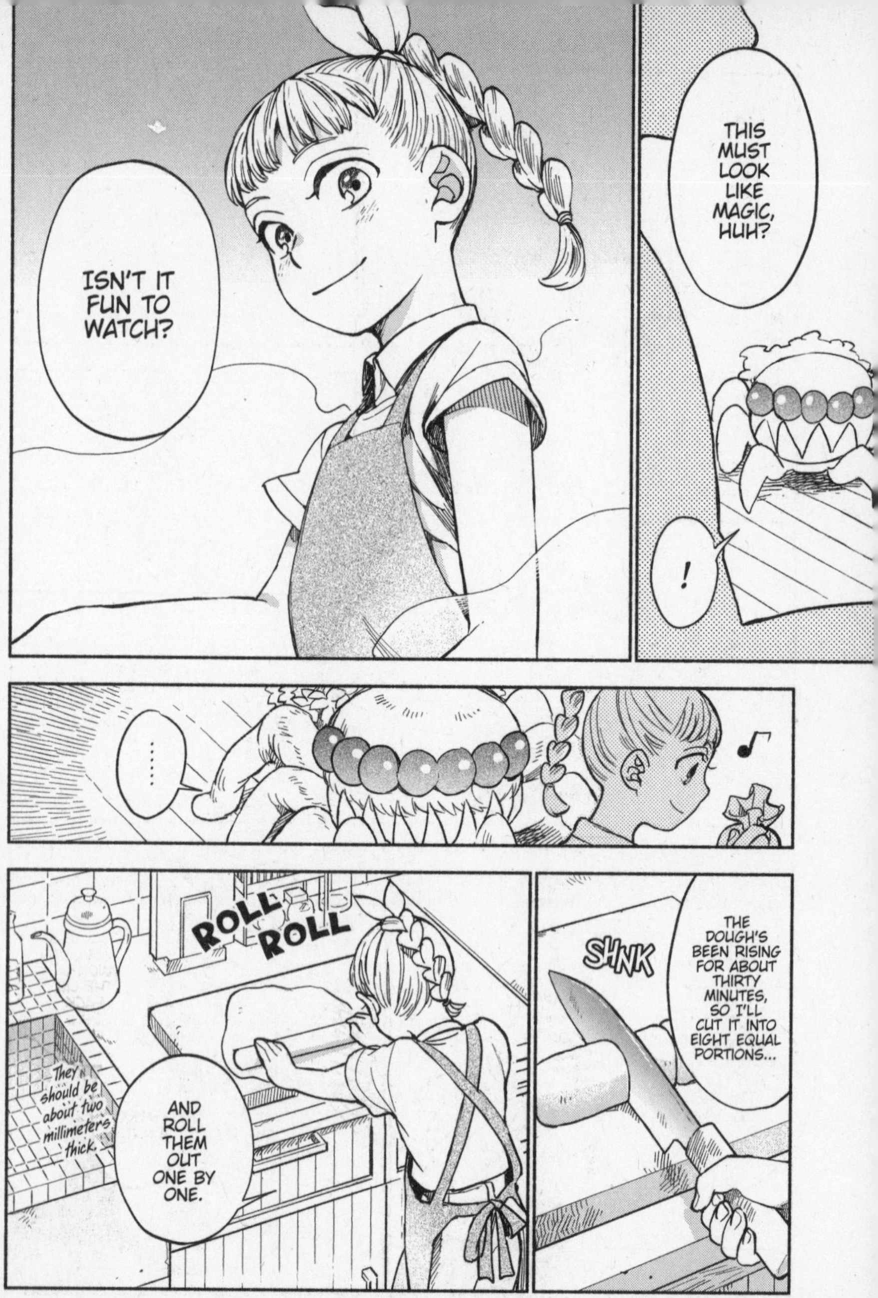
THIS MUST LOOK LIKE MAGIC, HUH?
!
ISN'T IT FUN TO WATCH?
......
SHNK
THE DOUGH'S BEEN RISING FOR ABOUT THIRTY MINUTES, SO I'LL CUT IT INTO EIGHT EQUAL PORTIONS...
ROLL
ROLL
AND ROLL THEM OUT ONE BY ONE.
They should be about two millimeters thick.

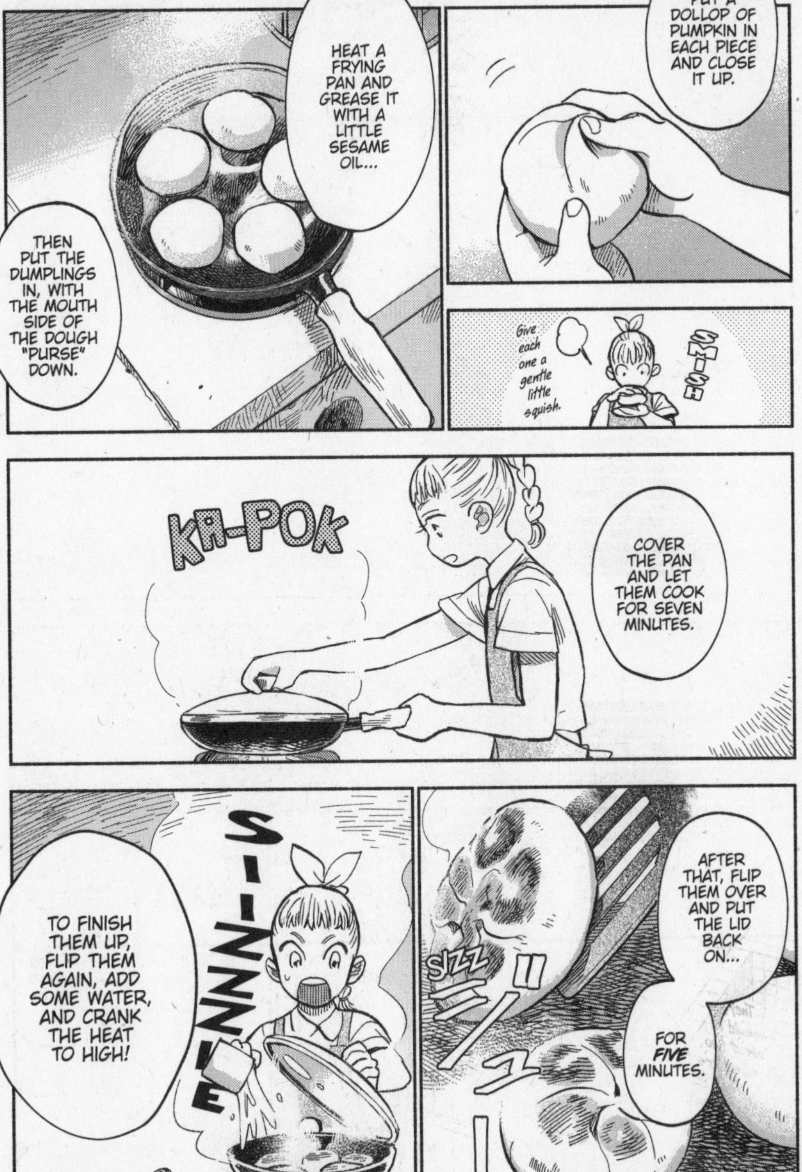
PUT A DOLLOP OF PUMPKIN IN EACH PIECE AND CLOSE IT UP.
Give each one a gentle little squish.
SMISH
HEAT A FRYING PAN AND GREASE IT WITH A LITTLE SESAME OIL...
THEN PUT THE DUMPLINGS IN, WITH THE MOUTH SIDE OF THE DOUGH "PURSE" DOWN.
COVER THE PAN AND LET THEM COOK FOR SEVEN MINUTES.
KA-POK
AFTER THAT, FLIP THEM OVER AND PUT THE LID BACK ON...
SIZZ
FOR *FIVE* MINUTES.
SIIZZZLE
TO FINISH THEM UP, FLIP THEM AGAIN, ADD SOME WATER, AND CRANK THE HEAT TO HIGH!

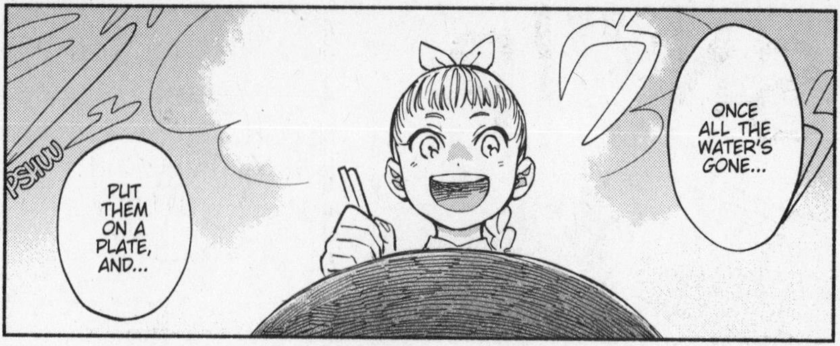
ONCE ALL THE WATER'S GONE...
PSHUU
PUT THEM ON A PLATE, AND...

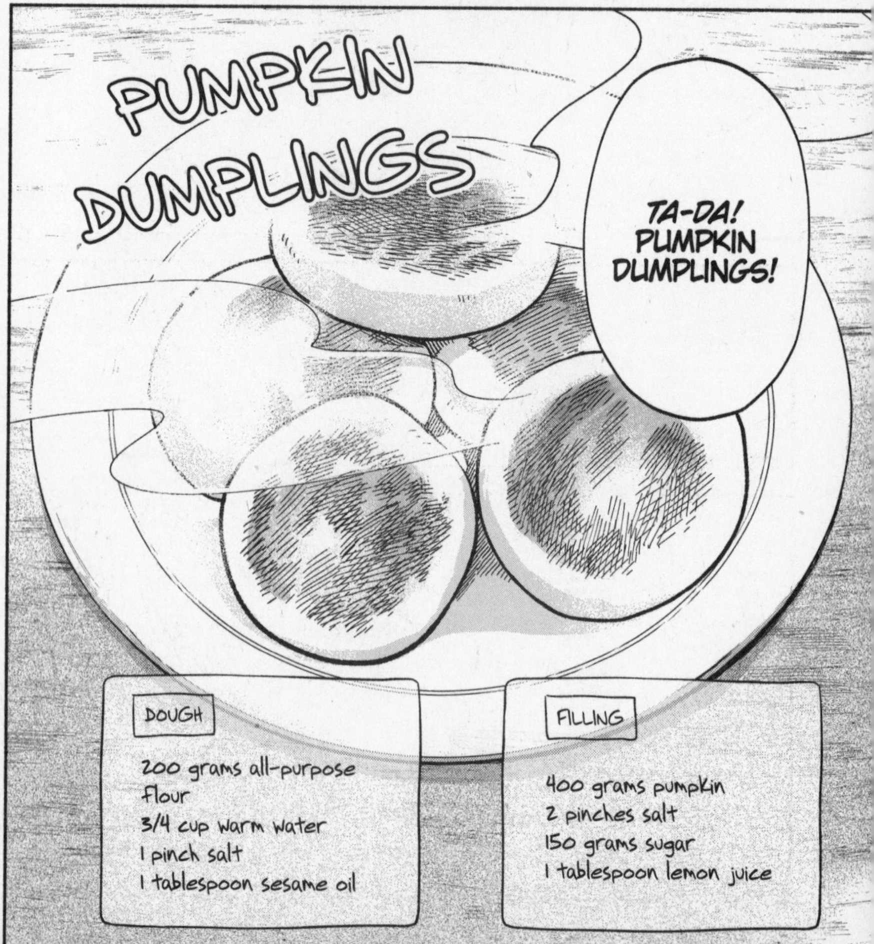
TA-DA! PUMPKIN DUMPLINGS!
PUMPKIN DUMPLINGS
DOUGH
200 grams all-purpose flour
3/4 cup warm water
1 pinch salt
1 tablespoon sesame oil
FILLING
400 grams pumpkin
2 pinches salt
150 grams sugar
1 tablespoon lemon juice

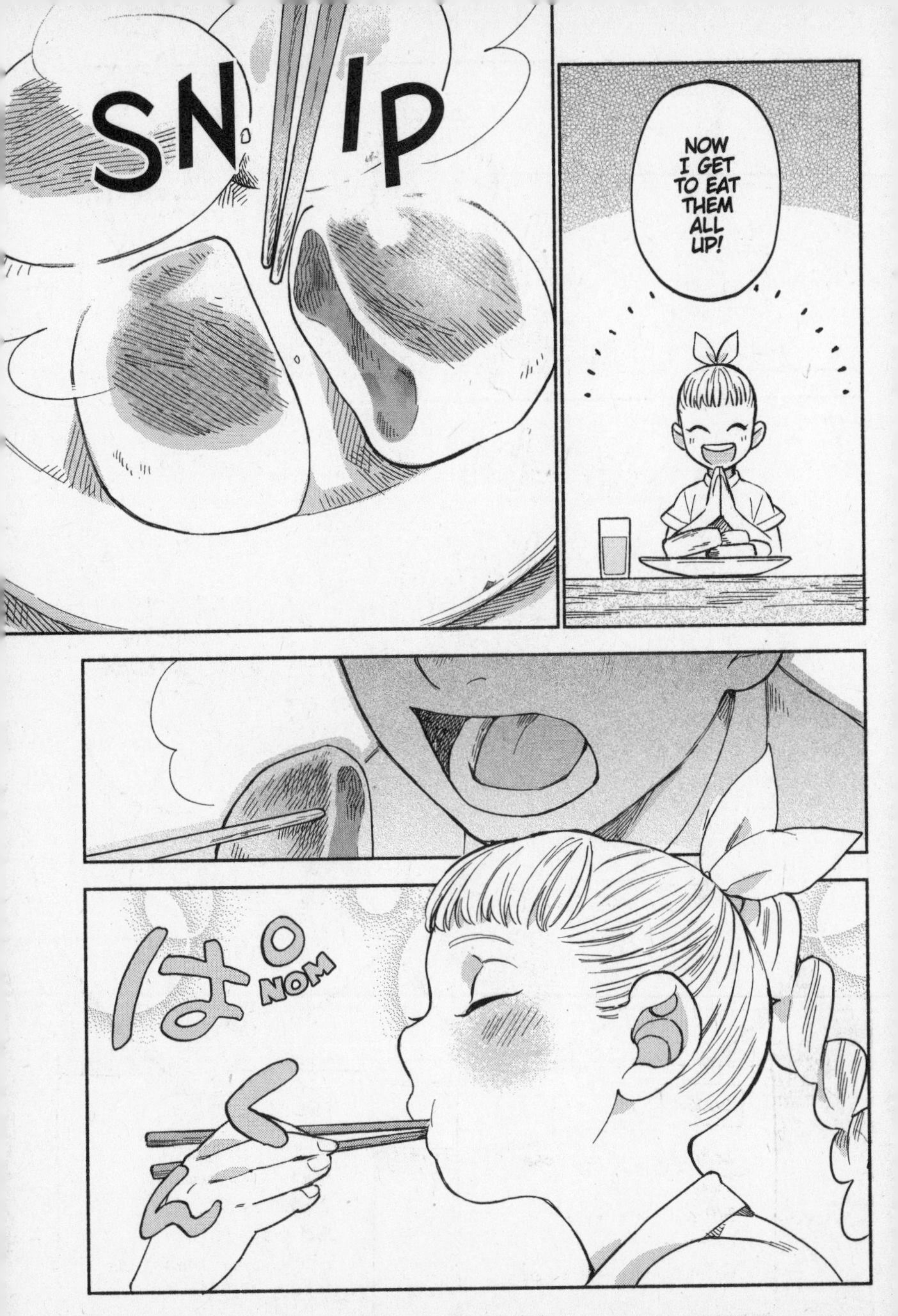
NOW I GET TO EAT THEM ALL UP!
SNIP
NOM

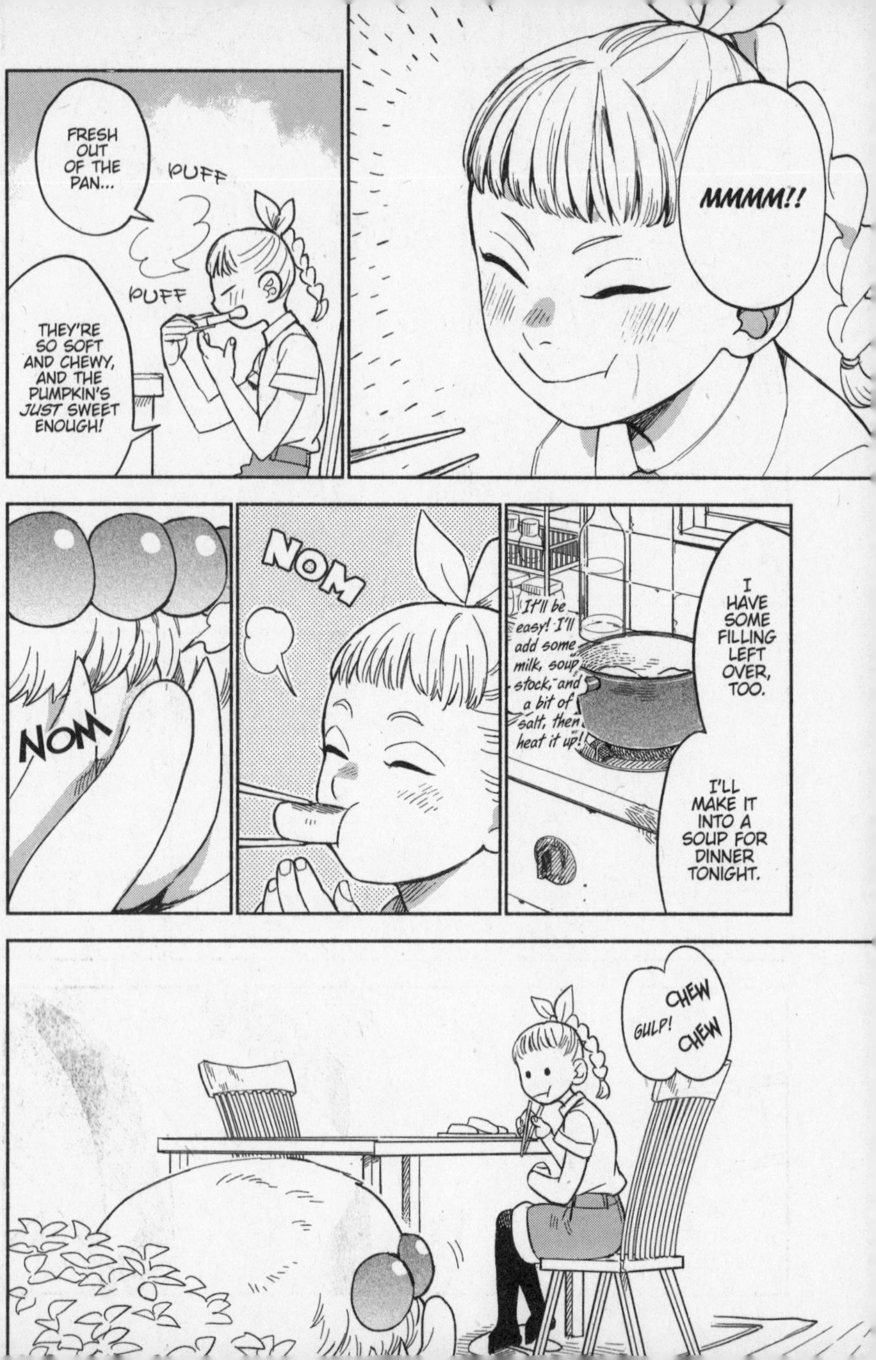
MMMM!!
FRESH OUT OF THE PAN...
PUFF
PUFF
THEY'RE SO SOFT AND CHEWY, AND THE PUMPKIN'S JUST SWEET ENOUGH!
I HAVE SOME FILLING LEFT OVER, TOO.
It'll be easy! I'll add some milk, soup stock, and a bit of salt, then heat it up!
I'LL MAKE IT INTO A SOUP FOR DINNER TONIGHT.
NOM
NOM
CHEW
GULP!
CHEW

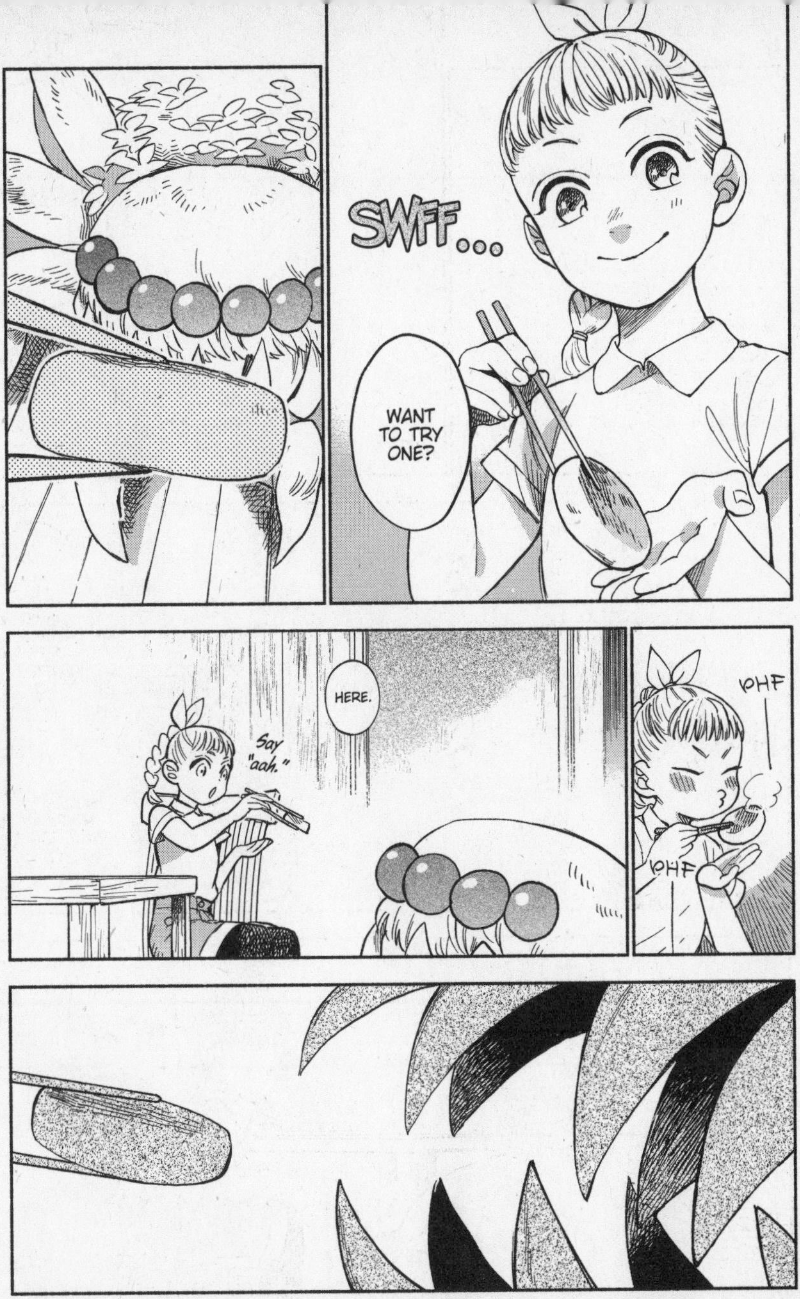
SWFF...
WANT TO TRY ONE?
UHF
UHF
HERE.
Say "aah."

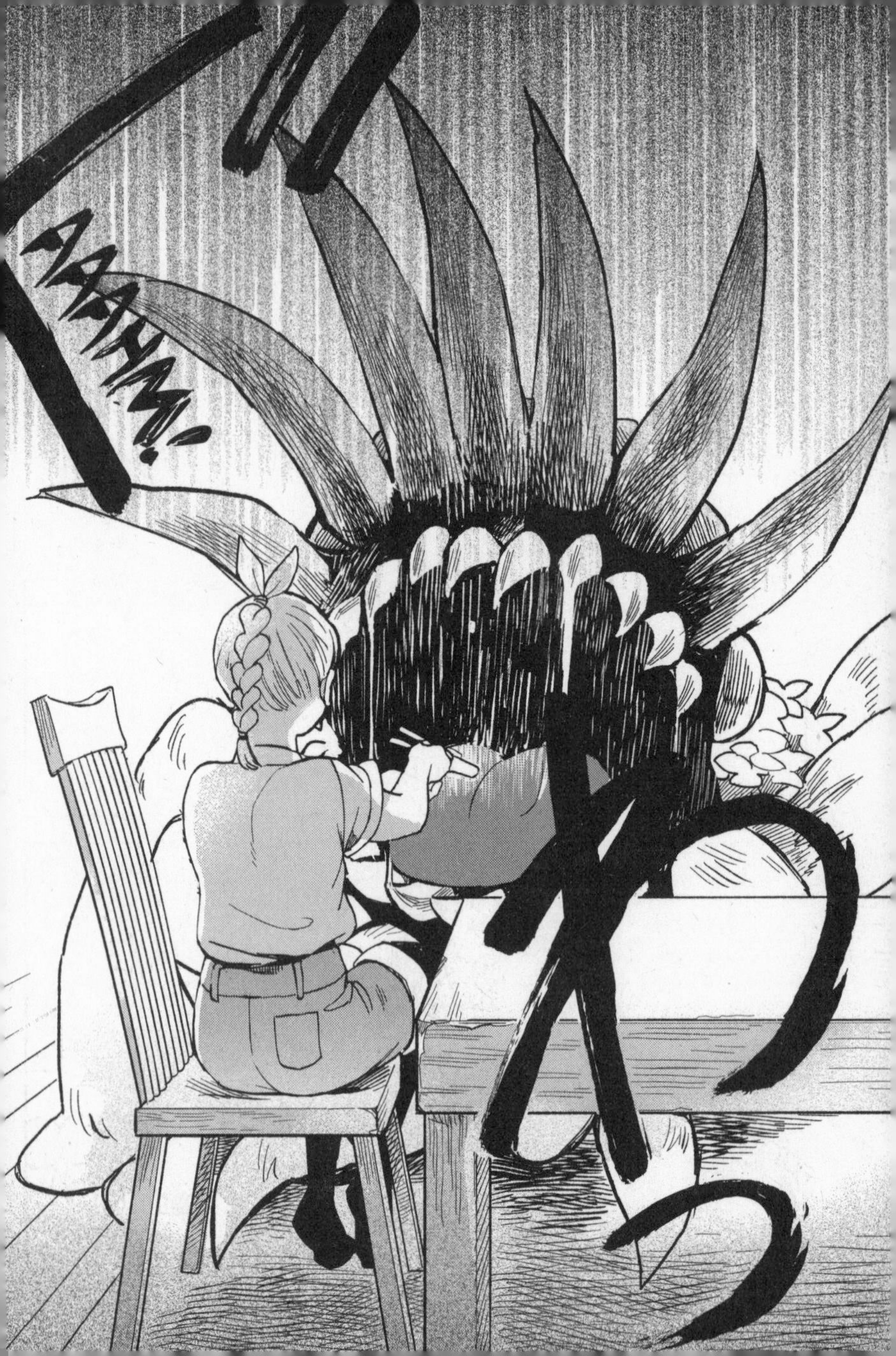
AAAHM!!

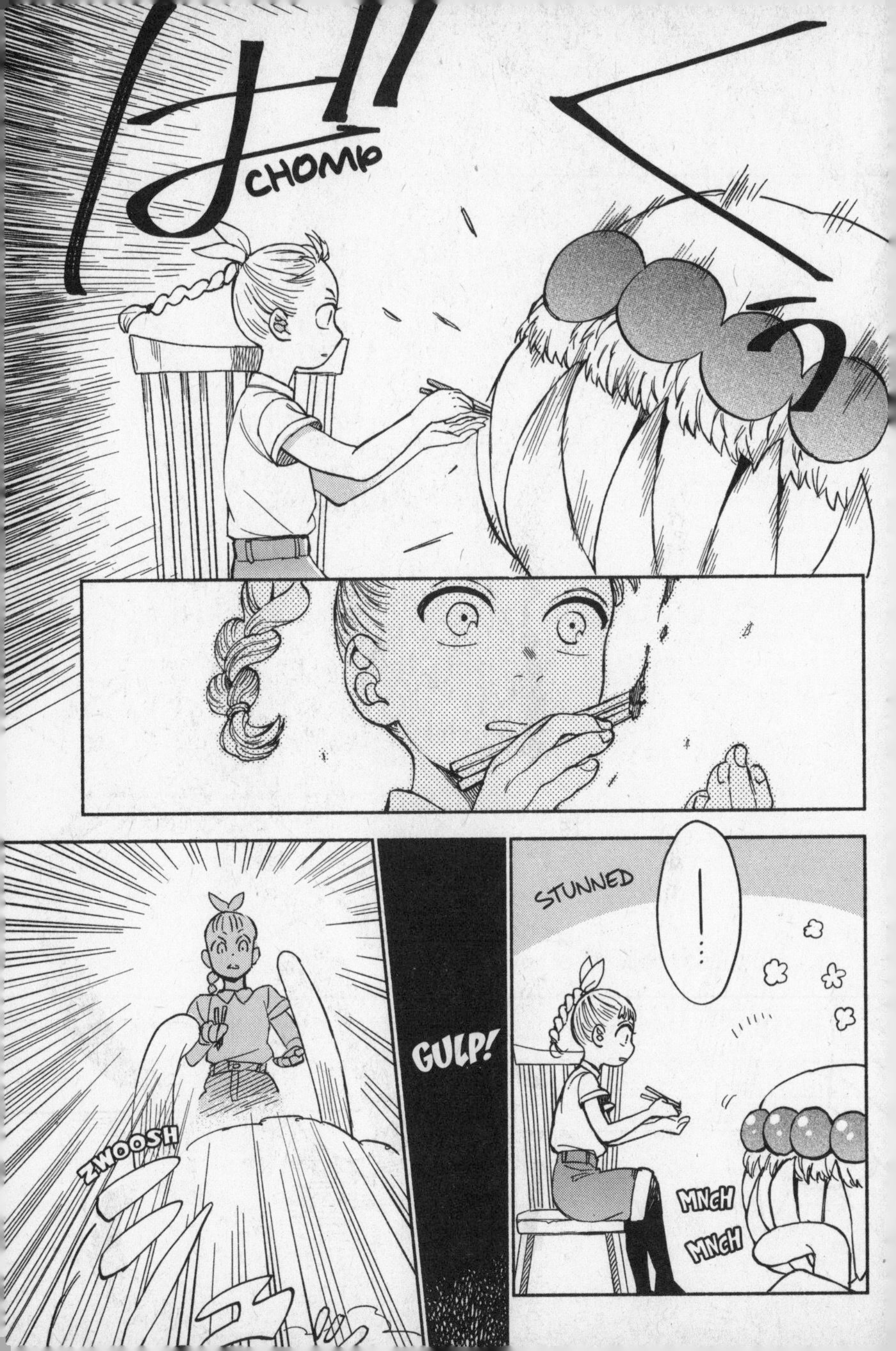
CHOMP
STUNNED
!...
MNCH
MNCH
GULP!
ZWOOSH

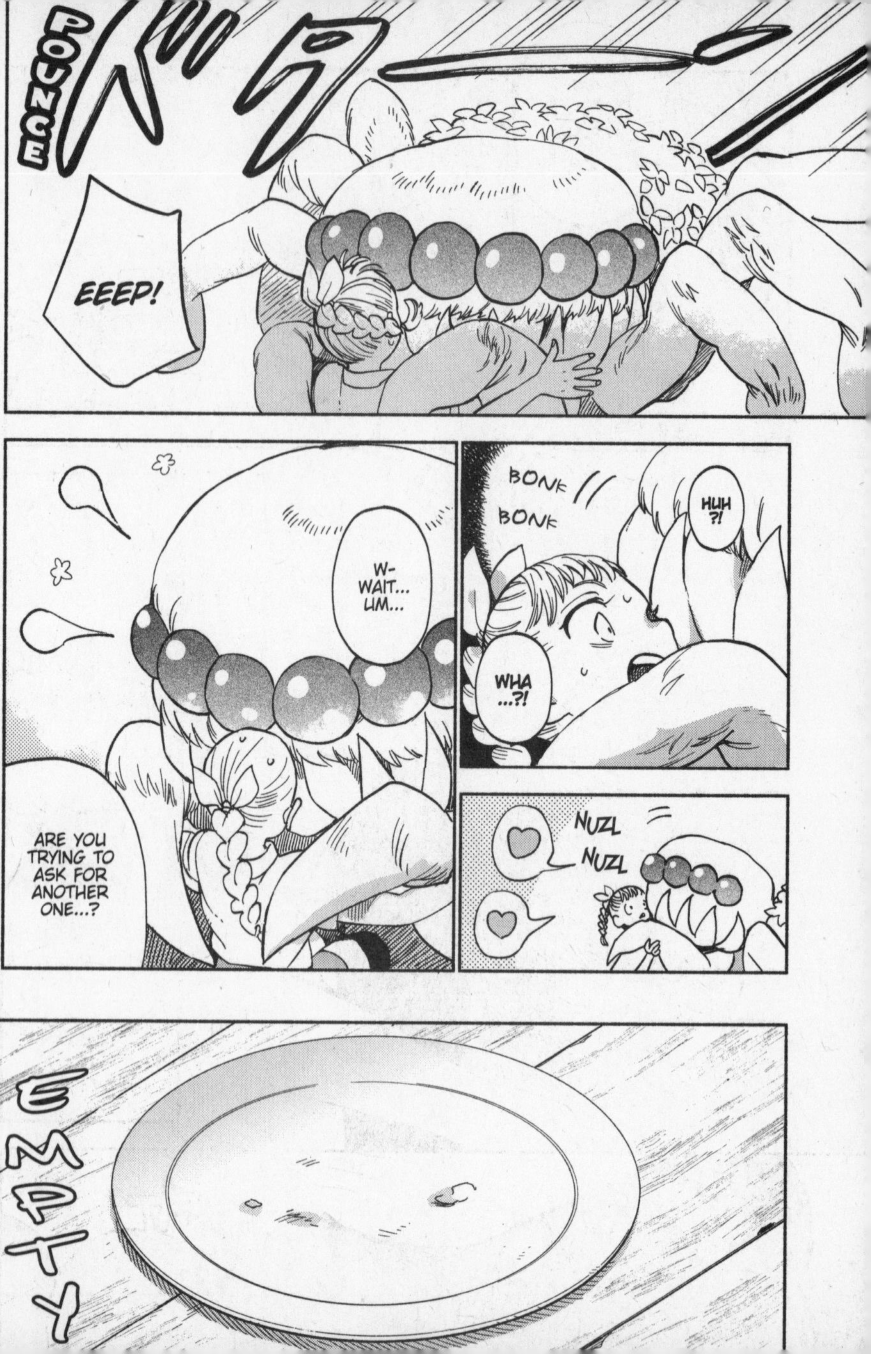
POUNCE
EEEP!
HUH ?!
BONK BONK
WHA ...?!
NUZL NUZL
W- WAIT... UM...
ARE YOU TRYING TO ASK FOR ANOTHER ONE...?
EMPTY

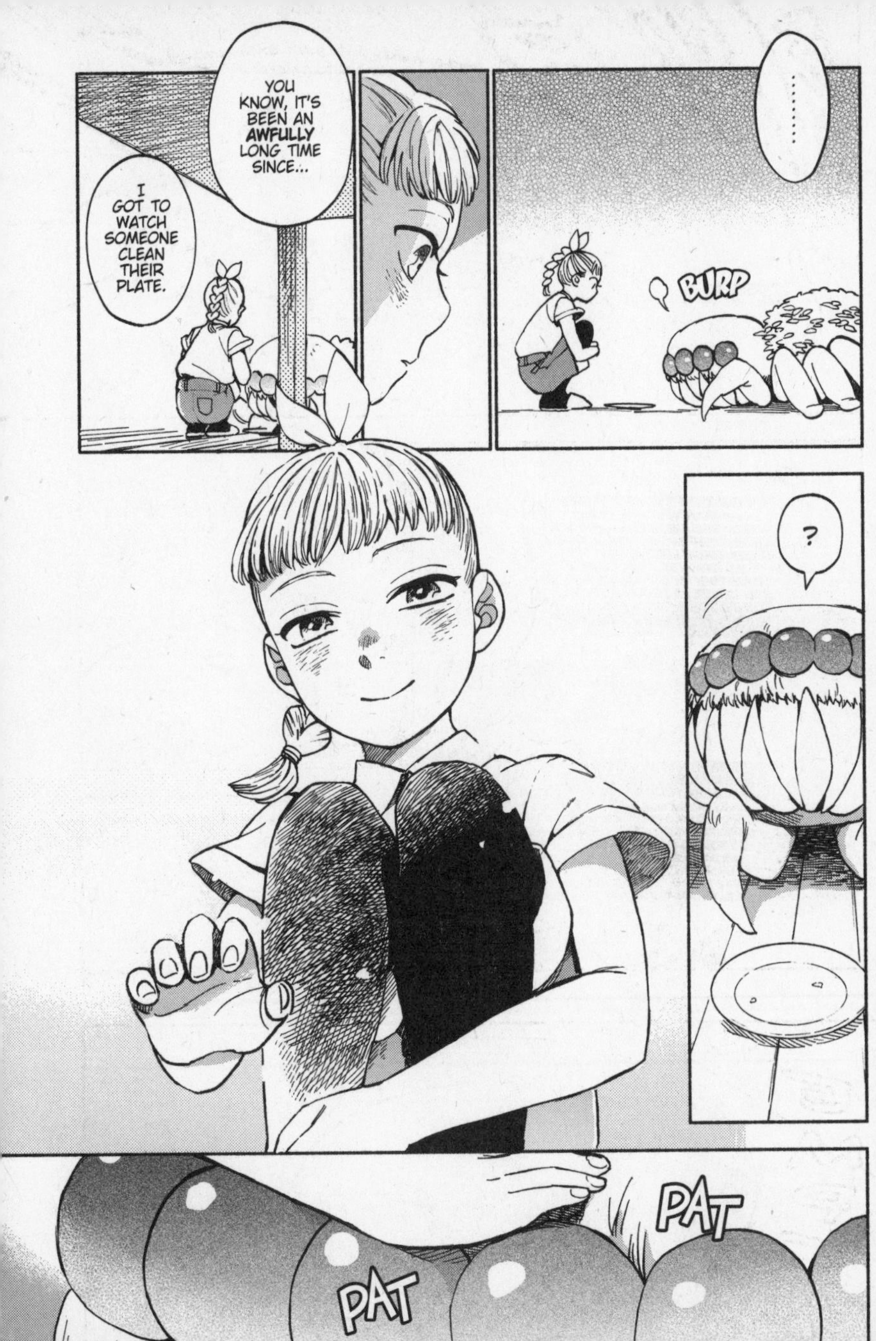
......
BURP
YOU KNOW, IT'S BEEN AN **AWFULLY** LONG TIME SINCE...
I GOT TO WATCH SOMEONE CLEAN THEIR PLATE.
?
PAT
PAT

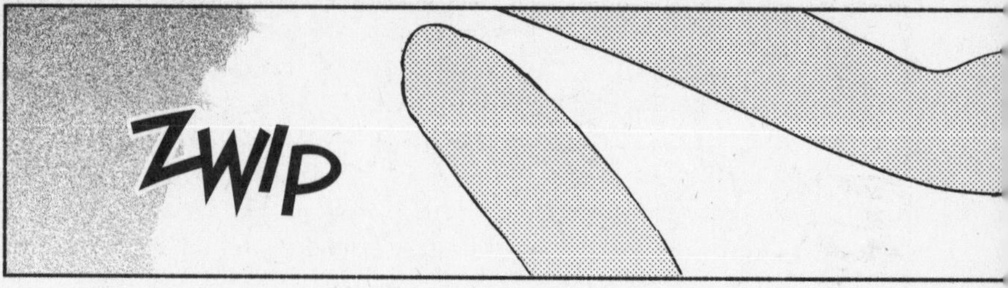
ZWIP
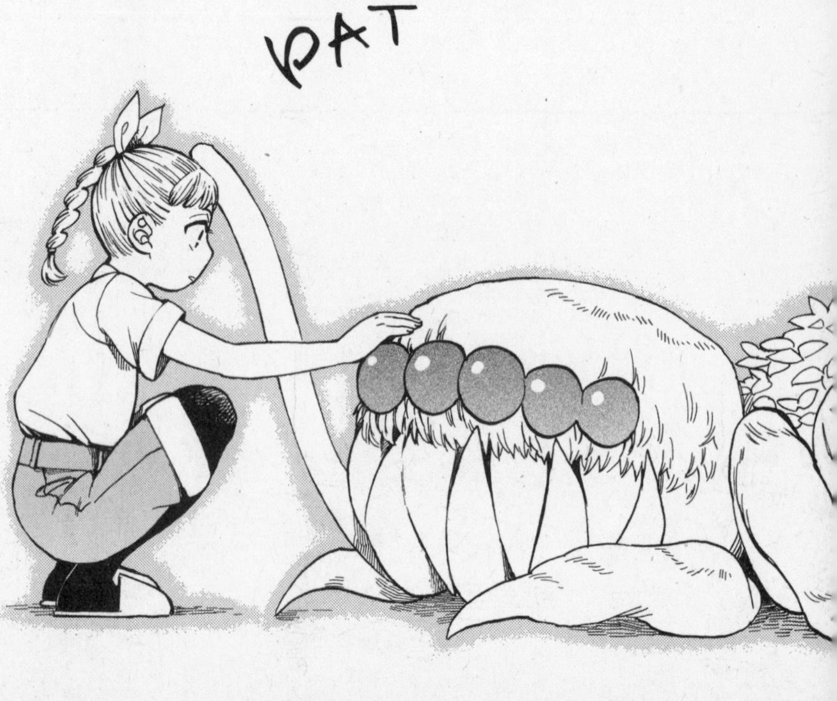
PAT

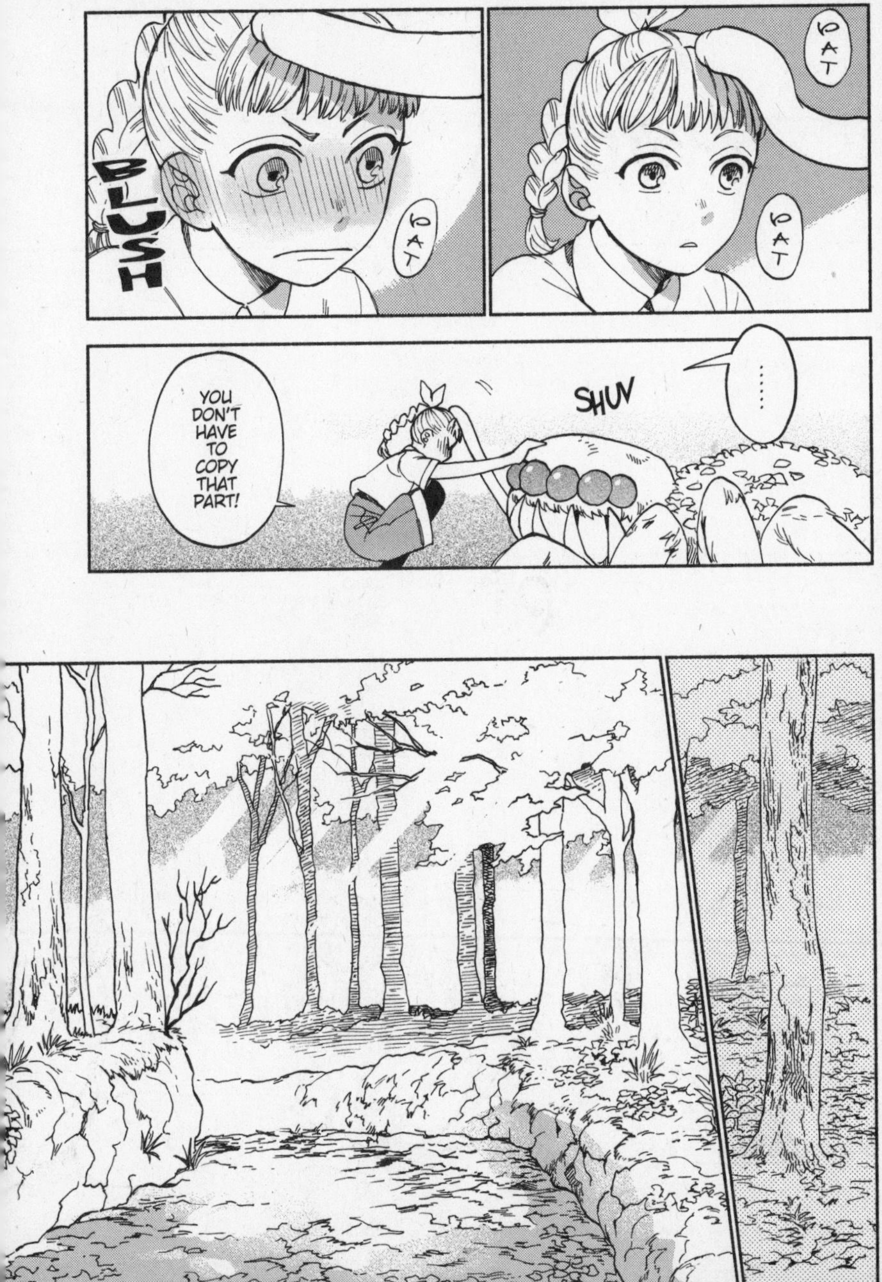
PAT
PAT
PAT
BLUSH
......
SHUV
YOU DON'T HAVE TO COPY THAT PART!

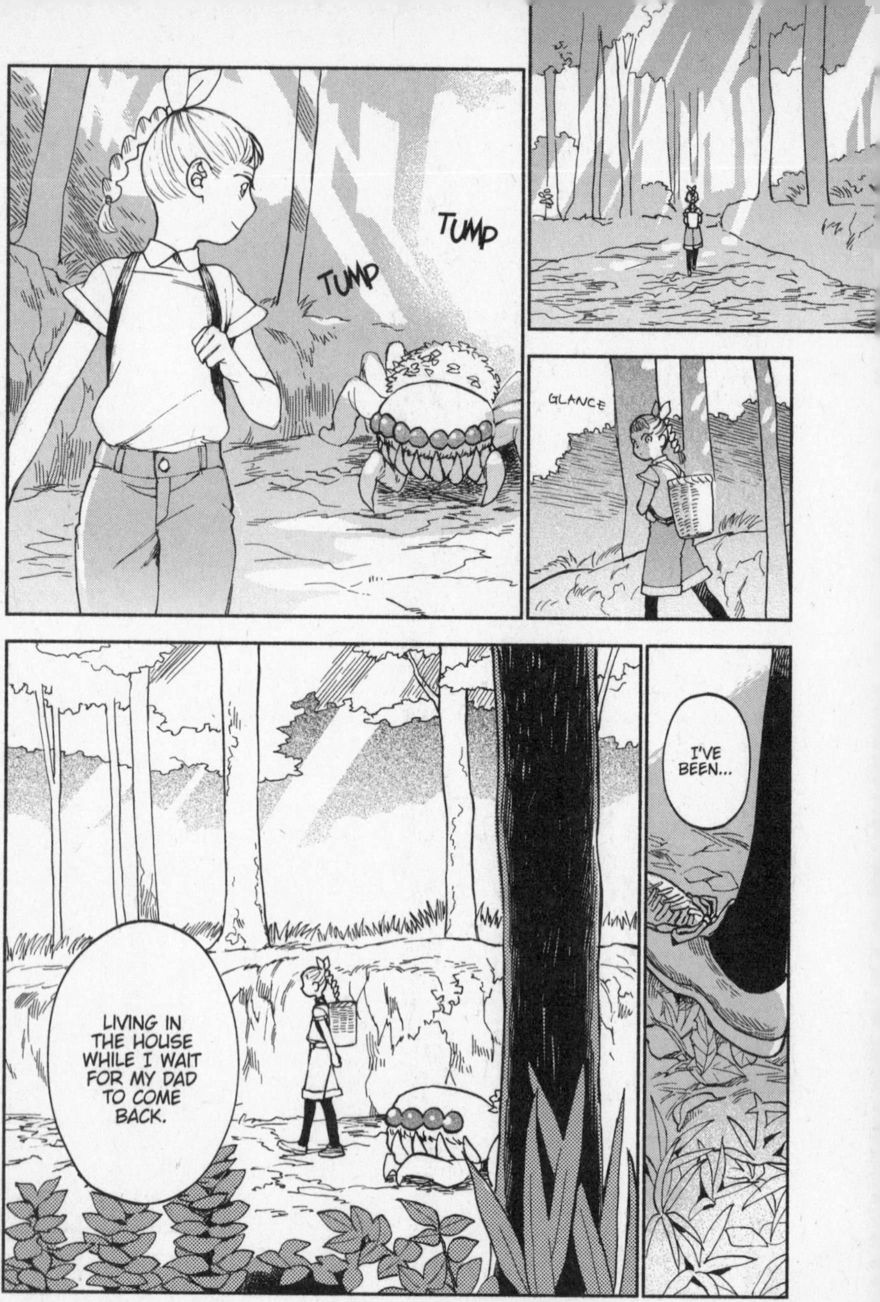
GLANCE
TUMP
TUMP
I'VE BEEN...
LIVING IN THE HOUSE WHILE I WAIT FOR MY DAD TO COME BACK.

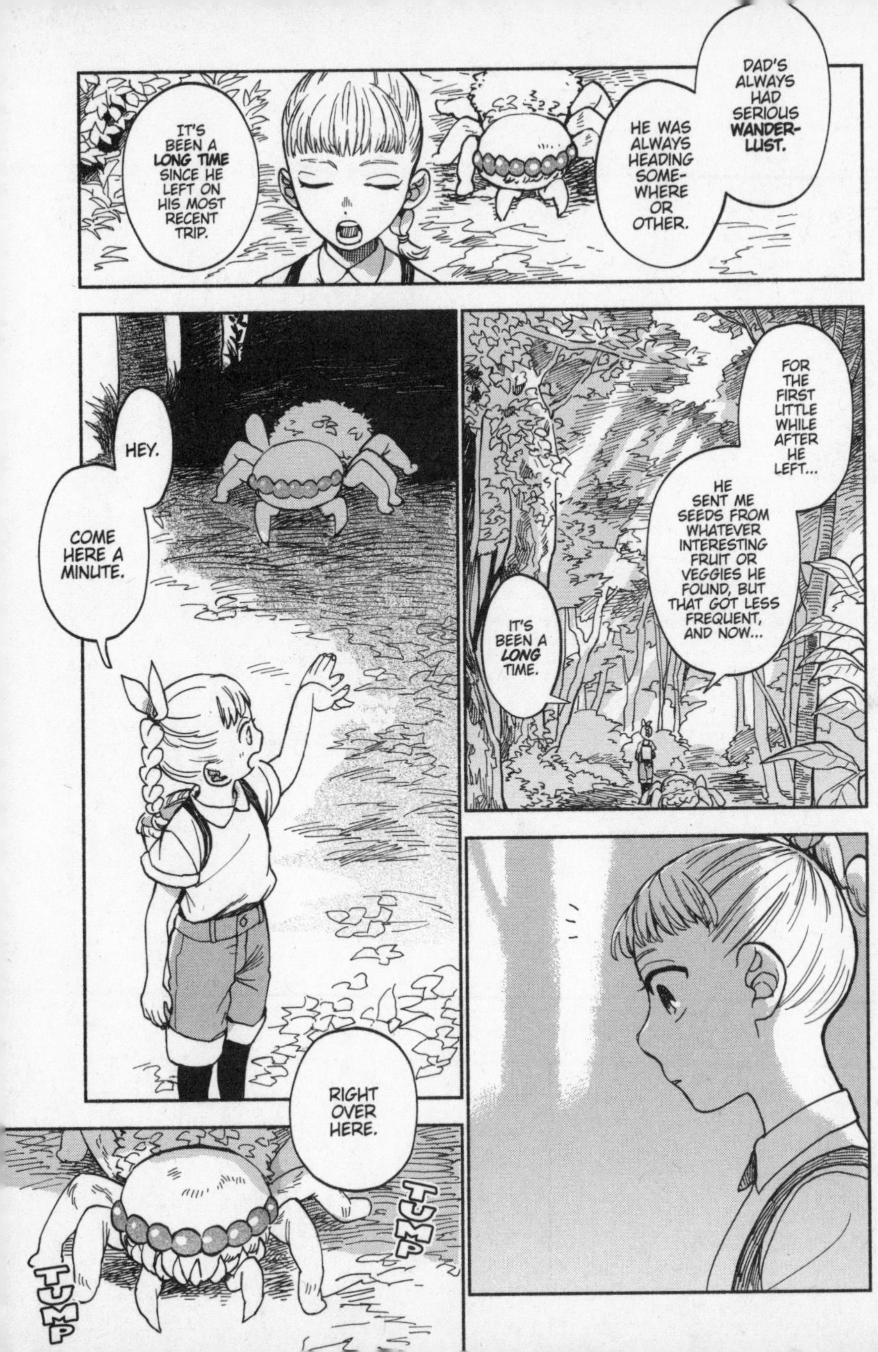
DAD'S ALWAYS HAD SERIOUS WANDER-LUST.
HE WAS ALWAYS HEADING SOME-WHERE OR OTHER.
IT'S BEEN A LONG TIME SINCE HE LEFT ON HIS MOST RECENT TRIP.
FOR THE FIRST LITTLE WHILE AFTER HE LEFT...
HE SENT ME SEEDS FROM WHATEVER INTERESTING FRUIT OR VEGGIES HE FOUND, BUT THAT GOT LESS FREQUENT, AND NOW...
IT'S BEEN A LONG TIME.
HEY.
COME HERE A MINUTE.
RIGHT OVER HERE.
TUMP
TUMP

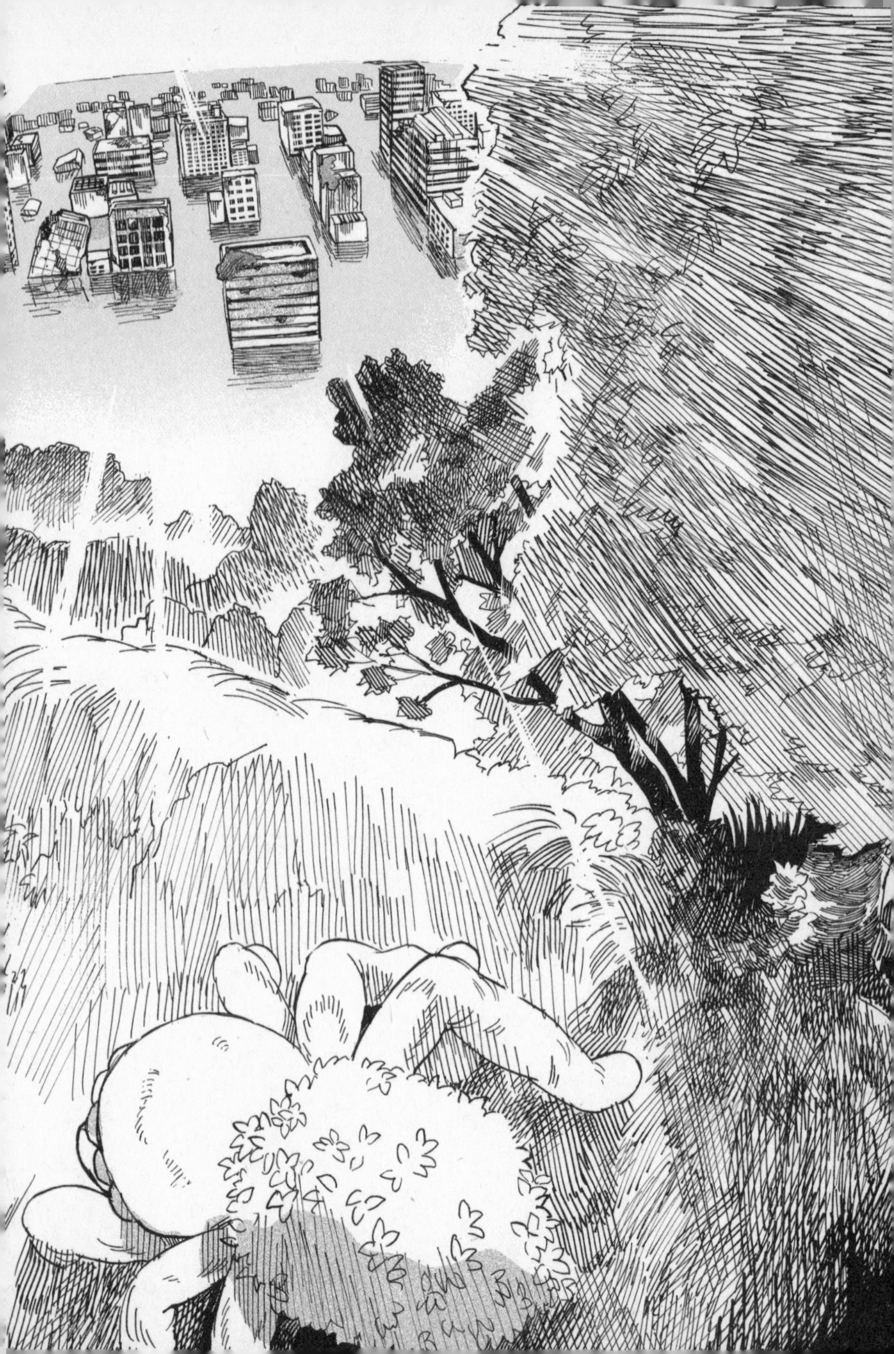

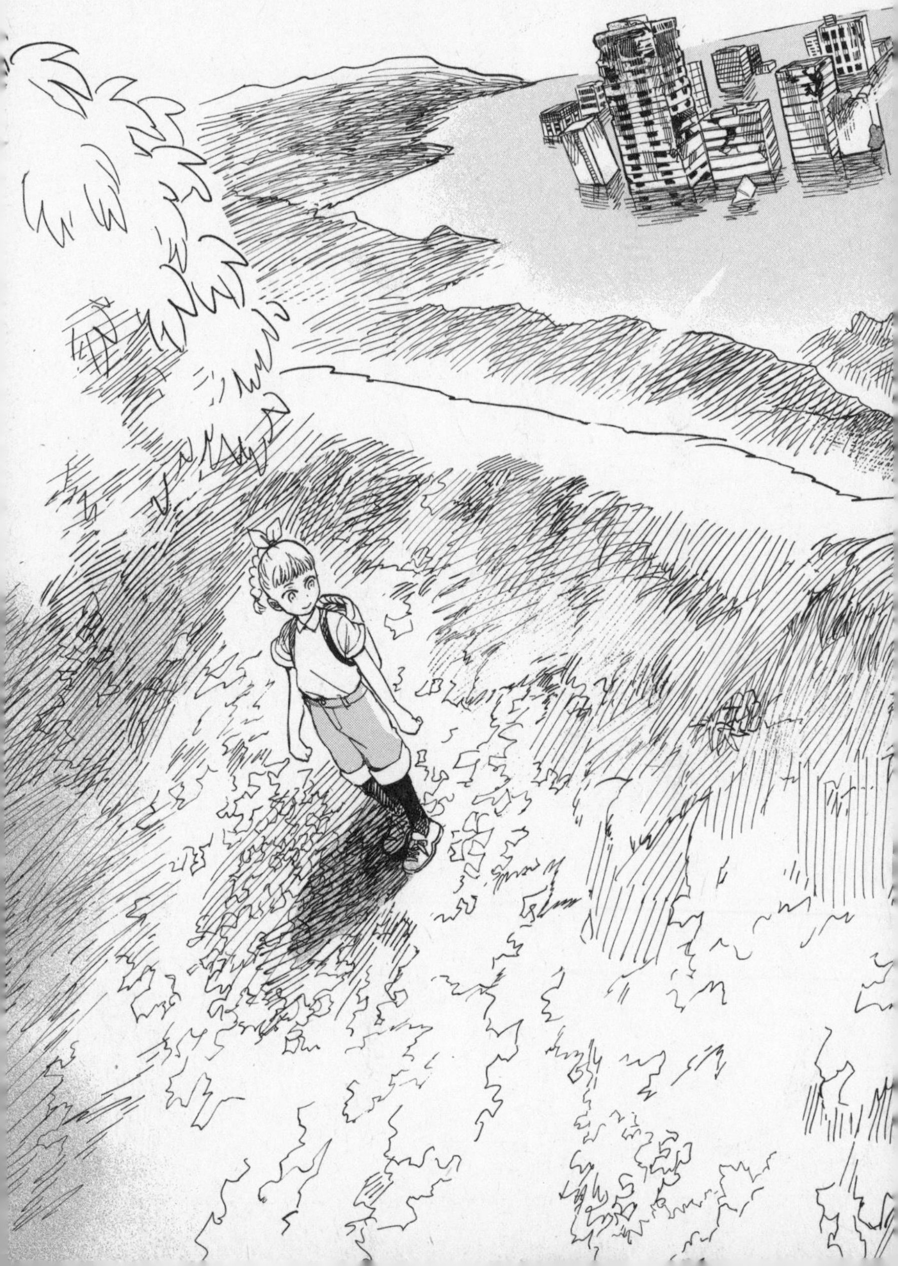

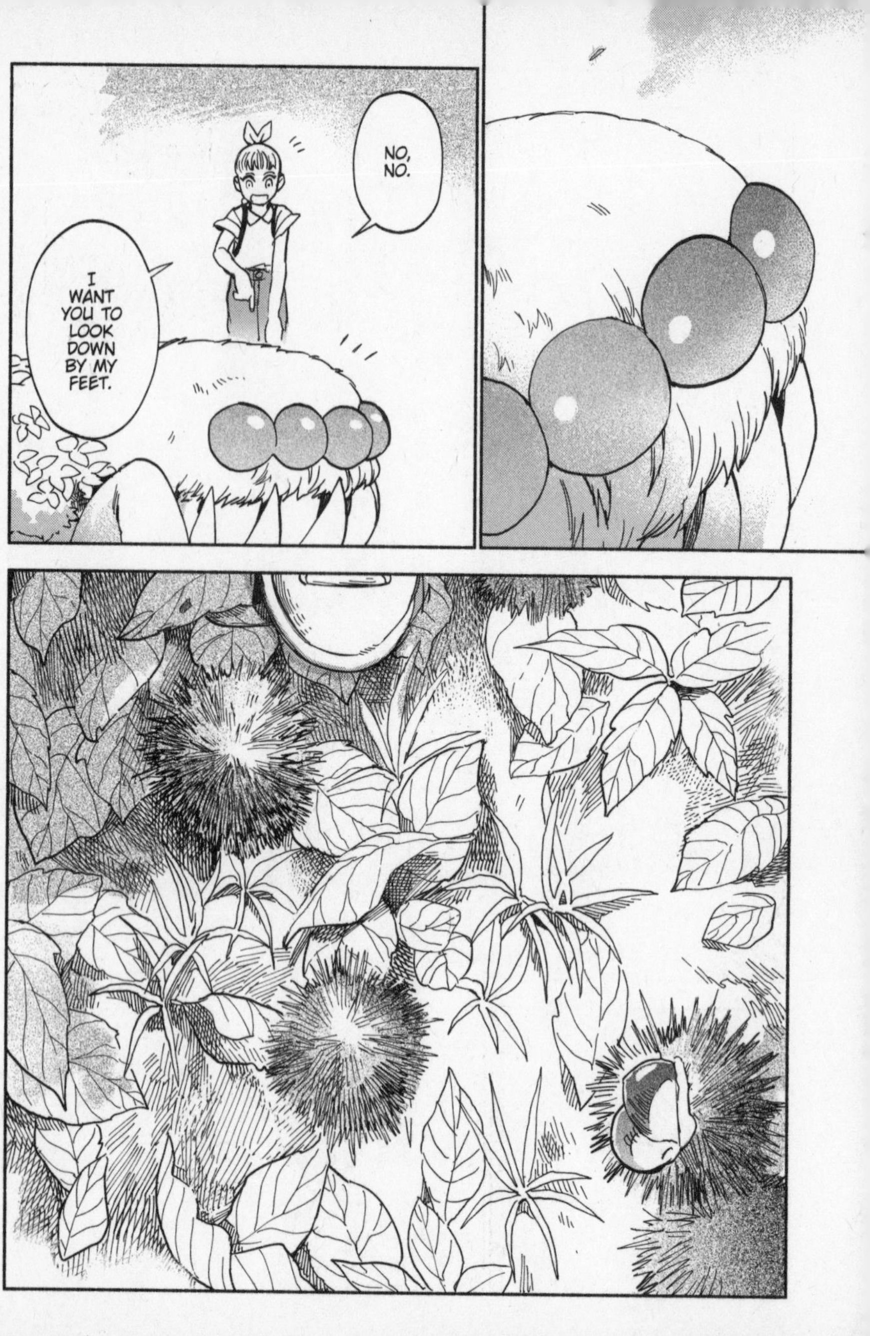
NO, NO.
I WANT YOU TO LOOK DOWN BY MY FEET.

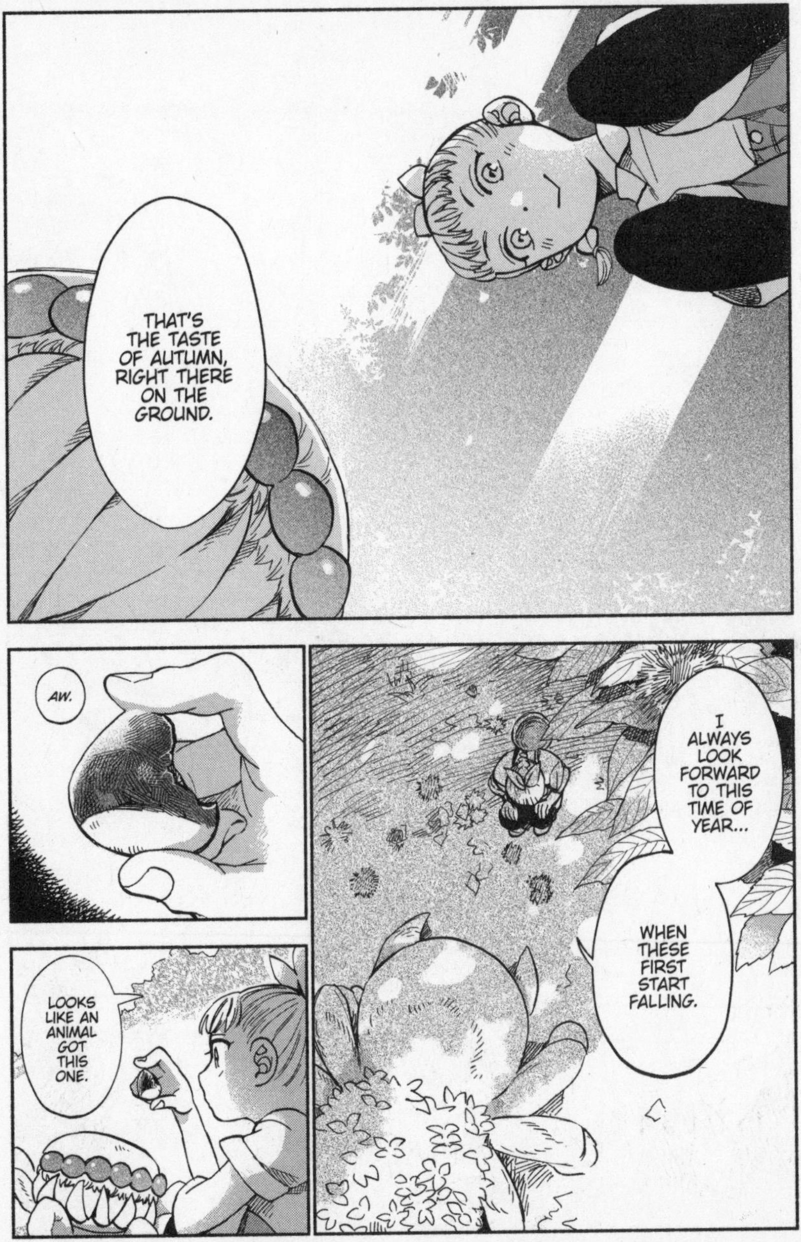
THAT'S THE TASTE OF AUTUMN, RIGHT THERE ON THE GROUND.
I ALWAYS LOOK FORWARD TO THIS TIME OF YEAR...
WHEN THESE FIRST START FALLING.
AW.
LOOKS LIKE AN ANIMAL GOT THIS ONE.

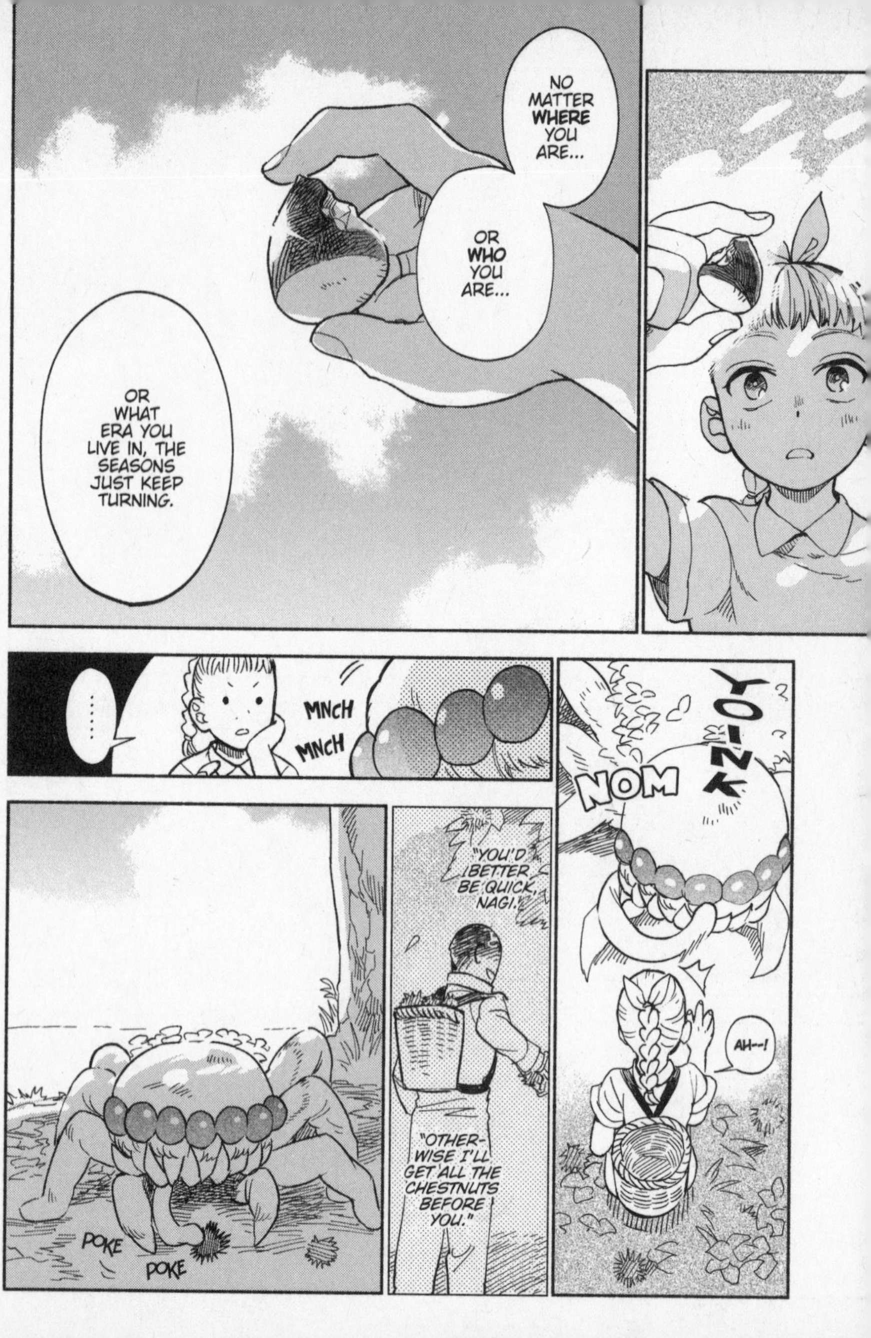
NO MATTER WHERE YOU ARE...
OR WHO YOU ARE...
OR WHAT ERA YOU LIVE IN, THE SEASONS JUST KEEP TURNING.
YOINK
NOM
AH--!
......
MNCH
MNCH
"YOU'D BETTER BE QUICK, NAGI."
"OTHER-WISE I'LL GET ALL THE CHESTNUTS BEFORE YOU."
POKE
POKE

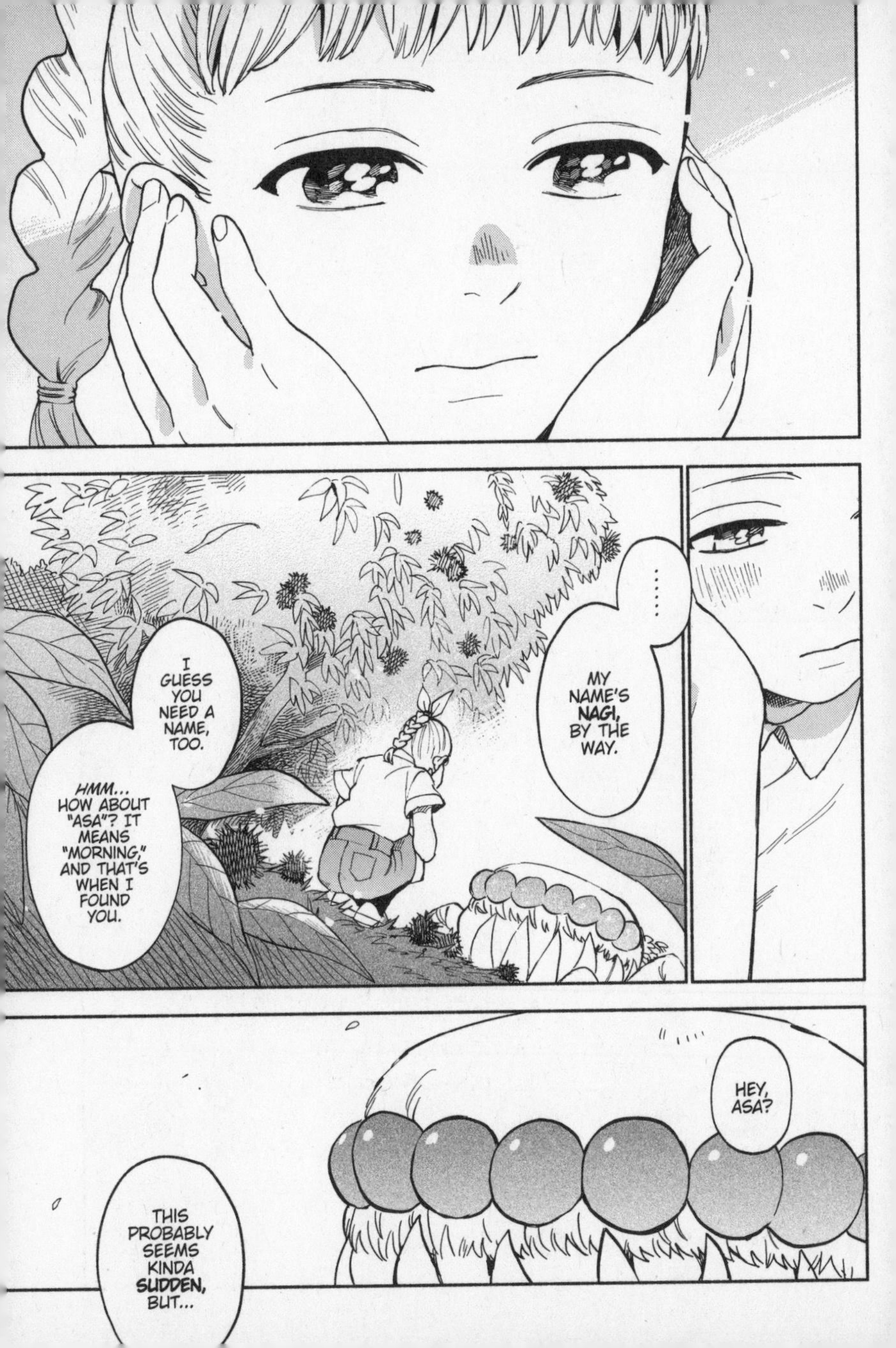
......
MY NAME'S **NAGI,** BY THE WAY.
I GUESS YOU NEED A NAME, TOO.
HMM... HOW ABOUT "ASA"? IT MEANS "MORNING," AND THAT'S WHEN I FOUND YOU.
HEY, ASA?
THIS PROBABLY SEEMS KINDA **SUDDEN,** BUT...

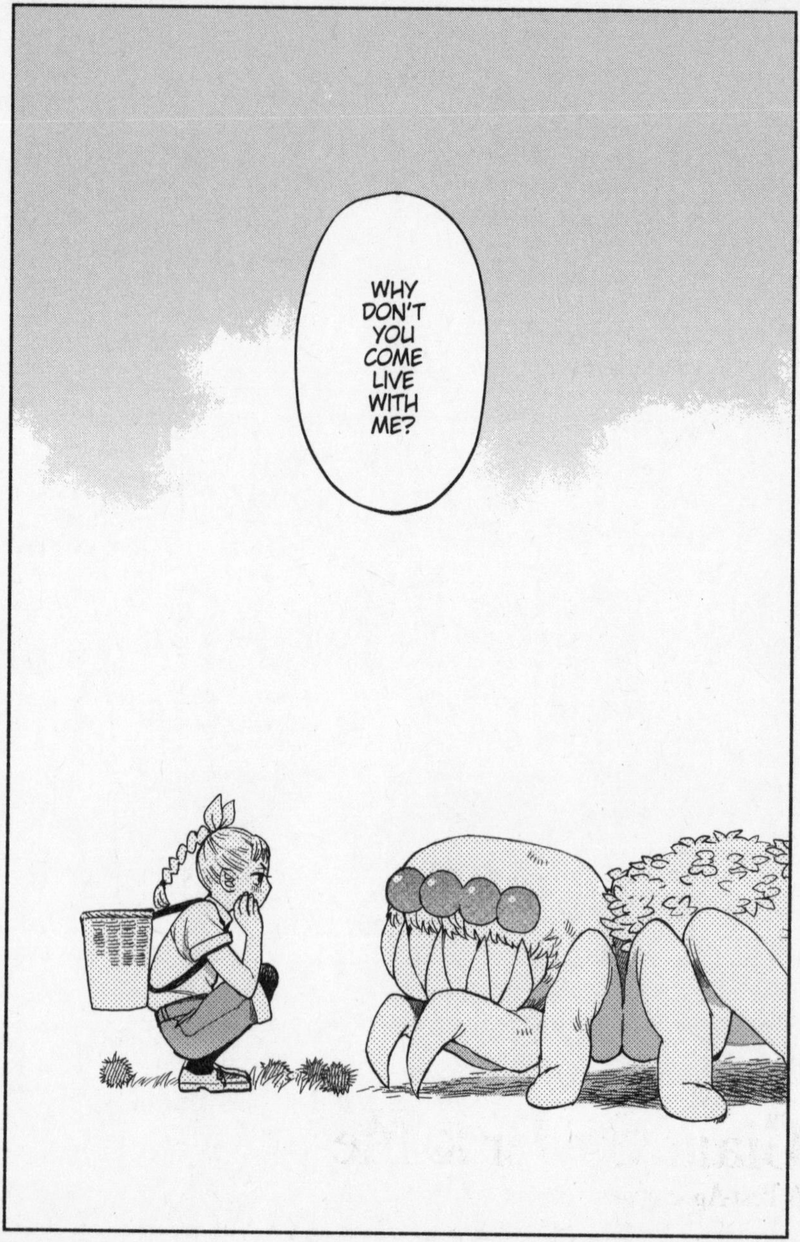
WHY DON'T YOU COME LIVE WITH ME?

Giant Spider & Me
A Post-Apocalyptic Tale

Giant Spider & Me
A Post-Apocalyptic Tale

Chapter 2: Running Errands & a Twist on Ratatouille

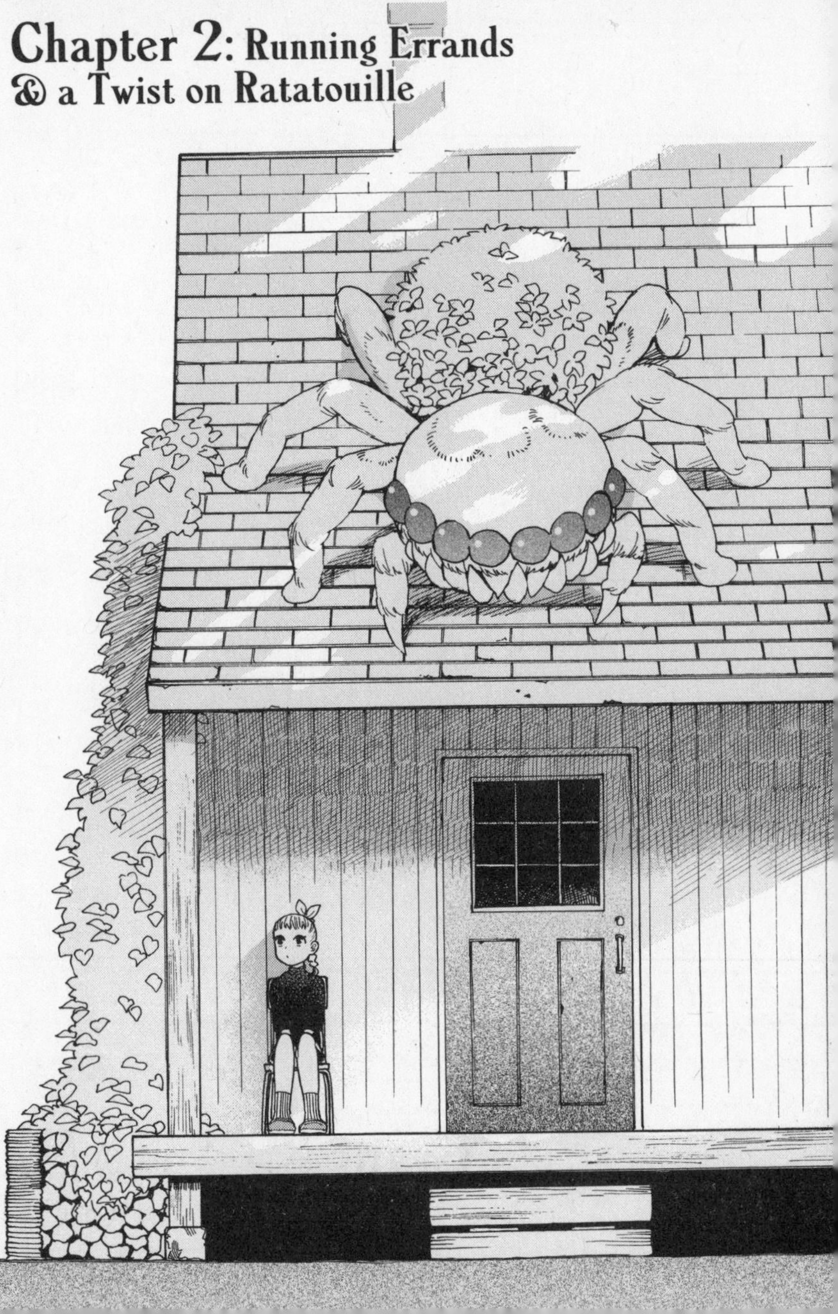

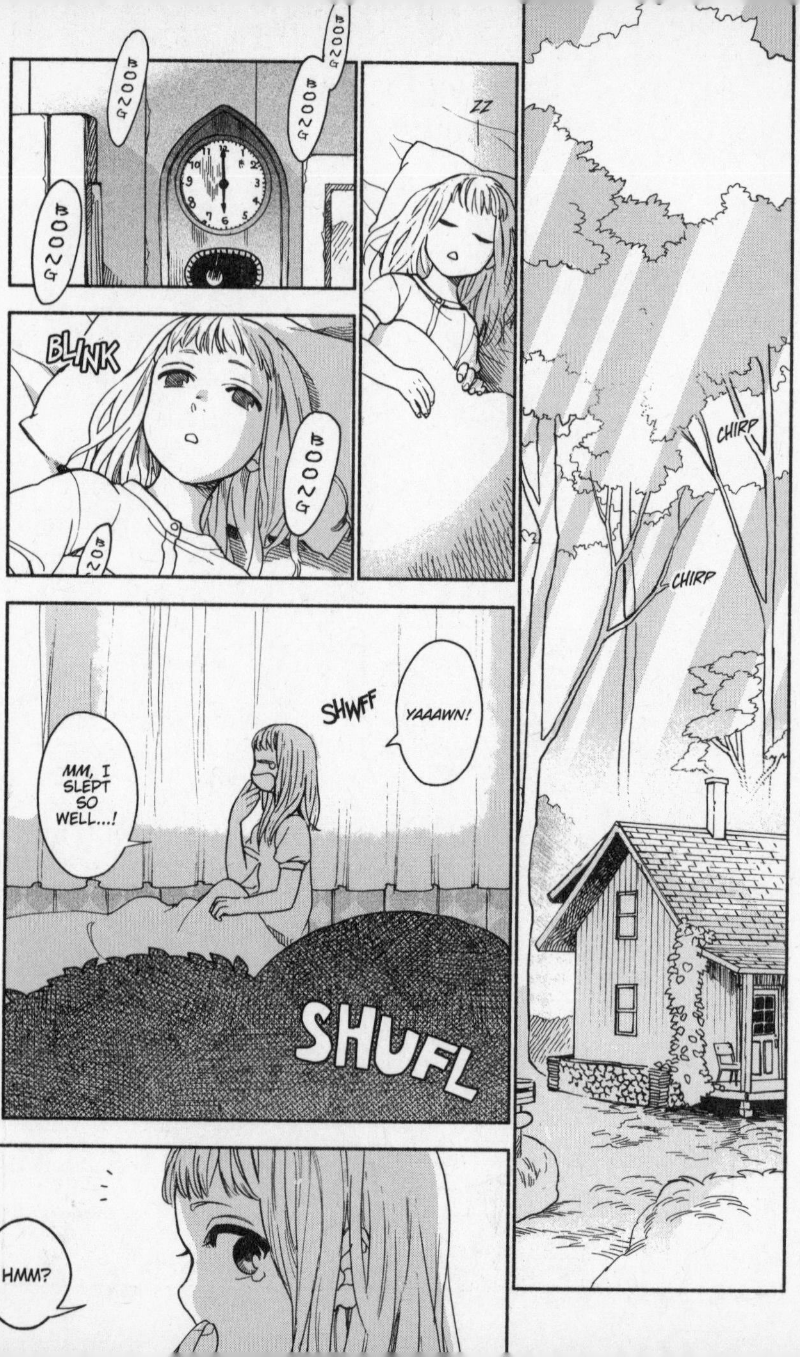

CHIRP
CHIRP
ZZ
BOONG
BOONG
BOONG
BOONG
BLINK
BOONG
YAAAWN!
SHWFF
MM, I SLEPT SO WELL...!
SHUFL
HMM?

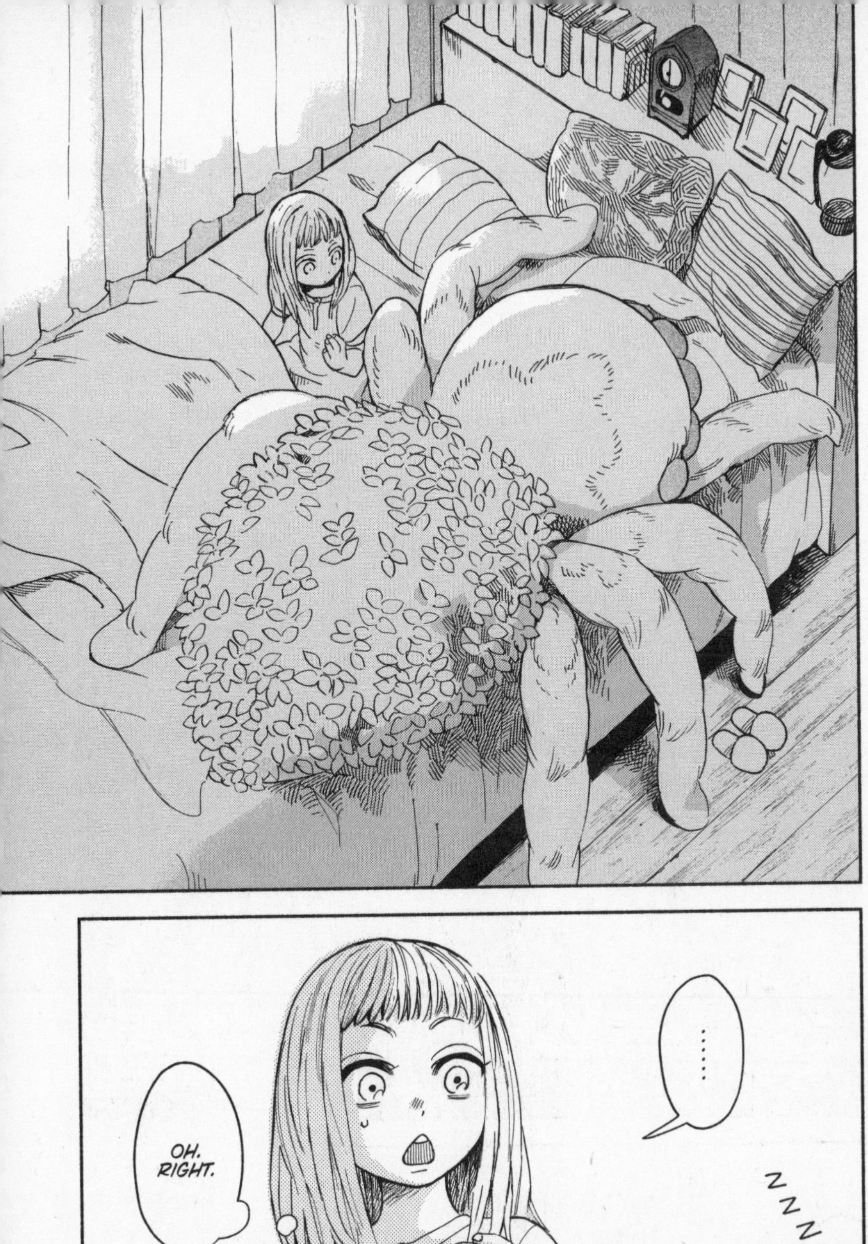
......
NNNNN
OH. RIGHT.

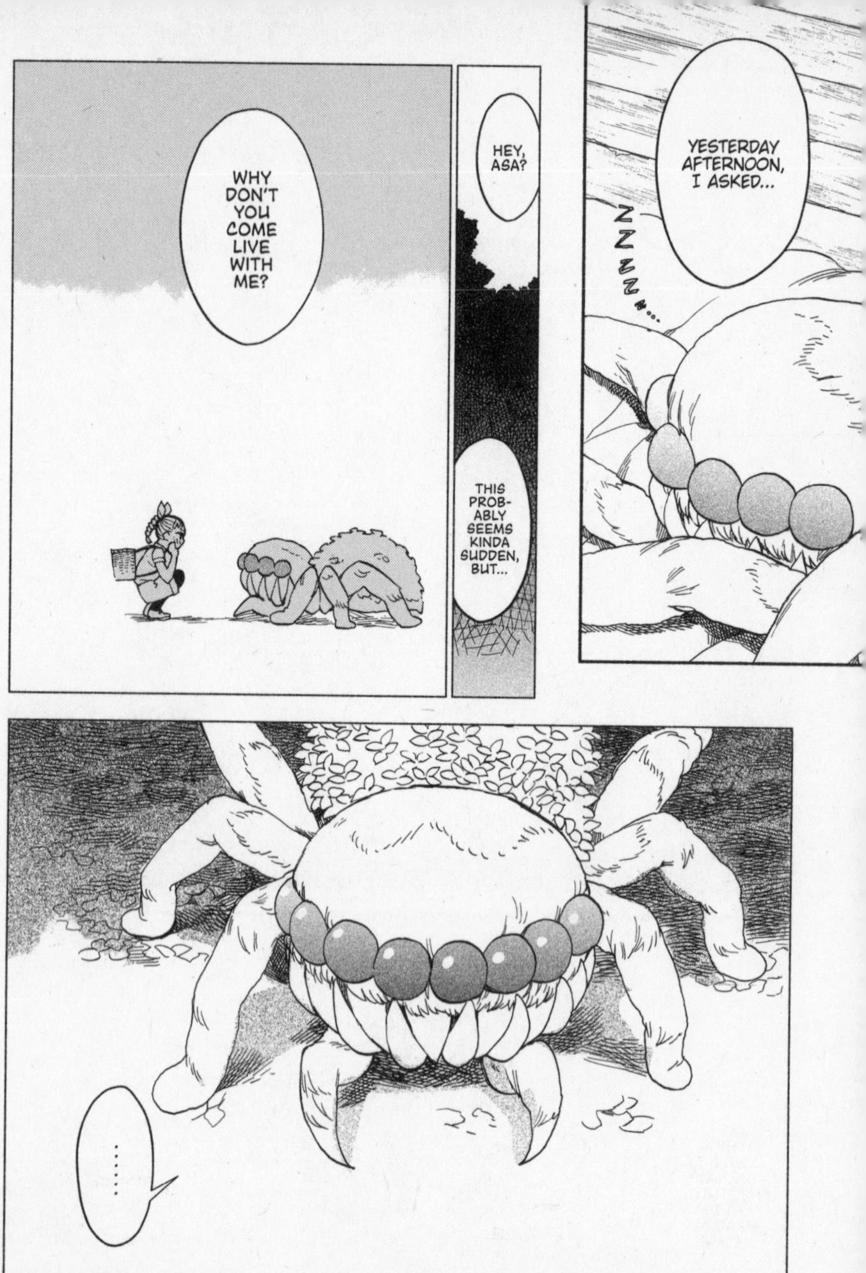
YESTERDAY AFTERNOON, I ASKED...
ZZZZZ...
HEY, ASA?
THIS PROBABLY SEEMS KINDA SUDDEN, BUT...
WHY DON'T YOU COME LIVE WITH ME?
......

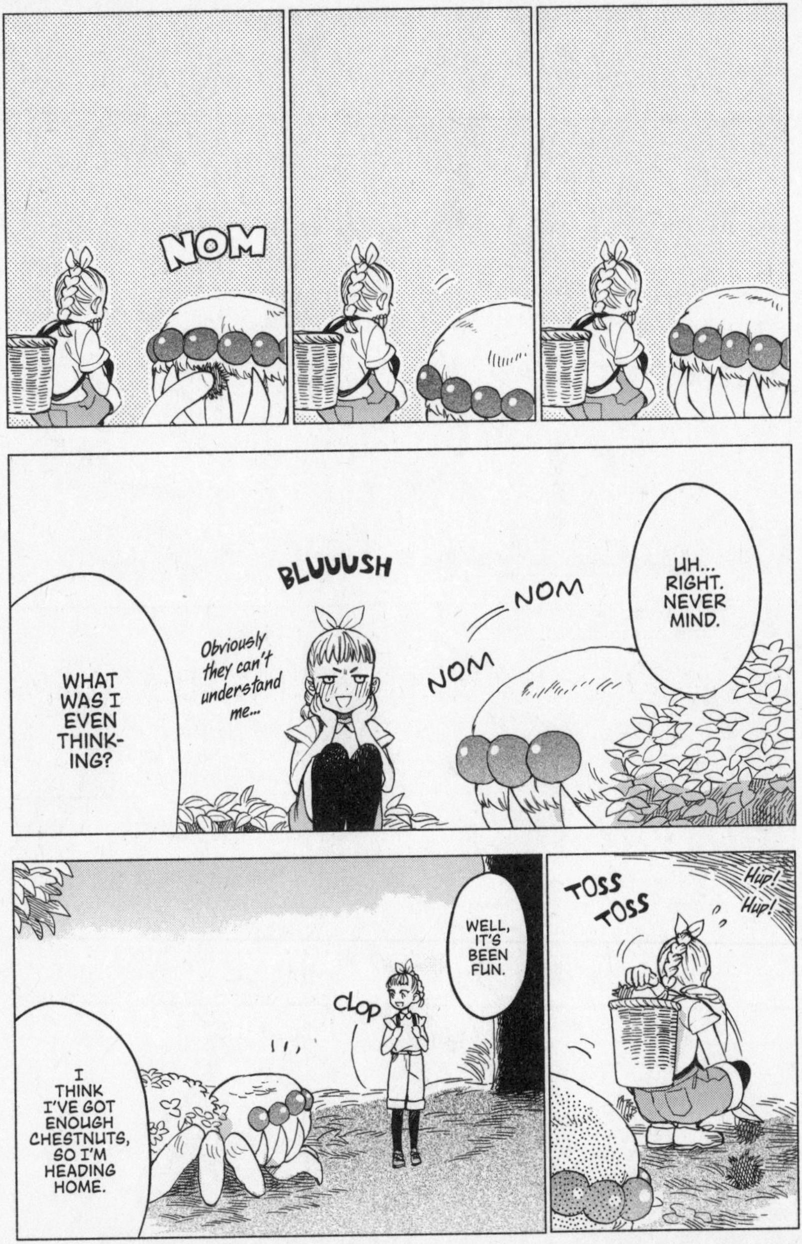
NOM
UH... RIGHT. NEVER MIND.
NOM
NOM
BLUUUSH
Obviously they can't understand me...
WHAT WAS I EVEN THINKING?
Hup!
Hup!
TOSS
TOSS
WELL, IT'S BEEN FUN.
CLOP
I THINK I'VE GOT ENOUGH CHESTNUTS, SO I'M HEADING HOME.

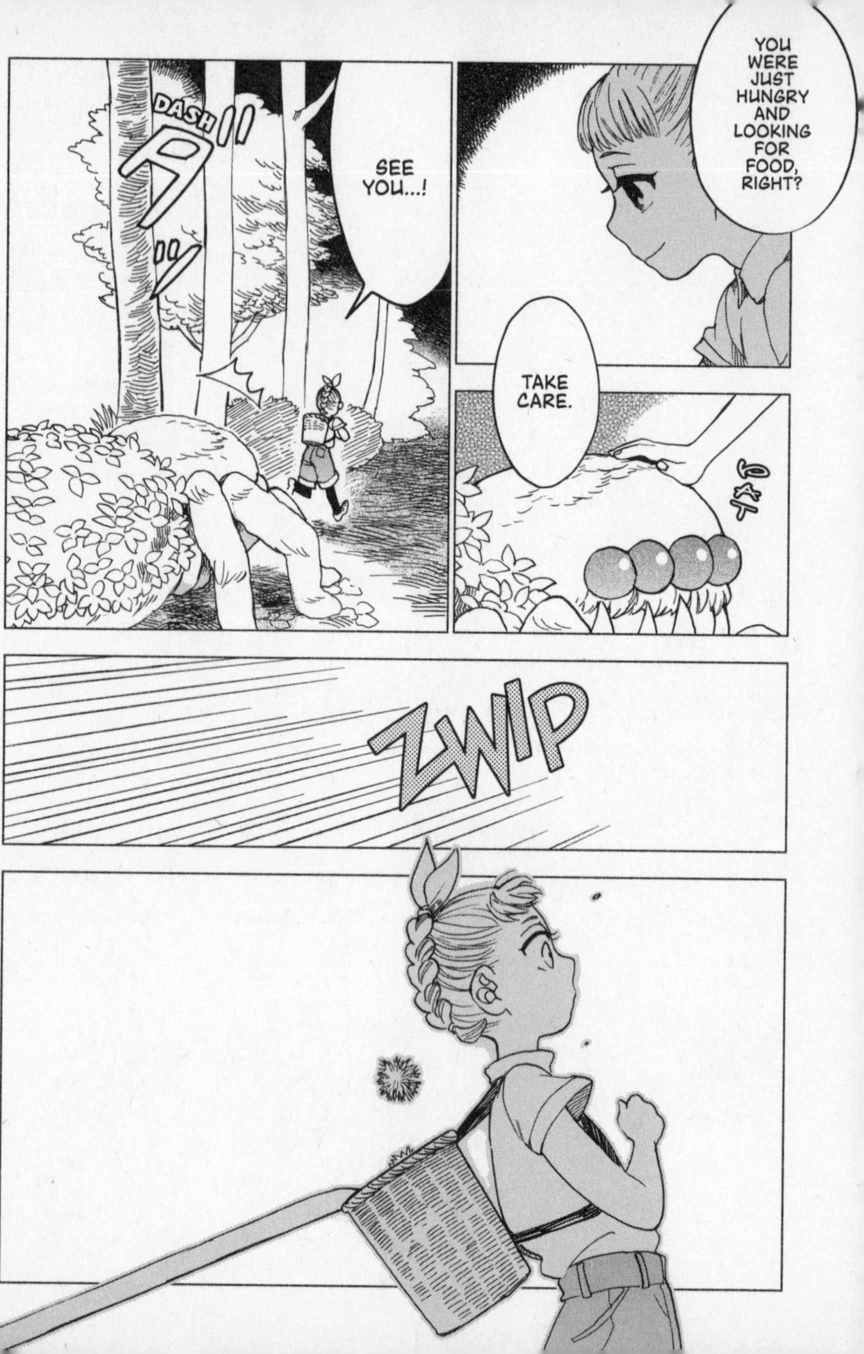
YOU WERE JUST HUNGRY AND LOOKING FOR FOOD, RIGHT?
TAKE CARE.
PAT
SEE YOU...!
DASH
ZWIP

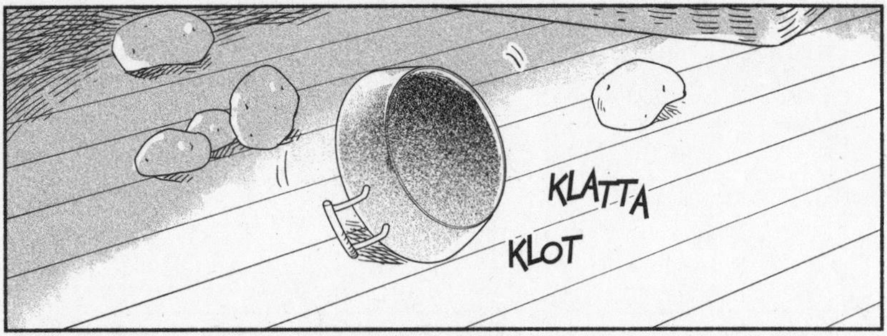
KLATTA
KLOT

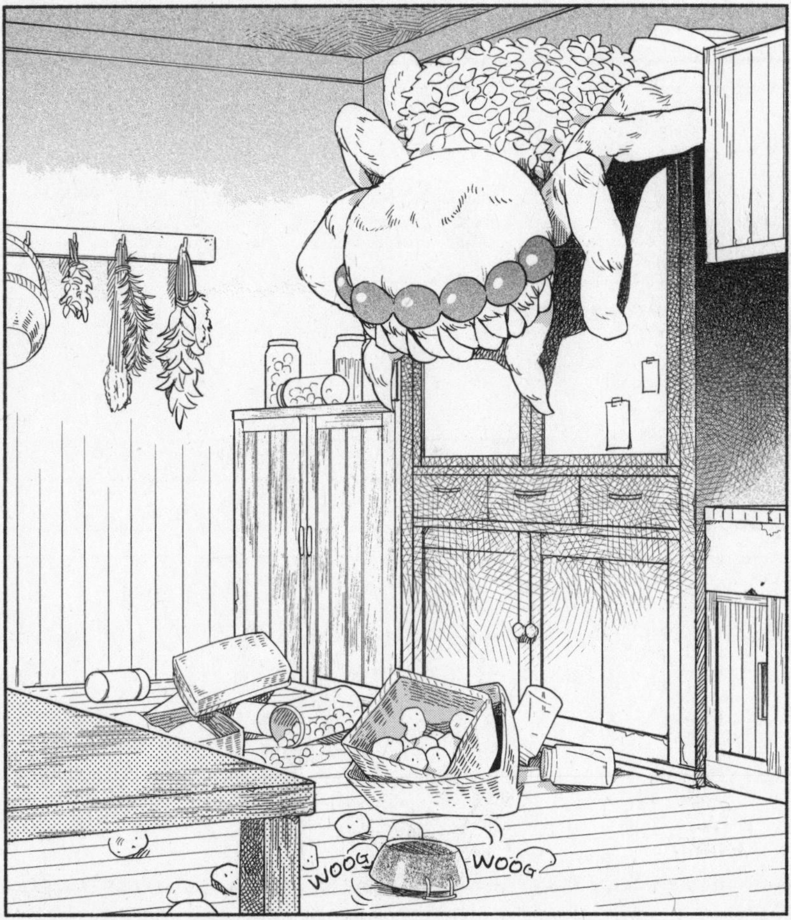
WOOG
WOOG

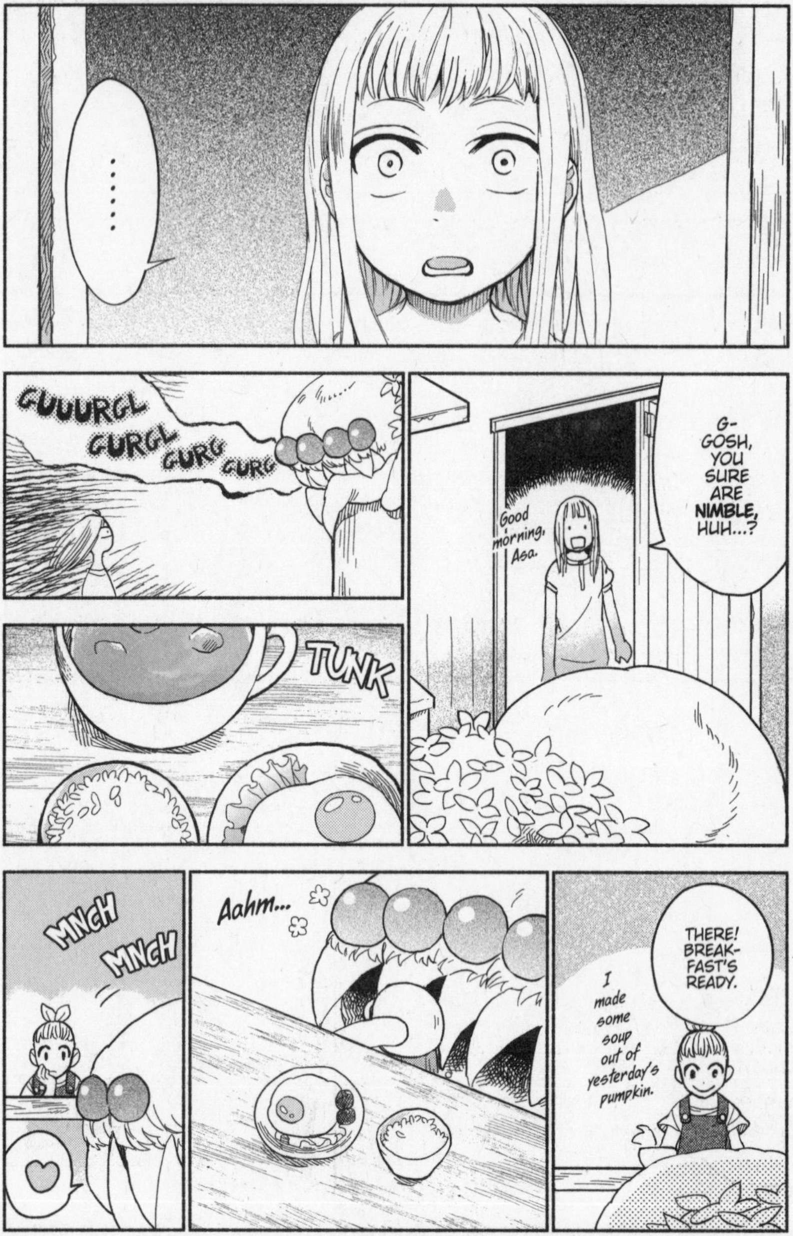
......
G-GOSH, YOU SURE ARE NIMBLE, HUH...?
Good morning, Asa.
GUUURGL GURGL GURG GURG
TUNK
THERE! BREAK-FAST'S READY.
I made some soup out of yesterday's pumpkin.
Aahm...
MNCH MNCH

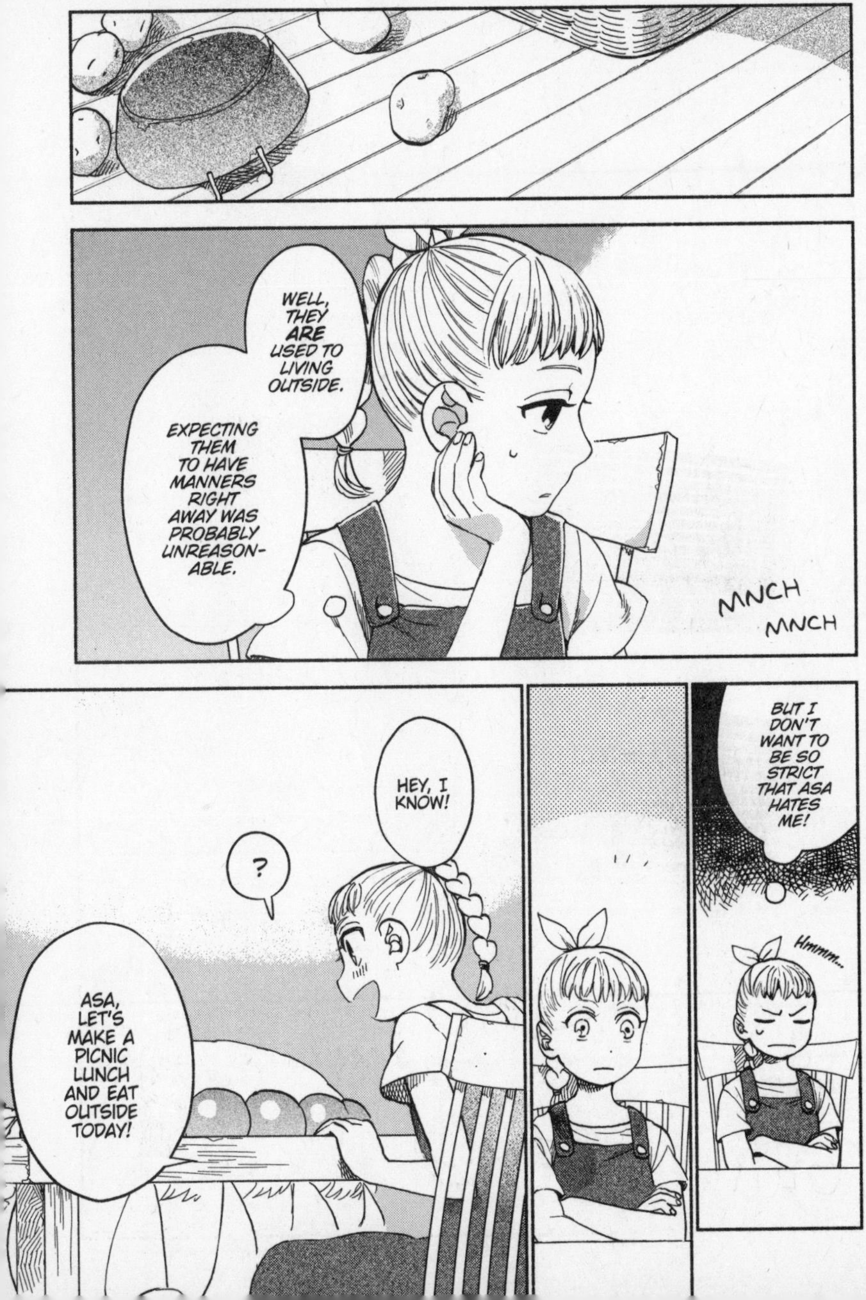

WELL, THEY ARE USED TO LIVING OUTSIDE.
EXPECTING THEM TO HAVE MANNERS RIGHT AWAY WAS PROBABLY UNREASON-ABLE.
MNCH
MNCH
Hmmm..
BUT I DON'T WANT TO BE SO STRICT THAT ASA HATES ME!
HEY, I KNOW!
?
ASA, LET'S MAKE A PICNIC LUNCH AND EAT OUTSIDE TODAY!

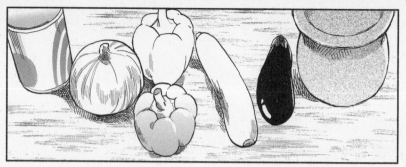

OKAY!

THIS IS IT FOR THE SUMMER VEGGIES, SO WE'LL GO OUT WITH A **BANG** AND USE THEM ALL UP!

Yeah!

CHOP

CHOP

CHOP

CHOP

CHOP

CHOP

FIRST, LET'S MINCE HALF AN ONION AND A CLOVE OF GARLIC.

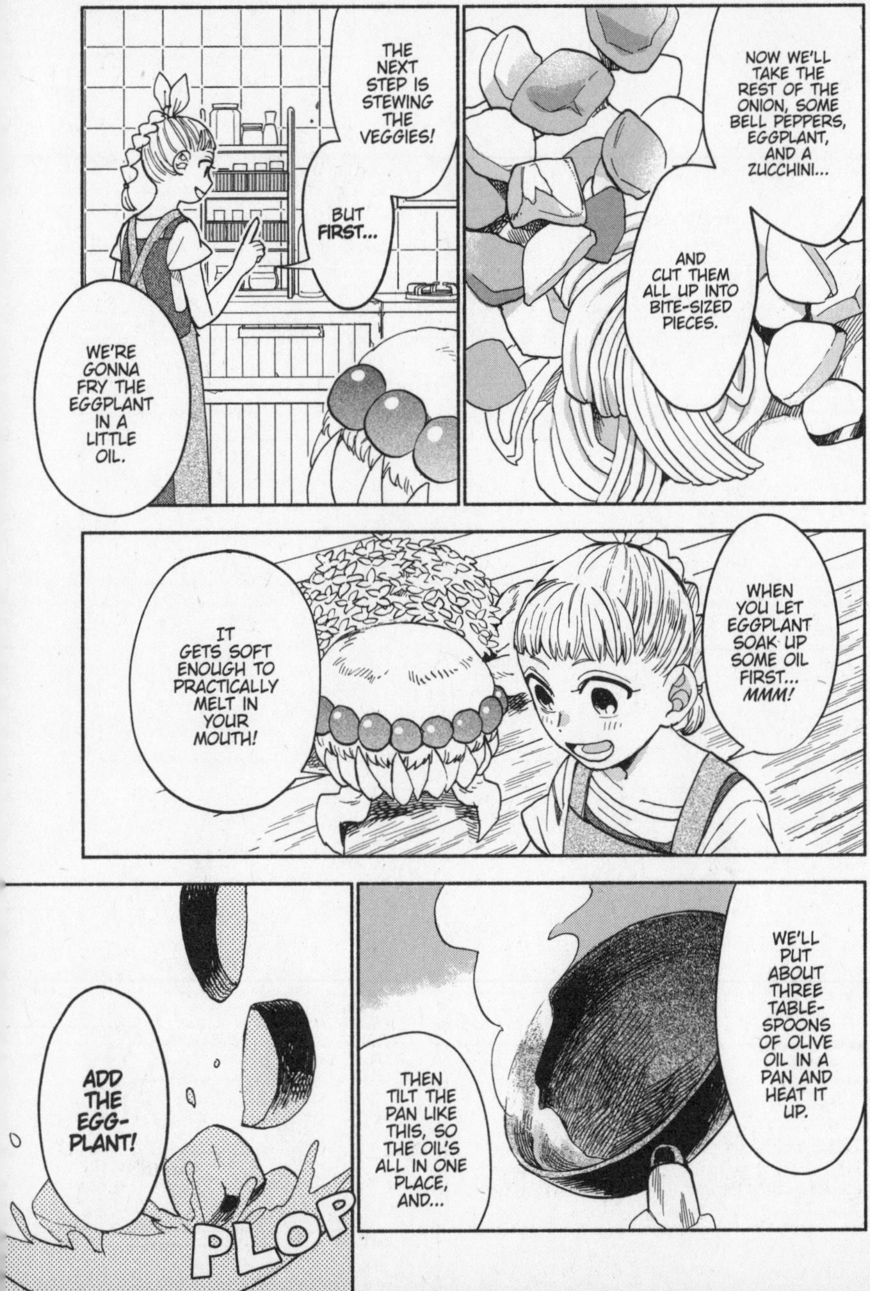
NOW WE'LL TAKE THE REST OF THE ONION, SOME BELL PEPPERS, EGGPLANT, AND A ZUCCHINI...
AND CUT THEM ALL UP INTO BITE-SIZED PIECES.
THE NEXT STEP IS STEWING THE VEGGIES!
BUT **FIRST...**
WE'RE GONNA FRY THE EGGPLANT IN A LITTLE OIL.
WHEN YOU LET EGGPLANT SOAK UP SOME OIL FIRST... *MMM!*
IT GETS SOFT ENOUGH TO PRACTICALLY MELT IN YOUR MOUTH!
WE'LL PUT ABOUT THREE TABLE-SPOONS OF OLIVE OIL IN A PAN AND HEAT IT UP.
THEN TILT THE PAN LIKE THIS, SO THE OIL'S ALL IN ONE PLACE, AND...
ADD THE EGG-PLANT!
PLOP

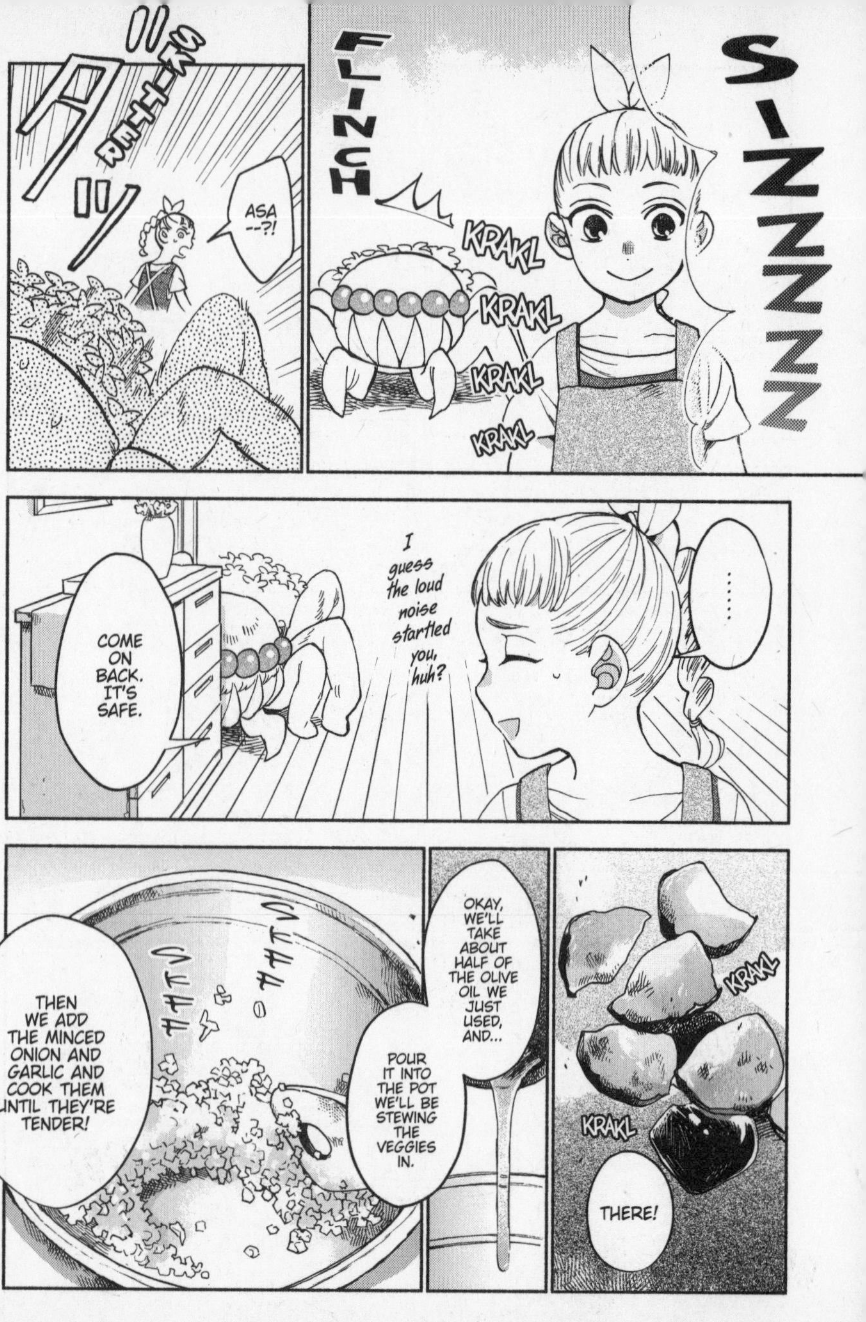
SIZZZZZ
FLINCH
KRAKL
KRAKL
KRAKL
KRAKL
SKITTER
ASA --?!
......
I guess the loud noise startled you, huh?
COME ON BACK. IT'S SAFE.
KRAKL
KRAKL
THERE!
OKAY, WE'LL TAKE ABOUT HALF OF THE OLIVE OIL WE JUST USED, AND...
POUR IT INTO THE POT WE'LL BE STEWING THE VEGGIES IN.
SFFF
SFFF
THEN WE ADD THE MINCED ONION AND GARLIC AND COOK THEM UNTIL THEY'RE TENDER!

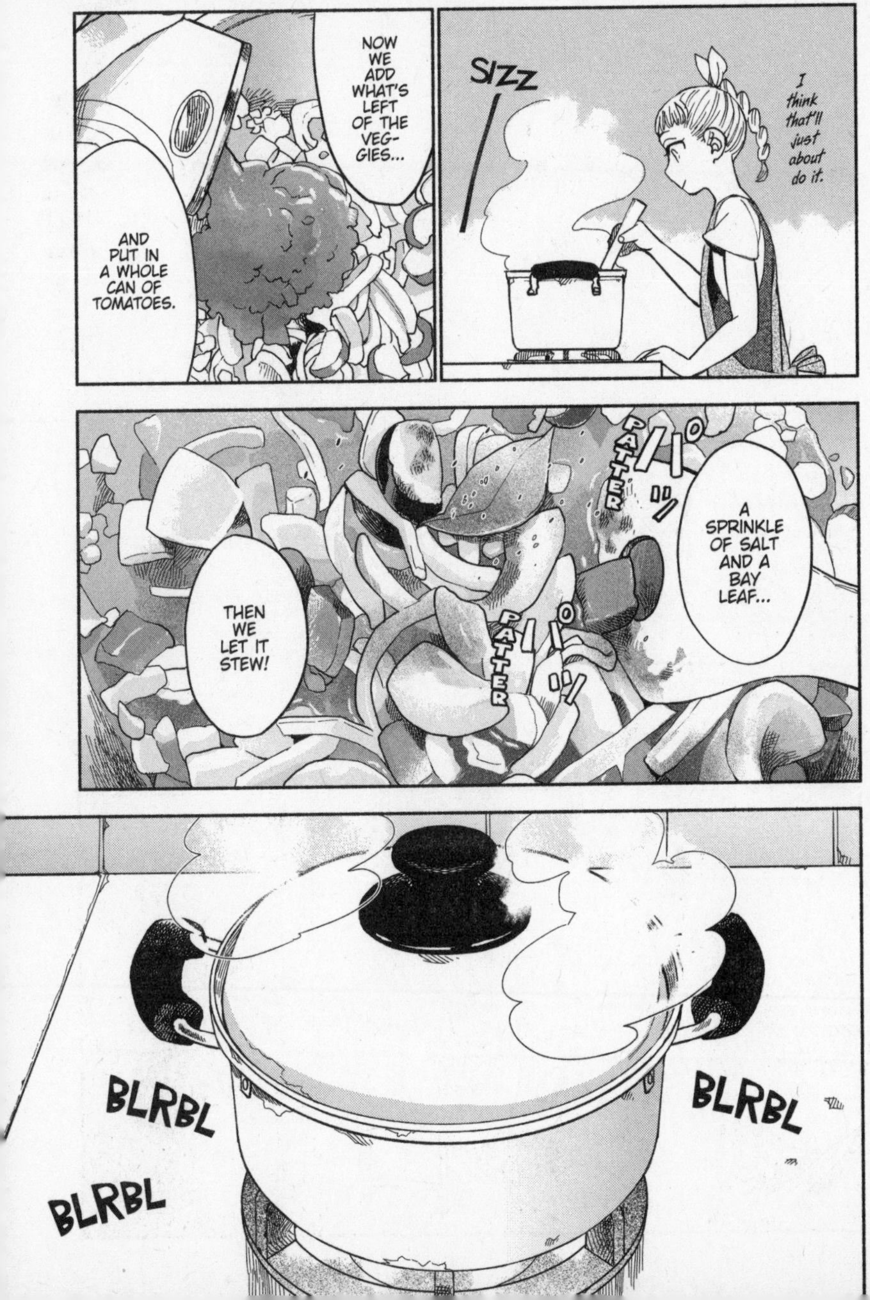
SIZZ
I think that'll just about do it.
NOW WE ADD WHAT'S LEFT OF THE VEG-GIES...
AND PUT IN A WHOLE CAN OF TOMATOES.
PATTER
A SPRINKLE OF SALT AND A BAY LEAF...
PATTER
THEN WE LET IT STEW!
BLRBL
BLRBL
BLRBL

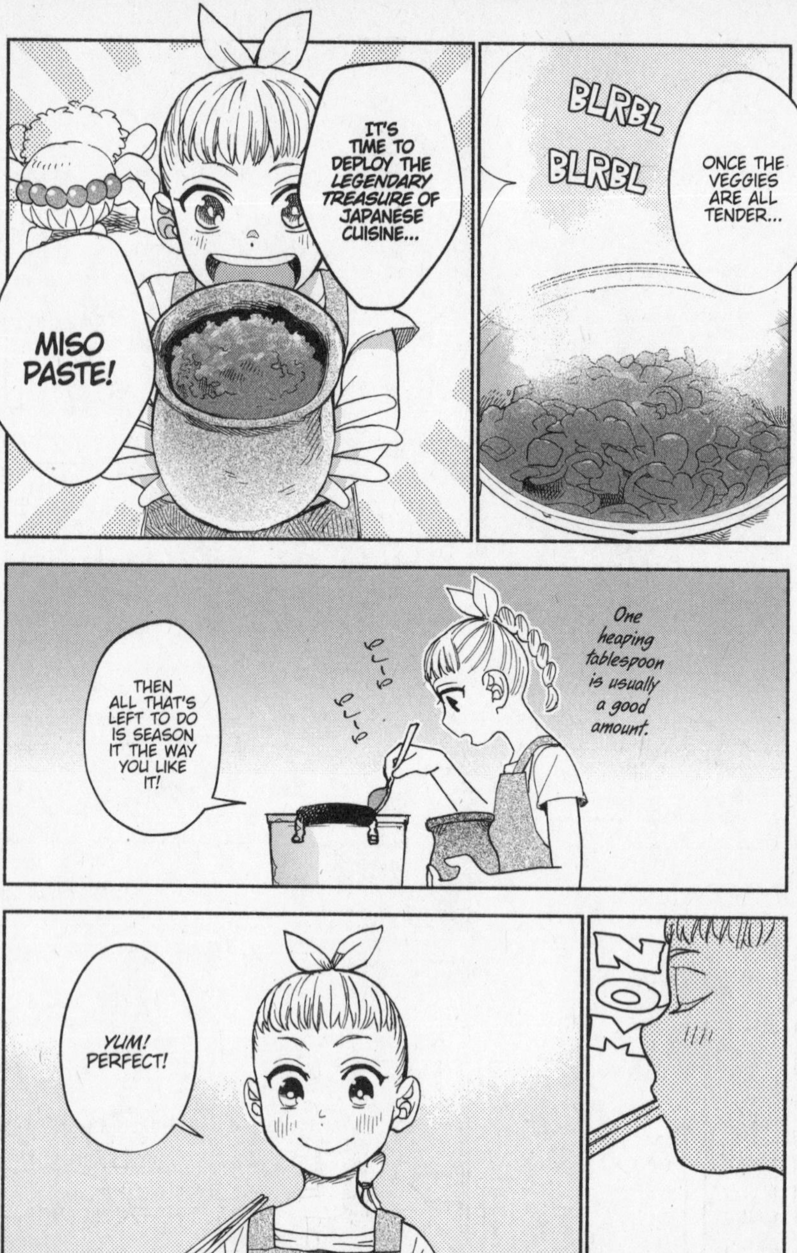
BLRBL
BLRBL
ONCE THE VEGGIES ARE ALL TENDER...
IT'S TIME TO DEPLOY THE *LEGENDARY TREASURE* OF JAPANESE CUISINE...
MISO PASTE!
One heaping tablespoon is usually a good amount.
THEN ALL THAT'S LEFT TO DO IS SEASON IT THE WAY YOU LIKE IT!
NOM
YUM! PERFECT!

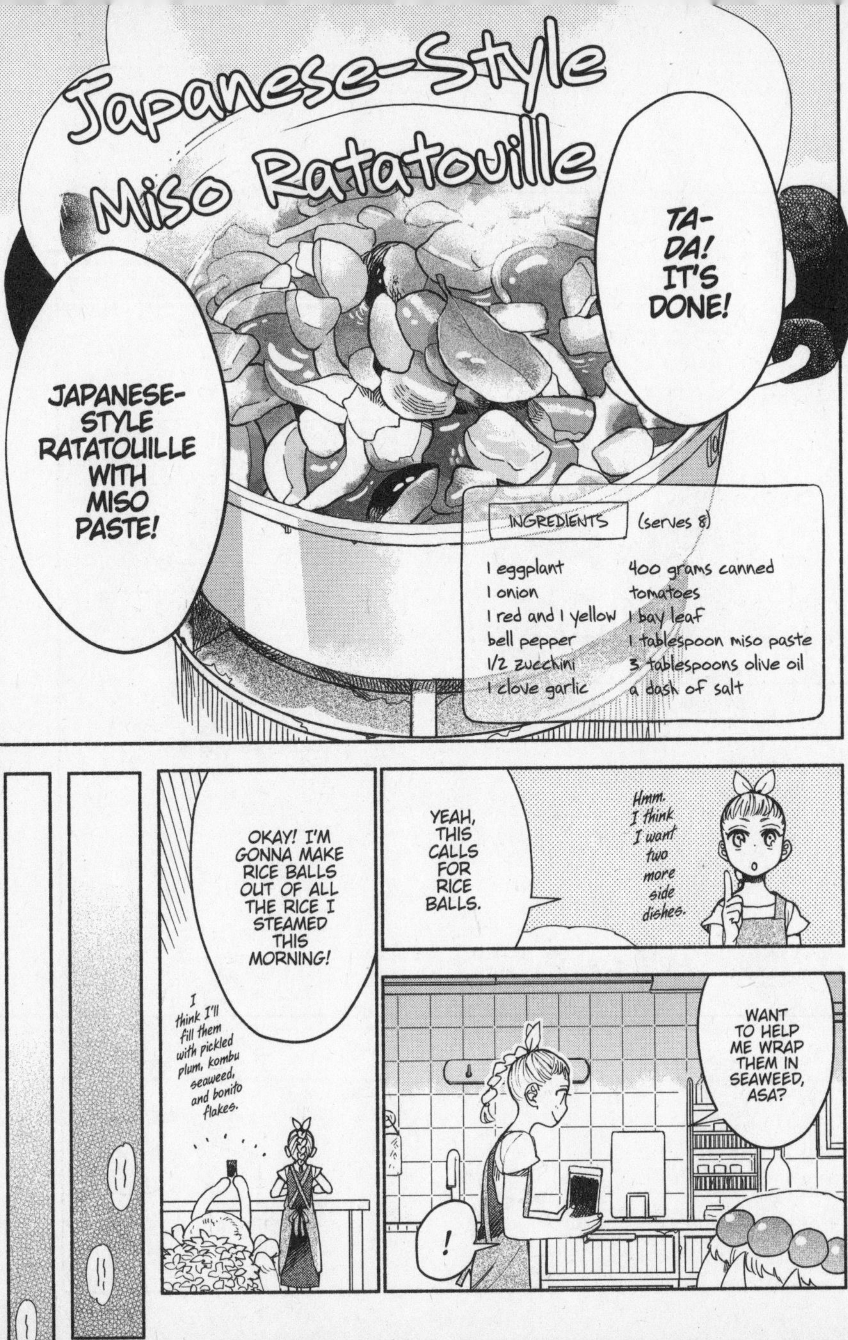

Japanese-Style Miso Ratatouille
TA-DA! IT'S DONE!
JAPANESE-STYLE RATATOUILLE WITH MISO PASTE!
INGREDIENTS (serves 8)
1 eggplant
1 onion
1 red and 1 yellow bell pepper
1/2 zucchini
1 clove garlic
400 grams canned tomatoes
1 bay leaf
1 tablespoon miso paste
3 tablespoons olive oil
a dash of salt
Hmm. I think I want two more side dishes.
YEAH, THIS CALLS FOR RICE BALLS.
WANT TO HELP ME WRAP THEM IN SEAWEED, ASA?
!
OKAY! I'M GONNA MAKE RICE BALLS OUT OF ALL THE RICE I STEAMED THIS MORNING!
I think I'll fill them with pickled plum, kombu seaweed, and bonito flakes.
...!
!!
!!

IF I PUT THESE OVER HERE, AND...

HMM...

PACK PACK

THOSE IN THERE...

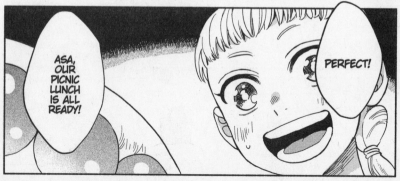

ASA, OUR PICNIC LUNCH IS ALL READY!

PERFECT!

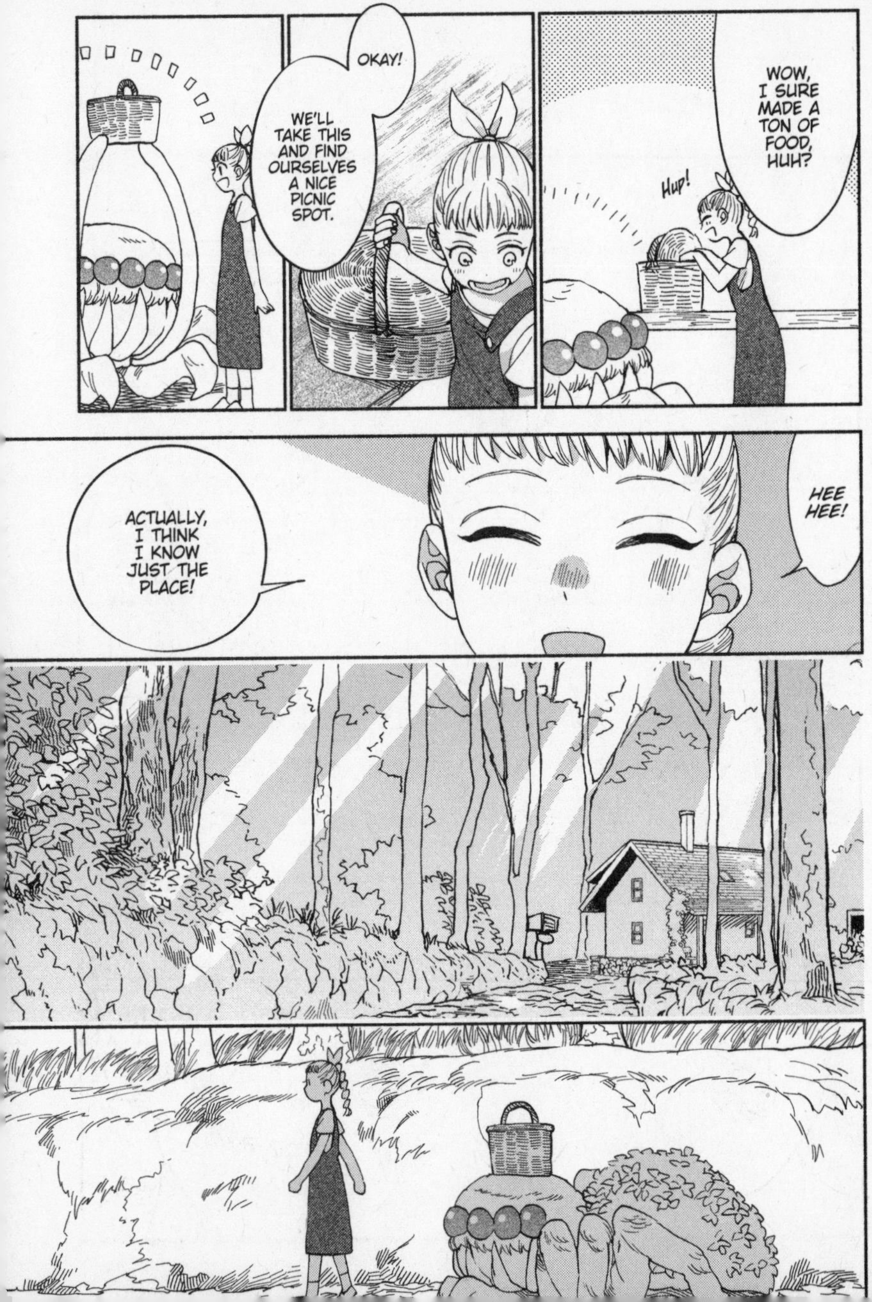
WOW, I SURE MADE A TON OF FOOD, HUH?
Hup!
OKAY!
WE'LL TAKE THIS AND FIND OURSELVES A NICE PICNIC SPOT.
HEE HEE!
ACTUALLY, I THINK I KNOW JUST THE PLACE!

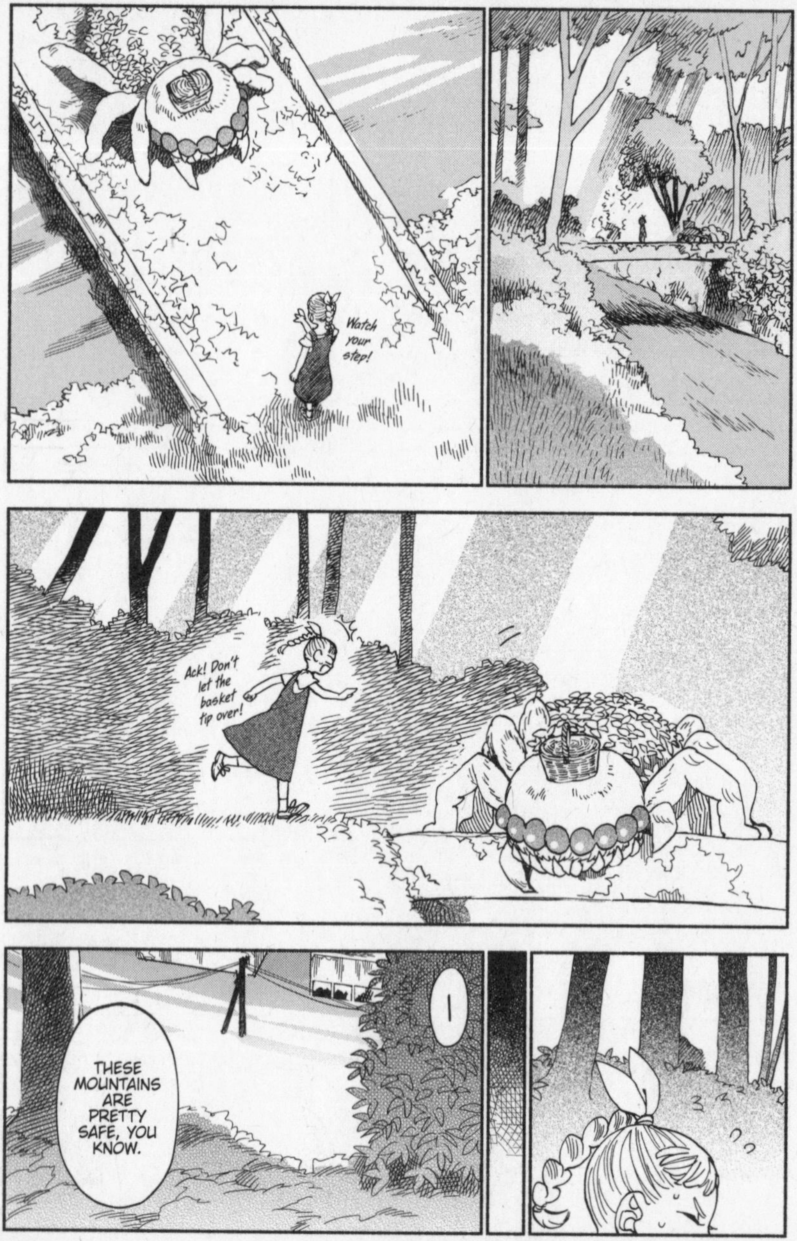

Watch your step!
Ack! Don't let the basket tip over!
!
THESE MOUNTAINS ARE PRETTY SAFE, YOU KNOW.

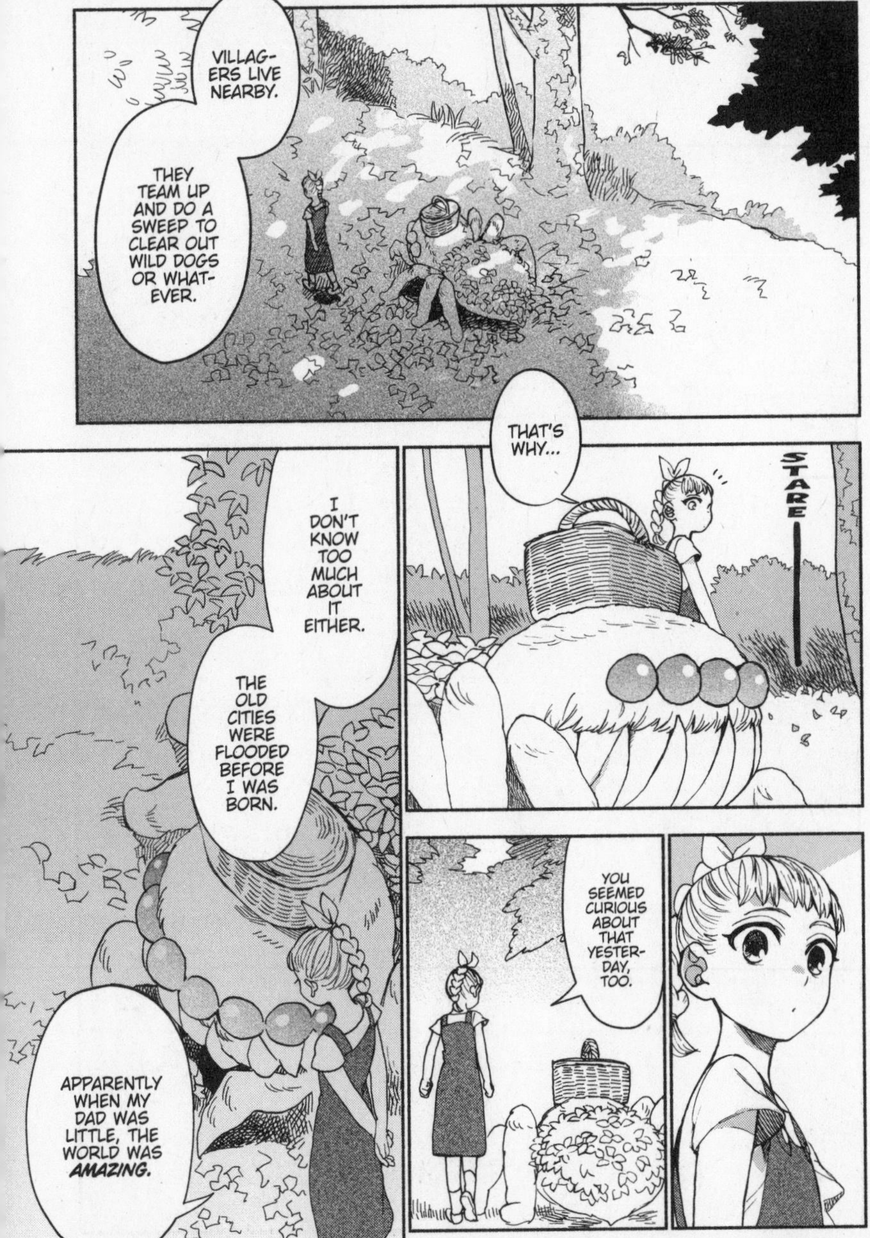
VILLAG-
ERS LIVE
NEARBY.
THEY TEAM UP AND DO A SWEEP TO CLEAR OUT WILD DOGS OR WHAT-EVER.
THAT'S WHY...
STARE
YOU SEEMED CURIOUS ABOUT THAT YESTER-DAY, TOO.
I DON'T KNOW TOO MUCH ABOUT IT EITHER.
THE OLD CITIES WERE FLOODED BEFORE I WAS BORN.
APPARENTLY WHEN MY DAD WAS LITTLE, THE WORLD WAS ***AMAZING.***

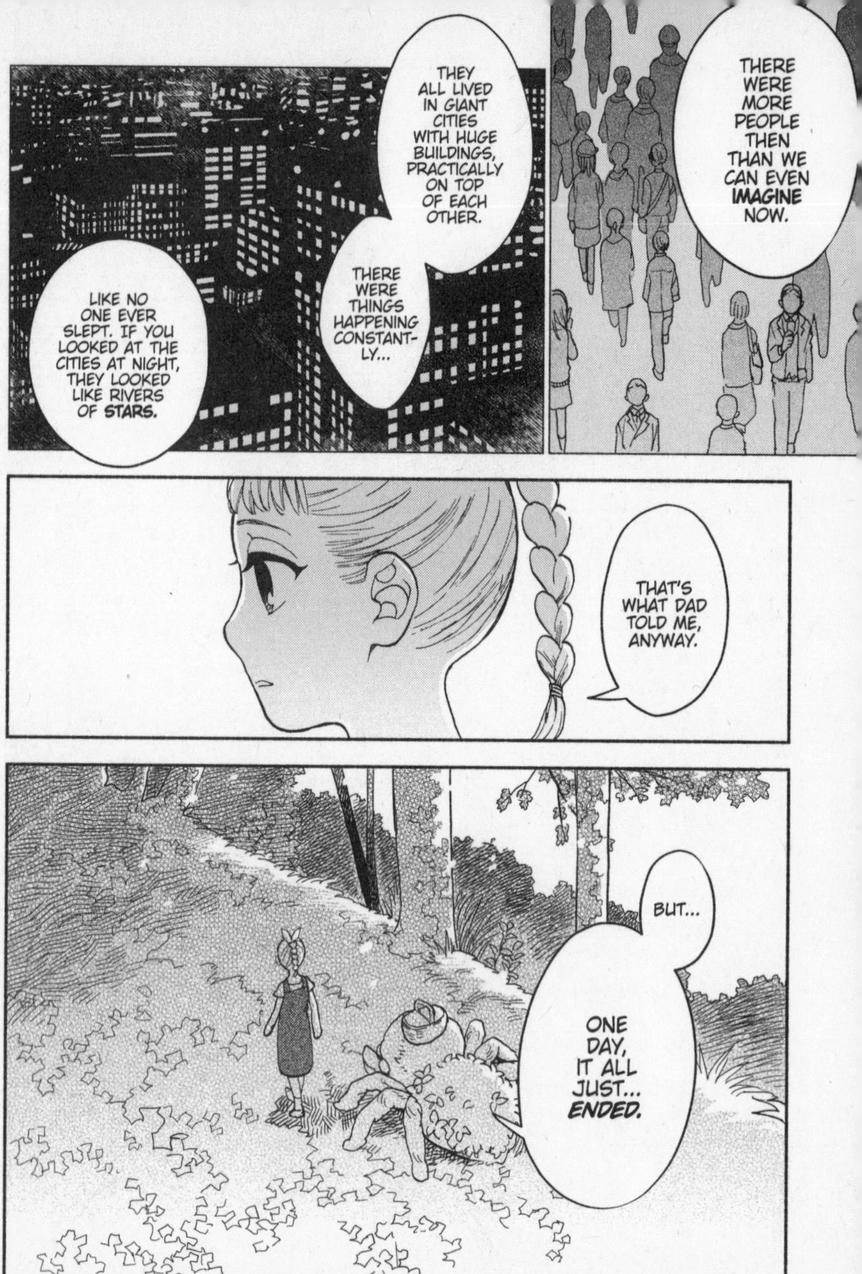
THERE WERE MORE PEOPLE THEN THAN WE CAN EVEN **IMAGINE** NOW.
THEY ALL LIVED IN GIANT CITIES WITH HUGE BUILDINGS, PRACTICALLY ON TOP OF EACH OTHER.
THERE WERE THINGS HAPPENING CONSTANT-LY...
LIKE NO ONE EVER SLEPT. IF YOU LOOKED AT THE CITIES AT NIGHT, THEY LOOKED LIKE RIVERS OF **STARS.**
THAT'S WHAT DAD TOLD ME, ANYWAY.
BUT...
ONE DAY, IT ALL JUST... ***ENDED.***

AHA!

......

ASA, WE'RE HERE!

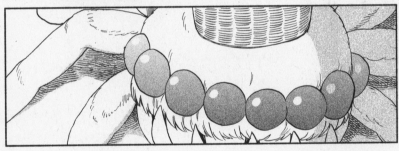

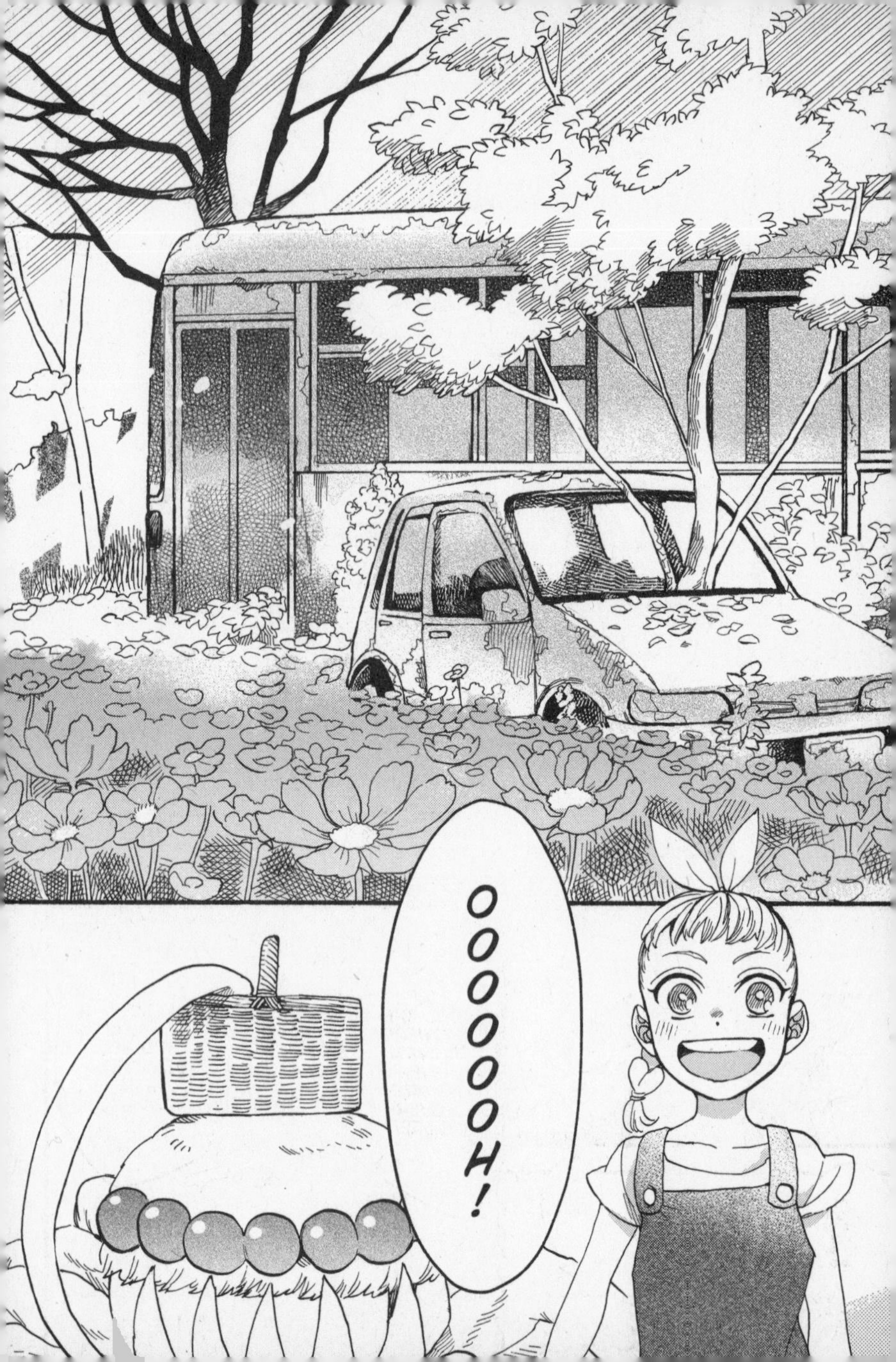
OOOOOOOH!

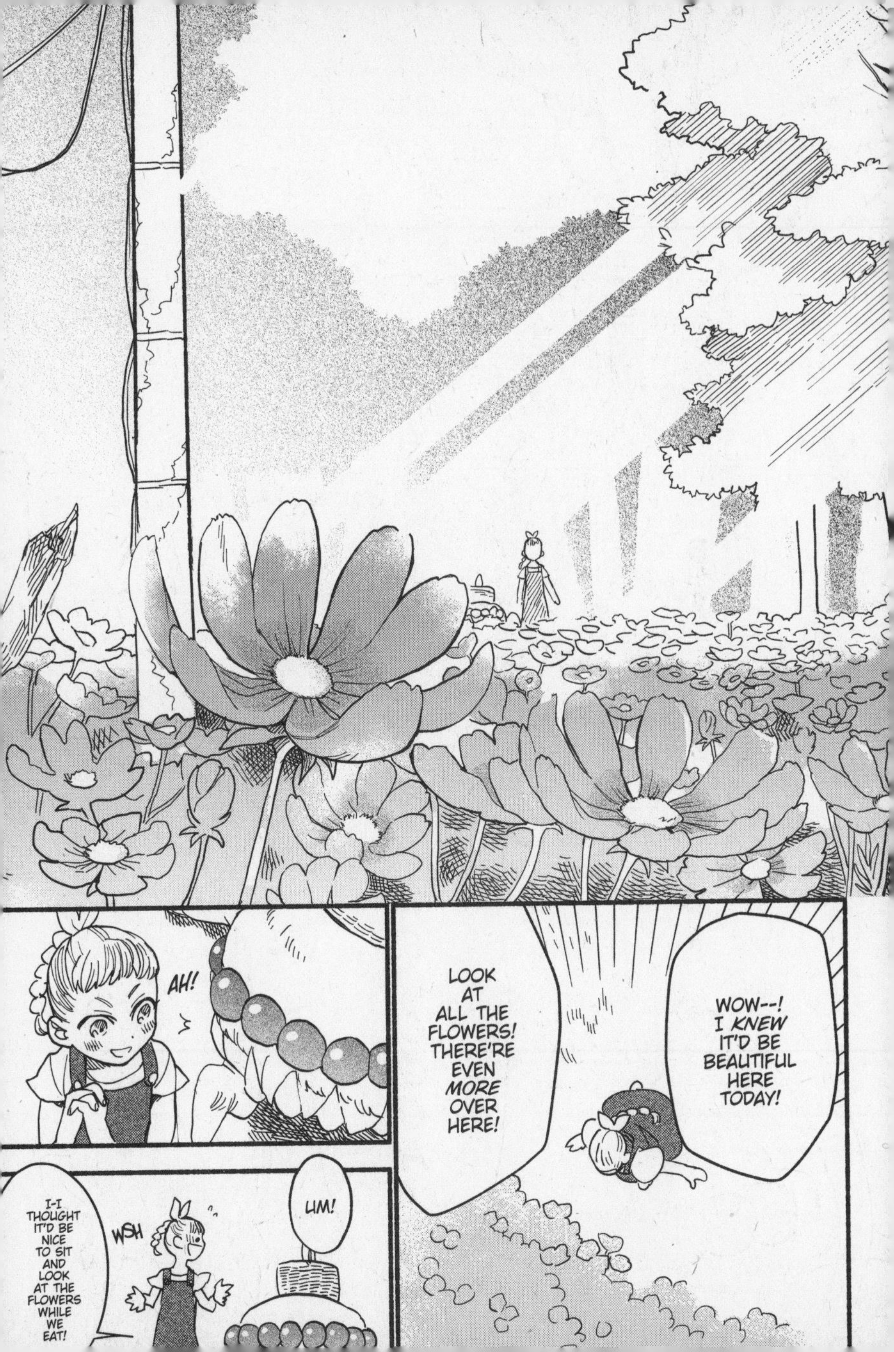
WOW--! I KNEW IT'D BE BEAUTIFUL HERE TODAY!
LOOK AT ALL THE FLOWERS! THERE'RE EVEN MORE OVER HERE!
AH!
UM!
WSH
I-I THOUGHT IT'D BE NICE TO SIT AND LOOK AT THE FLOWERS WHILE WE EAT!

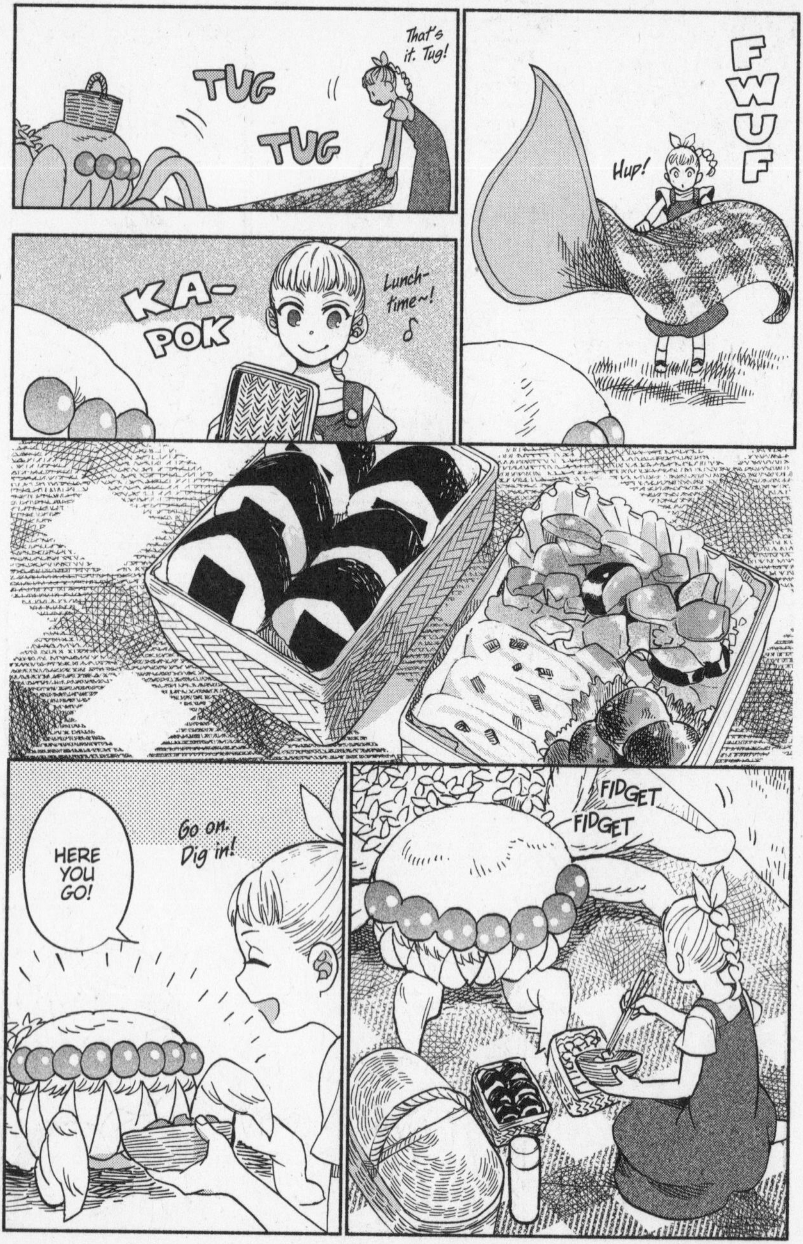
That's it. Tug!
TUG
TUG
FWUF
Hup!
KA-POK
Lunch-time~! ♪
HERE YOU GO!
Go on. Dig in!
FIDGET
FIDGET

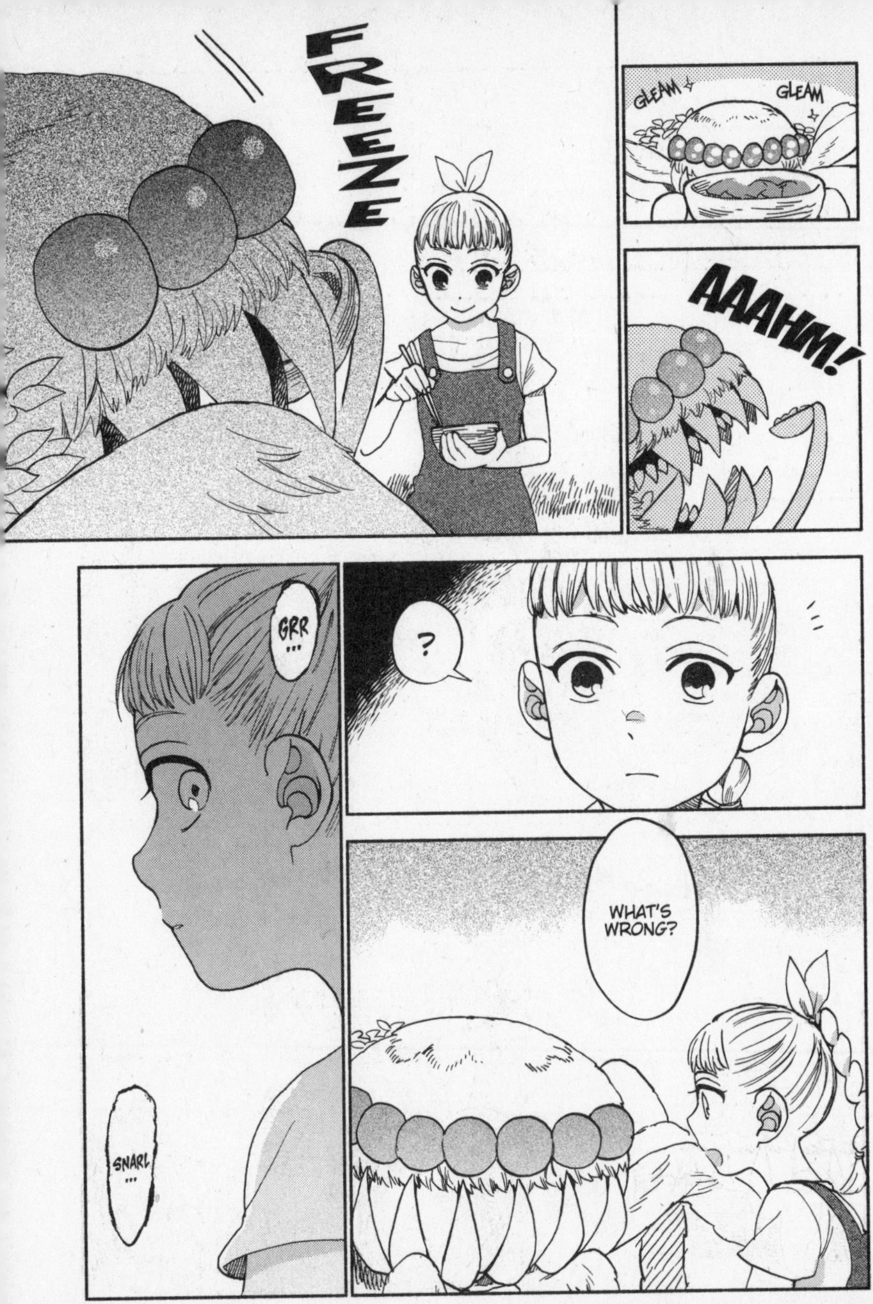
GLEAM
GLEAM
AAAHM!
FREEZE
?
WHAT'S WRONG?
GRR...
SNARL...

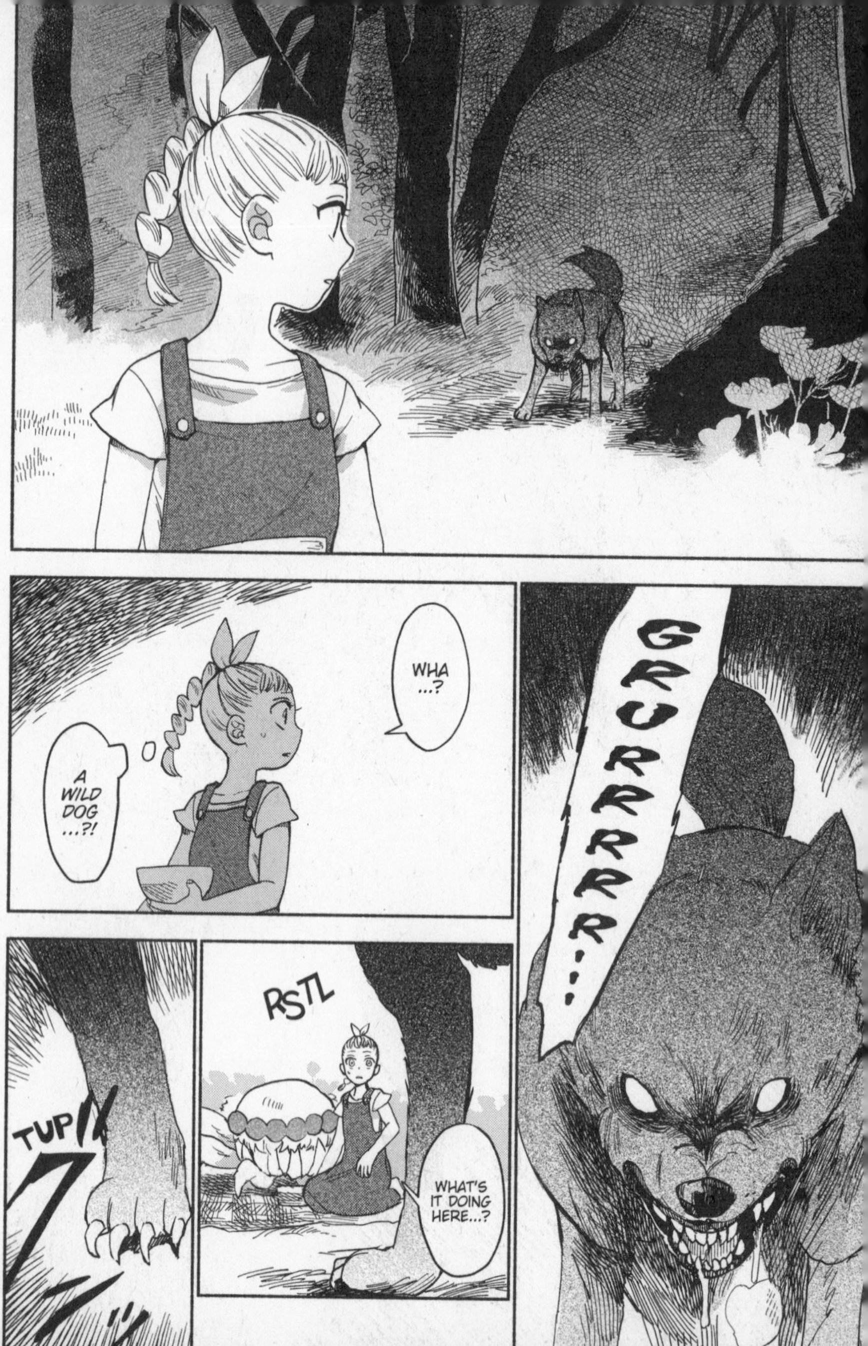
GRURRRRR...
WHA ...?
A WILD DOG ...?!
RSTL
WHAT'S IT DOING HERE...?
TUP

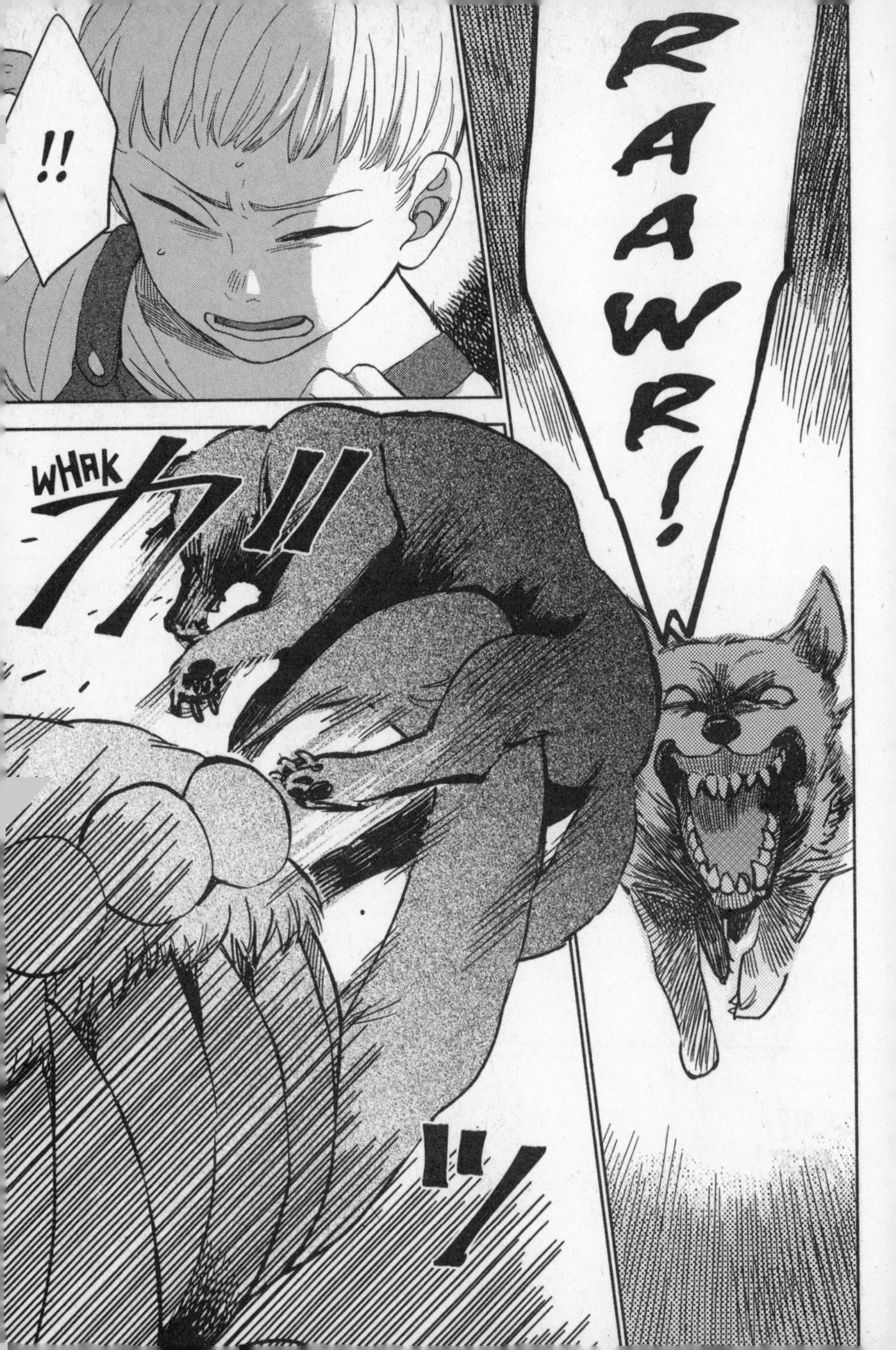
RAWR!
!!
WHAK

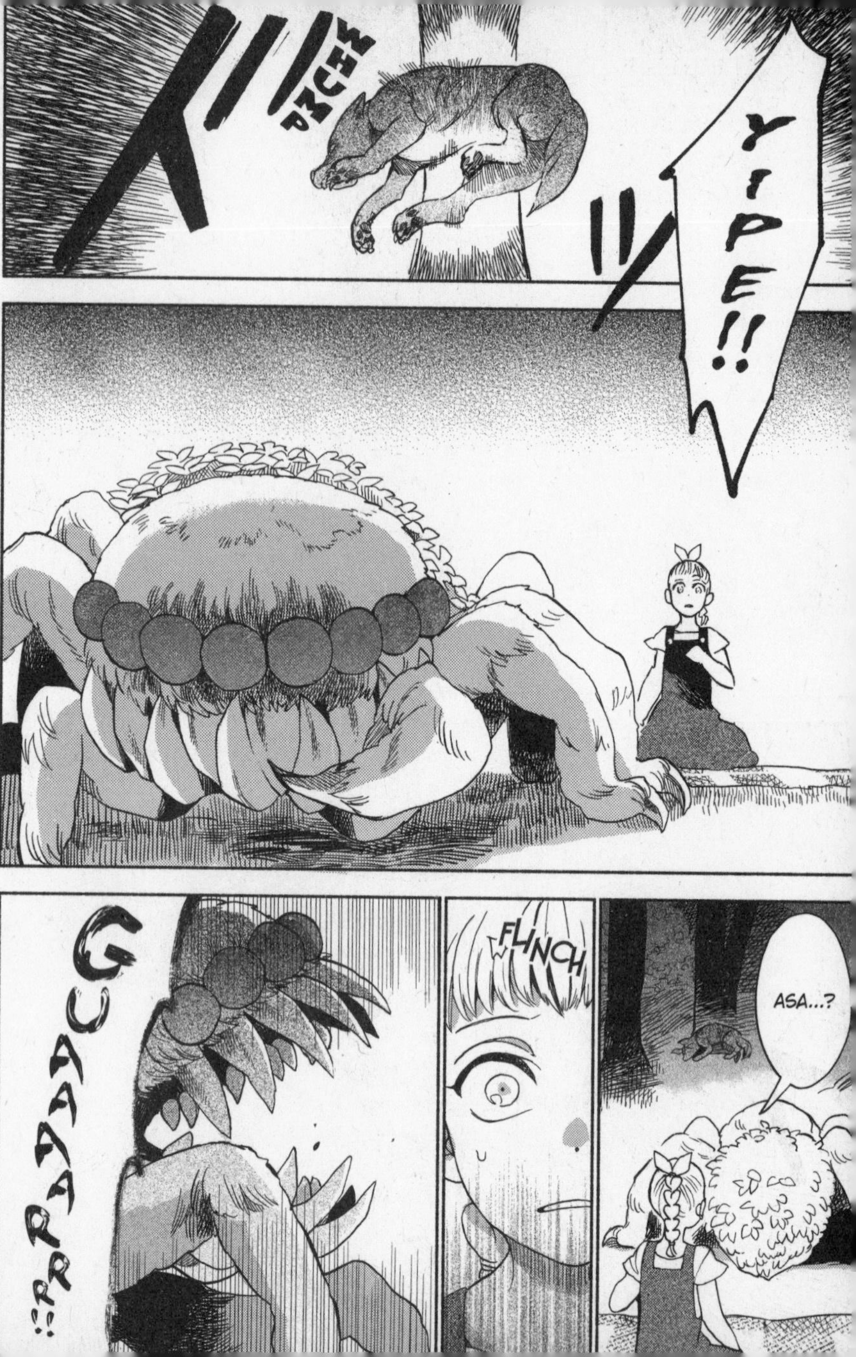
YIPE!!
WHUMP
ASA...?
FLINCH
GUAAAAAARRR!!

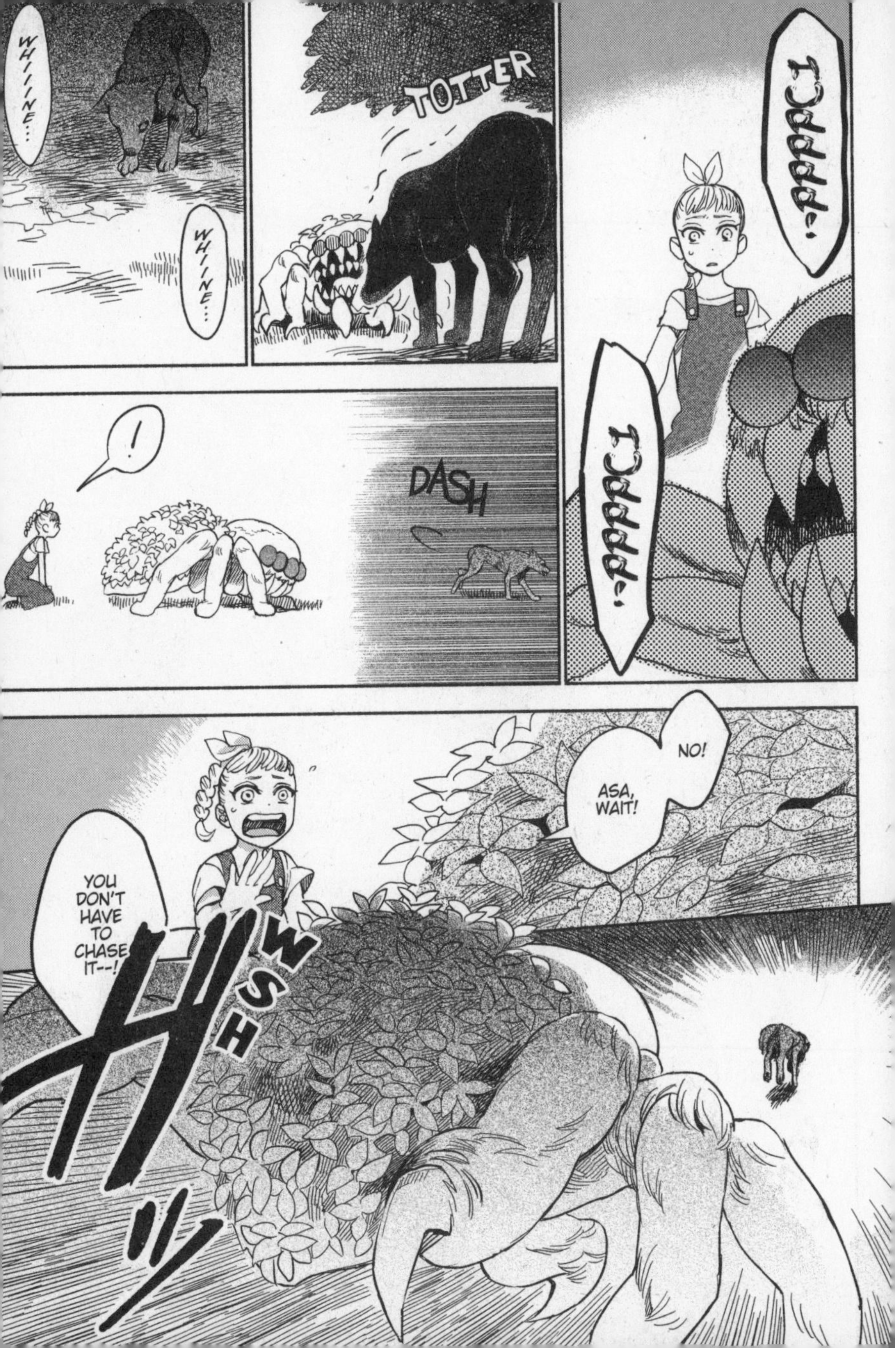
TOTTER
WHIIINE...
WHIINE...
DASH
!
NO!
ASA, WAIT!
YOU DON'T HAVE TO CHASE IT--!
WSH

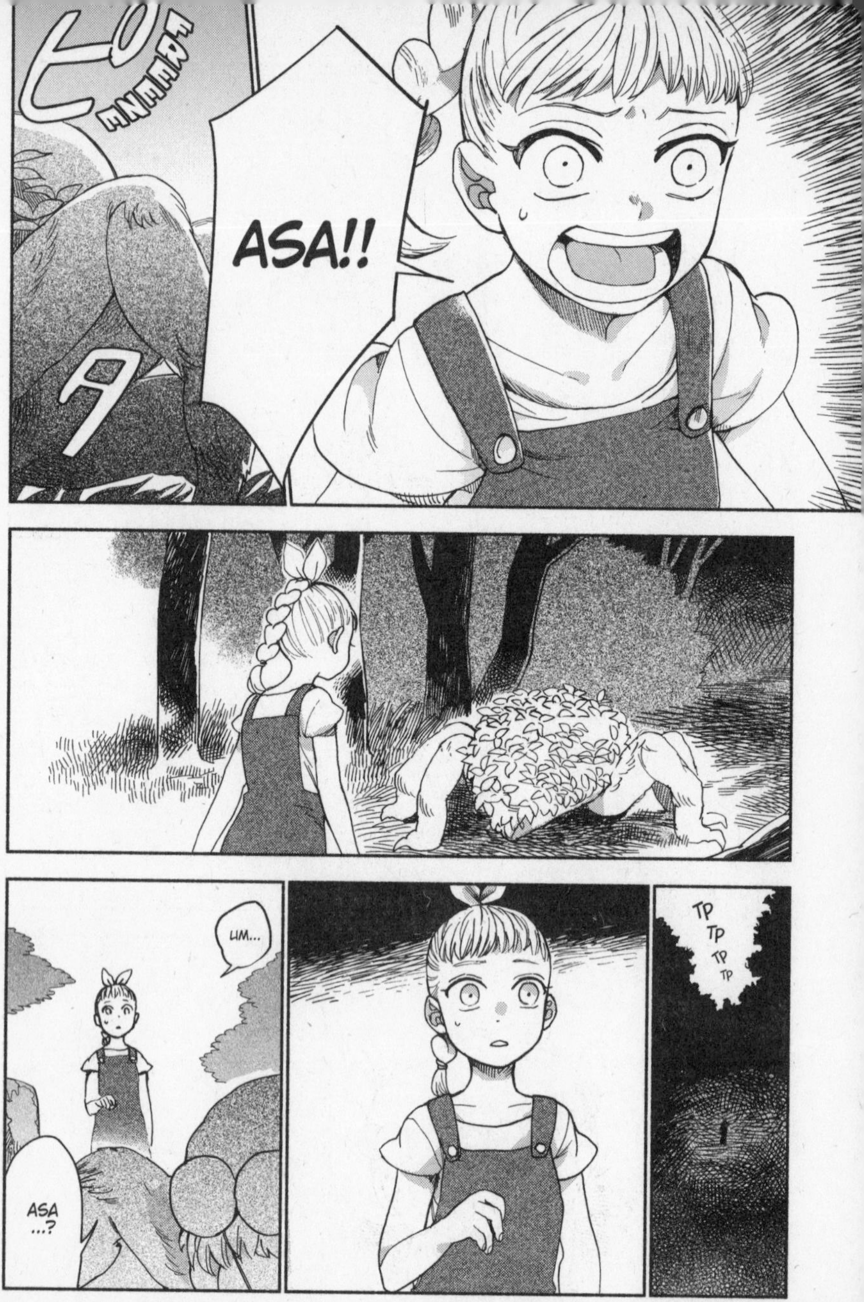
ASA!!
TP TP TP TP
UM...
ASA ...?

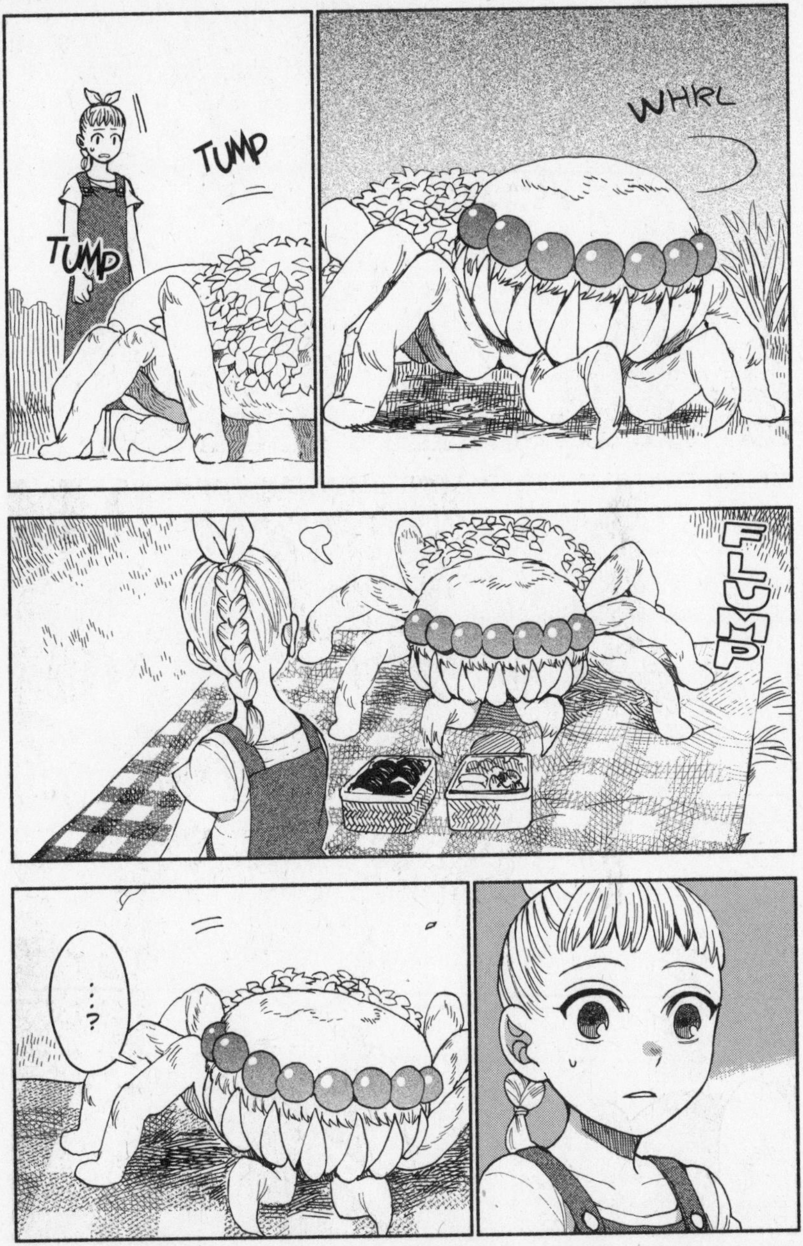
WHRL
TUMP
TUMP
FLUMP
...?

SLUMP

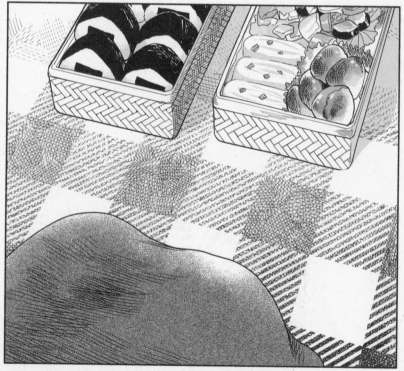

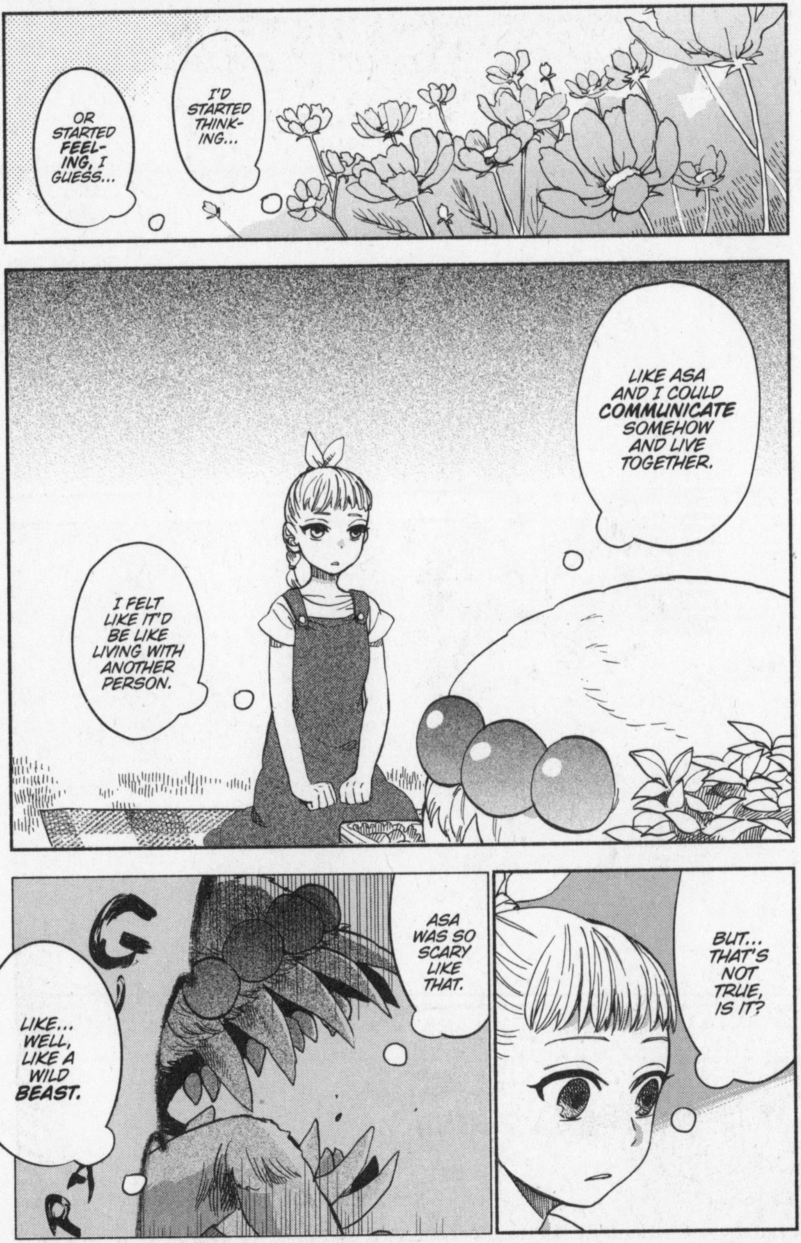
I'D STARTED THINKING...
OR STARTED FEELING, I GUESS...
LIKE ASA AND I COULD COMMUNICATE SOMEHOW AND LIVE TOGETHER.
I FELT LIKE IT'D BE LIKE LIVING WITH ANOTHER PERSON.
BUT... THAT'S NOT TRUE, IS IT?
ASA WAS SO SCARY LIKE THAT.
LIKE... WELL, LIKE A WILD BEAST.

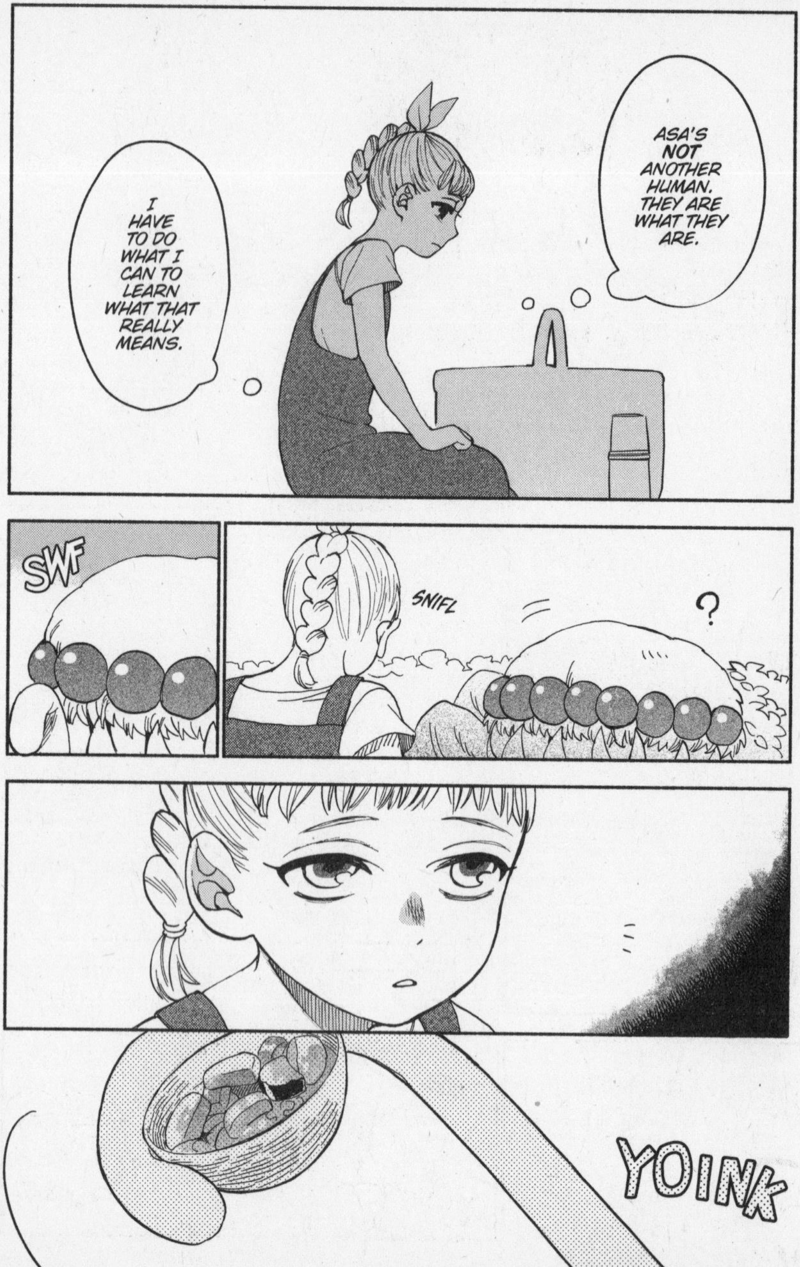
ASA'S NOT ANOTHER HUMAN. THEY ARE WHAT THEY ARE.
I HAVE TO DO WHAT I CAN TO LEARN WHAT THAT REALLY MEANS.
SNIFL
?
SWF
YOINK

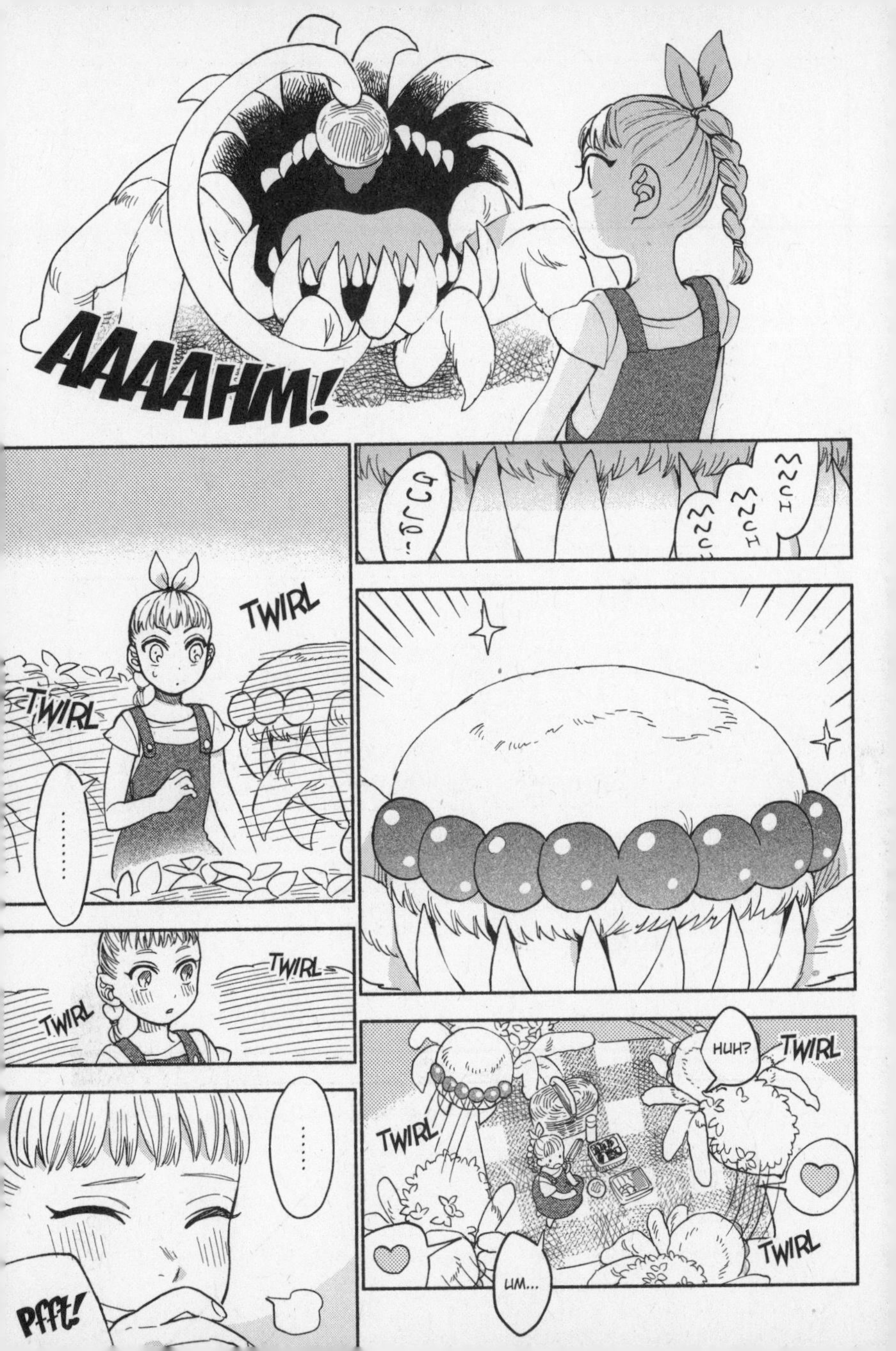
AAAAHM!
MNCH
MNCH
MNCH
GULP!
TWIRL
TWIRL
......
HUH?
TWIRL
TWIRL
TWIRL
UM...
TWIRL
TWIRL
......
Pfft!

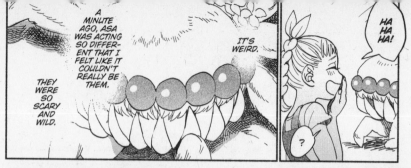

A MINUTE AGO, ASA WAS ACTING SO DIFFERENT THAT I FELT LIKE IT COULDN'T REALLY BE THEM.

THEY WERE SO SCARY AND WILD.

IT'S WEIRD.

HA HA HA!

BUT THIS ASA AND THAT ASA ARE THE SAME.

ASA IS JUST... ASA, AND THAT'S OKAY.

That was so funny!

COME ON. LET'S HAVE OUR PICNIC...

ASA.

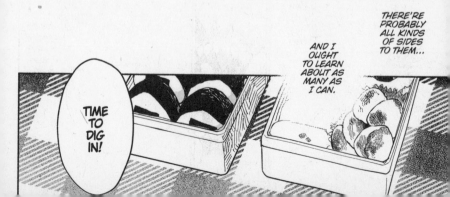

THERE'RE PROBABLY ALL KINDS OF SIDES TO THEM...

AND I OUGHT TO LEARN ABOUT AS MANY AS I CAN.

TIME TO DIG IN!

MMM!

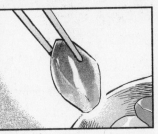

NOM

THE RATATOUILLE TURNED OUT SO WELL!

The miso paste really sets off the acidity of the tomatoes.

NOM NOM

FWIIIIISH

AAAHM!

And the eggplant is melt-in-your-mouth good!

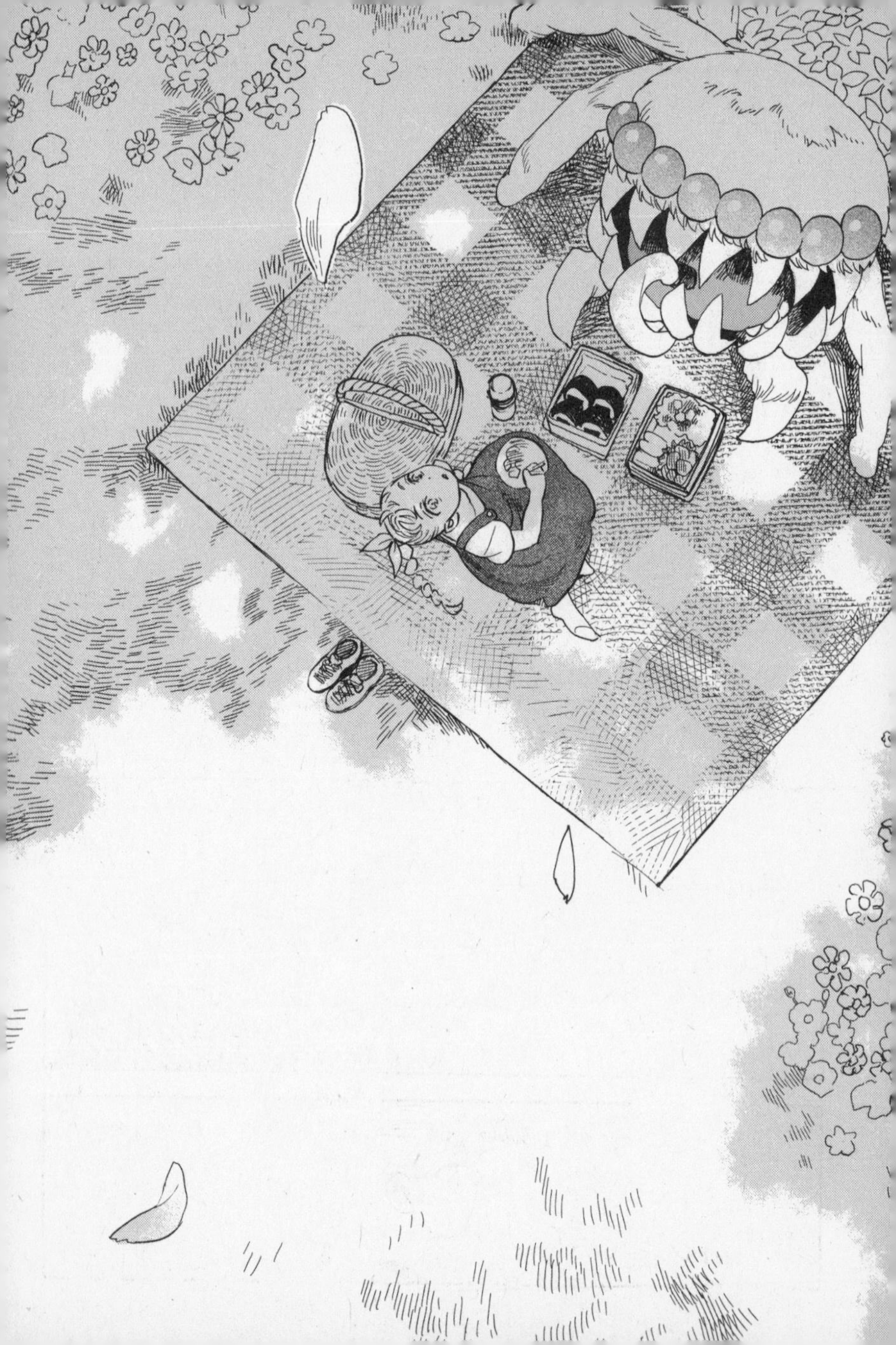

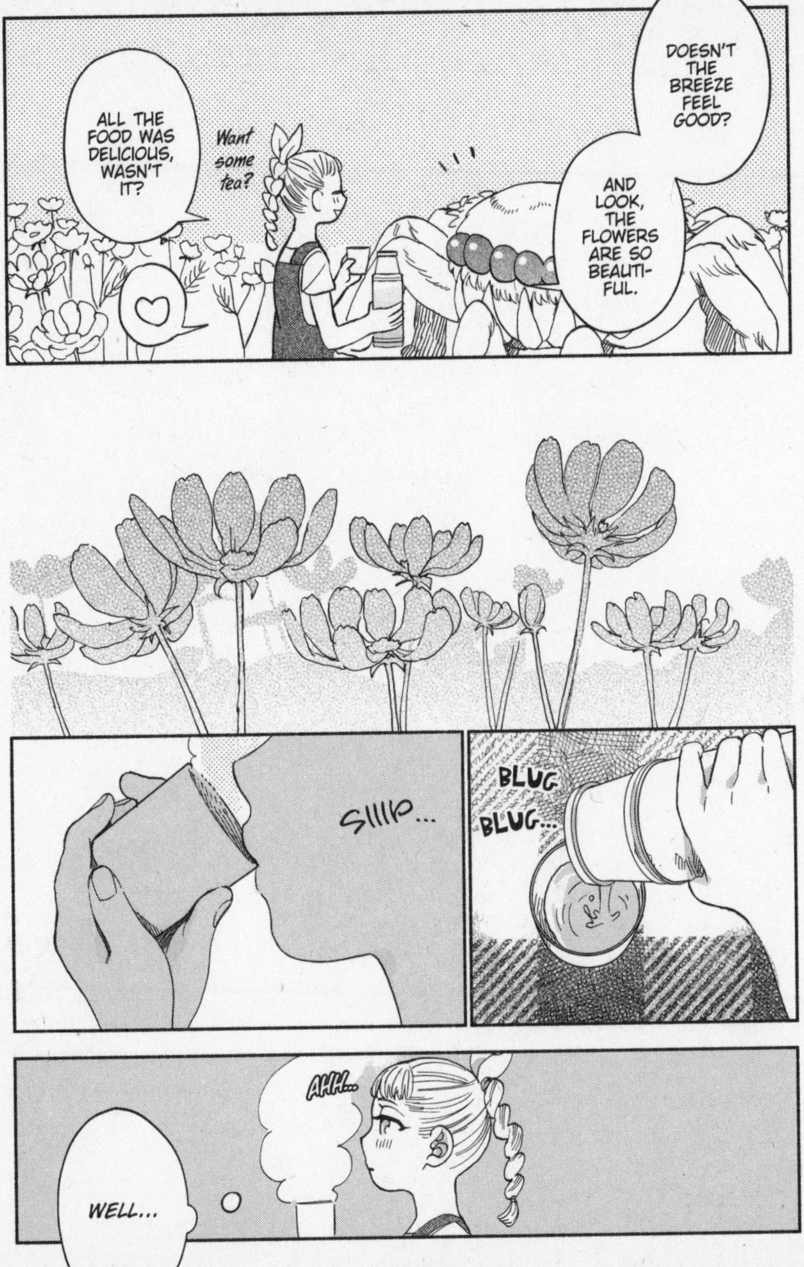
DOESN'T THE BREEZE FEEL GOOD?
AND LOOK, THE FLOWERS ARE SO BEAUTI-FUL.
Want some tea?
ALL THE FOOD WAS DELICIOUS, WASN'T IT?
BLUG BLUG...
SIIIP...
AHH...
WELL...

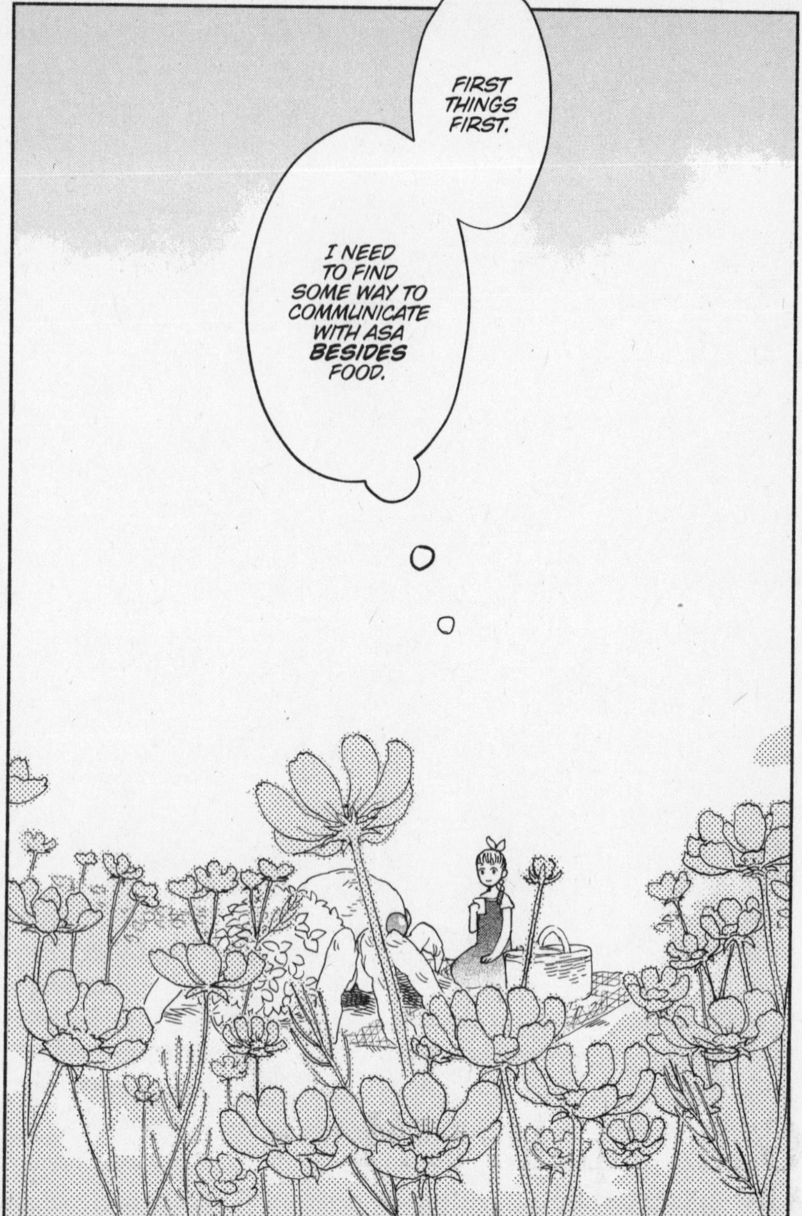
FIRST THINGS FIRST.
I NEED TO FIND SOME WAY TO COMMUNICATE WITH ASA **BESIDES** FOOD.

Giant Spider & Me
A Post-Apocalyptic Tale

Giant Spider & Me
A Post-Apocalyptic Tale

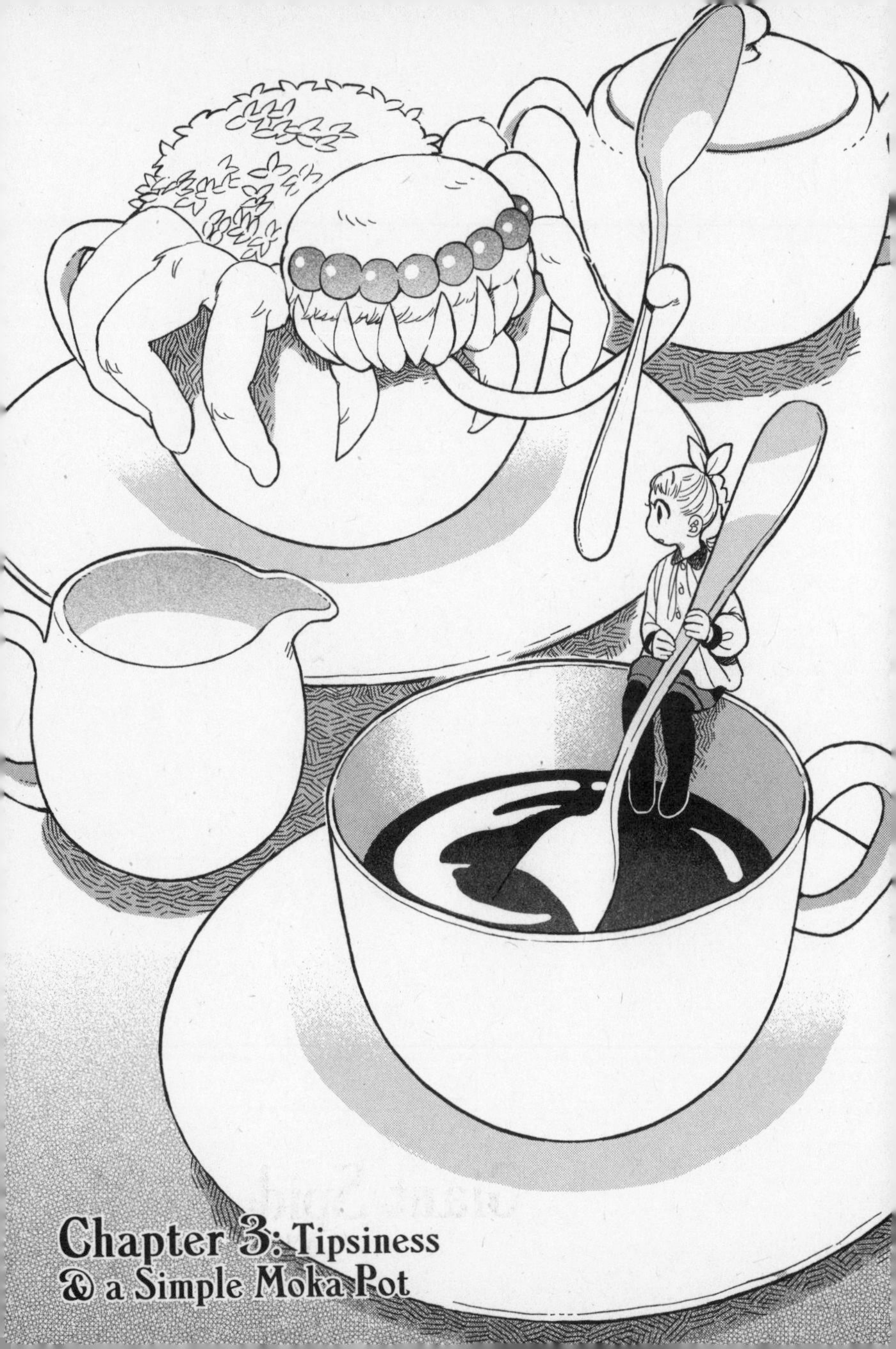

Chapter 3: Tipsiness & a Simple Moka Pot

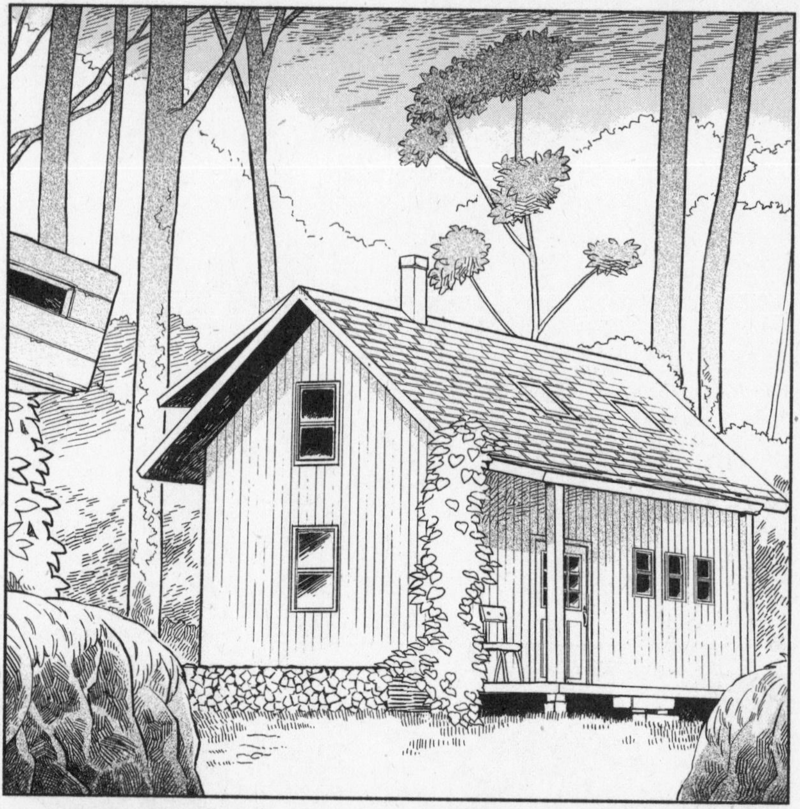
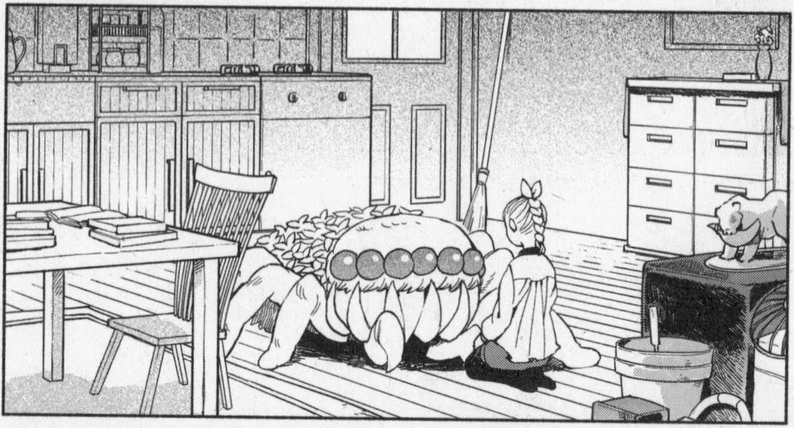

SHAKE, ASA. SHAKE!

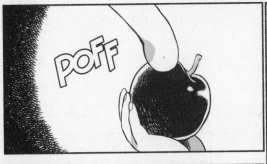

POFF

TUMP

TUMP

MNCH MNCH

Thank you.

· · · · · · ·

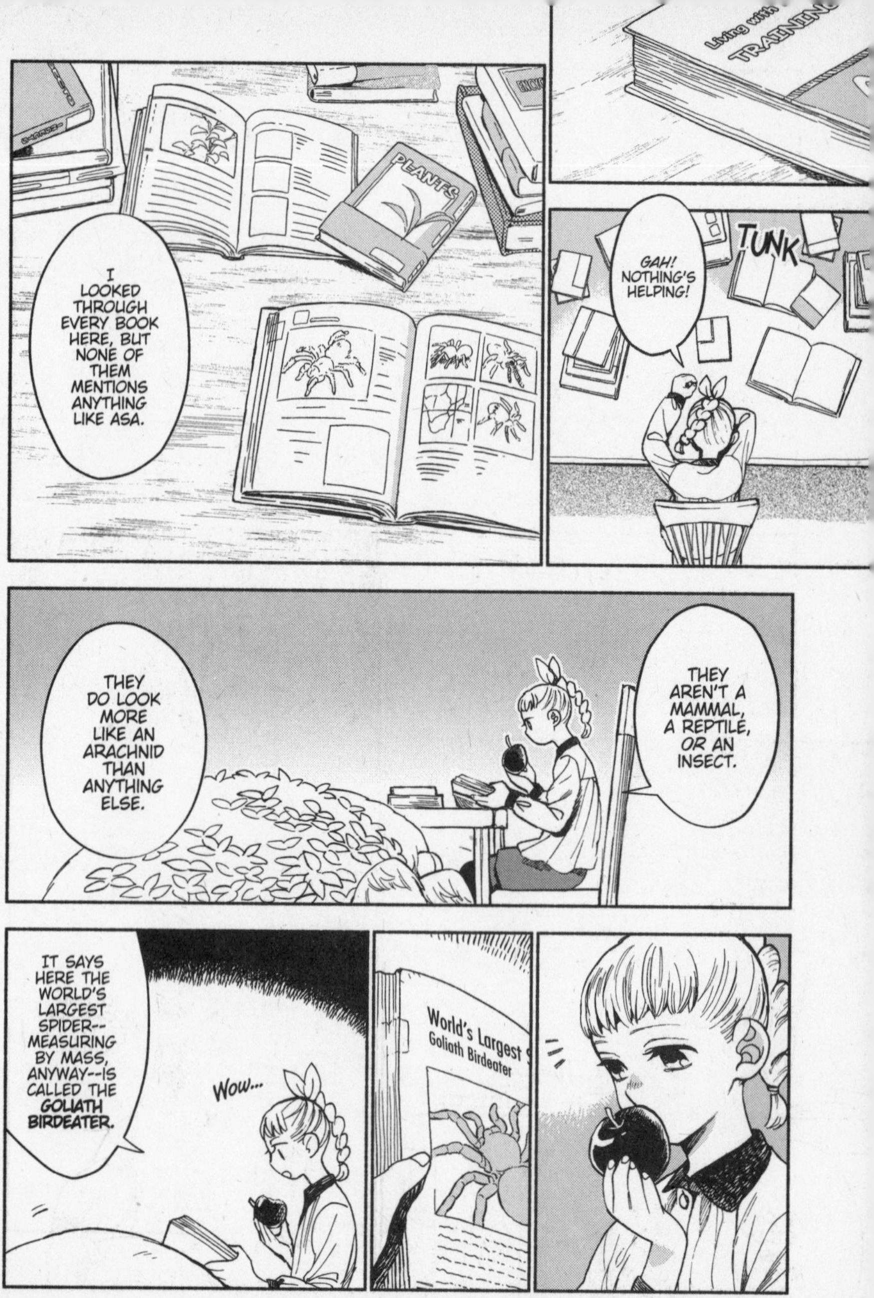
Living with TRAININ
TUNK
GAH! NOTHING'S HELPING!
PLANTS
I LOOKED THROUGH EVERY BOOK HERE, BUT NONE OF THEM MENTIONS ANYTHING LIKE ASA.
THEY AREN'T A MAMMAL, A REPTILE, OR AN INSECT.
THEY DO LOOK MORE LIKE AN ARACHNID THAN ANYTHING ELSE.
World's Largest
Goliath Birdeater
IT SAYS HERE THE WORLD'S LARGEST SPIDER--MEASURING BY MASS, ANYWAY--IS CALLED THE **GOLIATH BIRDEATER.**
Wow...

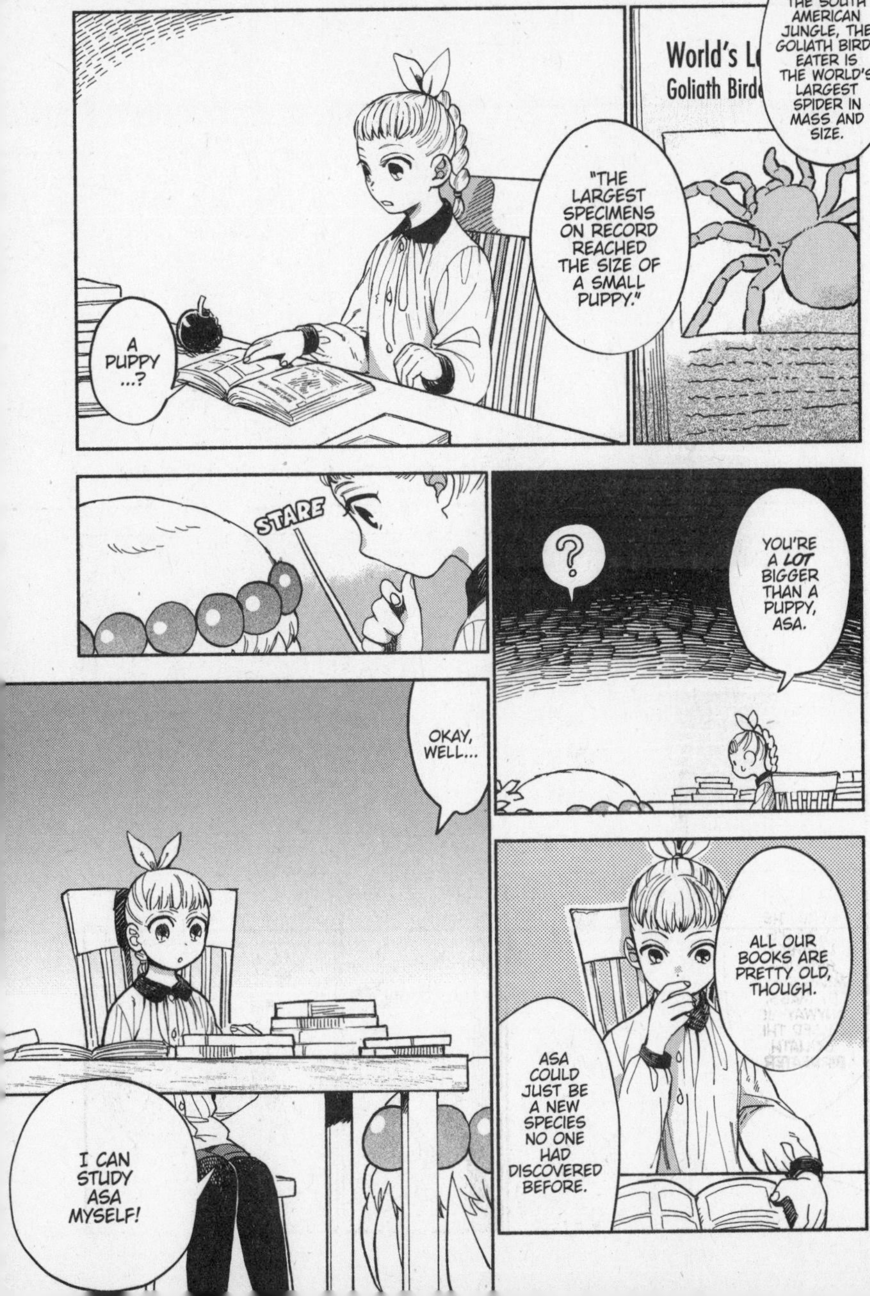
"NATIVE TO THE SOUTH AMERICAN JUNGLE, THE GOLIATH BIRD-EATER IS THE WORLD'S LARGEST SPIDER IN MASS AND SIZE.
"THE LARGEST SPECIMENS ON RECORD REACHED THE SIZE OF A SMALL PUPPY."
A PUPPY ...?
?
YOU'RE A *LOT* BIGGER THAN A PUPPY, ASA.
STARE
ALL OUR BOOKS ARE PRETTY OLD, THOUGH.
ASA COULD JUST BE A NEW SPECIES NO ONE HAD DISCOVERED BEFORE.
OKAY, WELL...
I CAN STUDY ASA MYSELF!

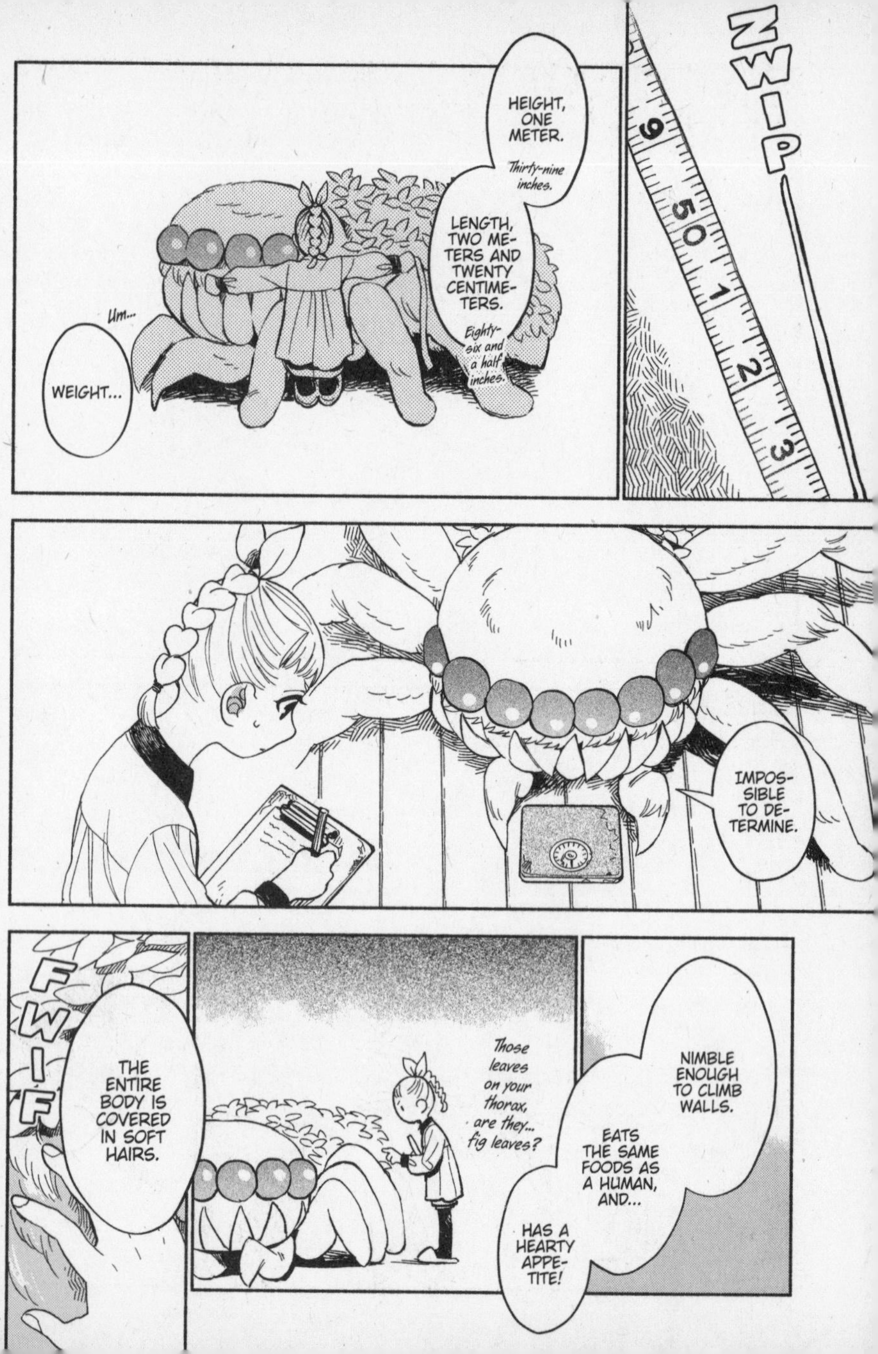
ZWIP
HEIGHT, ONE METER.
Thirty-nine inches.
LENGTH, TWO METERS AND TWENTY CENTIMETERS.
Eighty-six and a half inches.
Um...
WEIGHT...
IMPOSSIBLE TO DETERMINE.
NIMBLE ENOUGH TO CLIMB WALLS.
EATS THE SAME FOODS AS A HUMAN, AND...
HAS A HEARTY APPETITE!
Those leaves on your thorax, are they... fig leaves?
FWIF
THE ENTIRE BODY IS COVERED IN SOFT HAIRS.

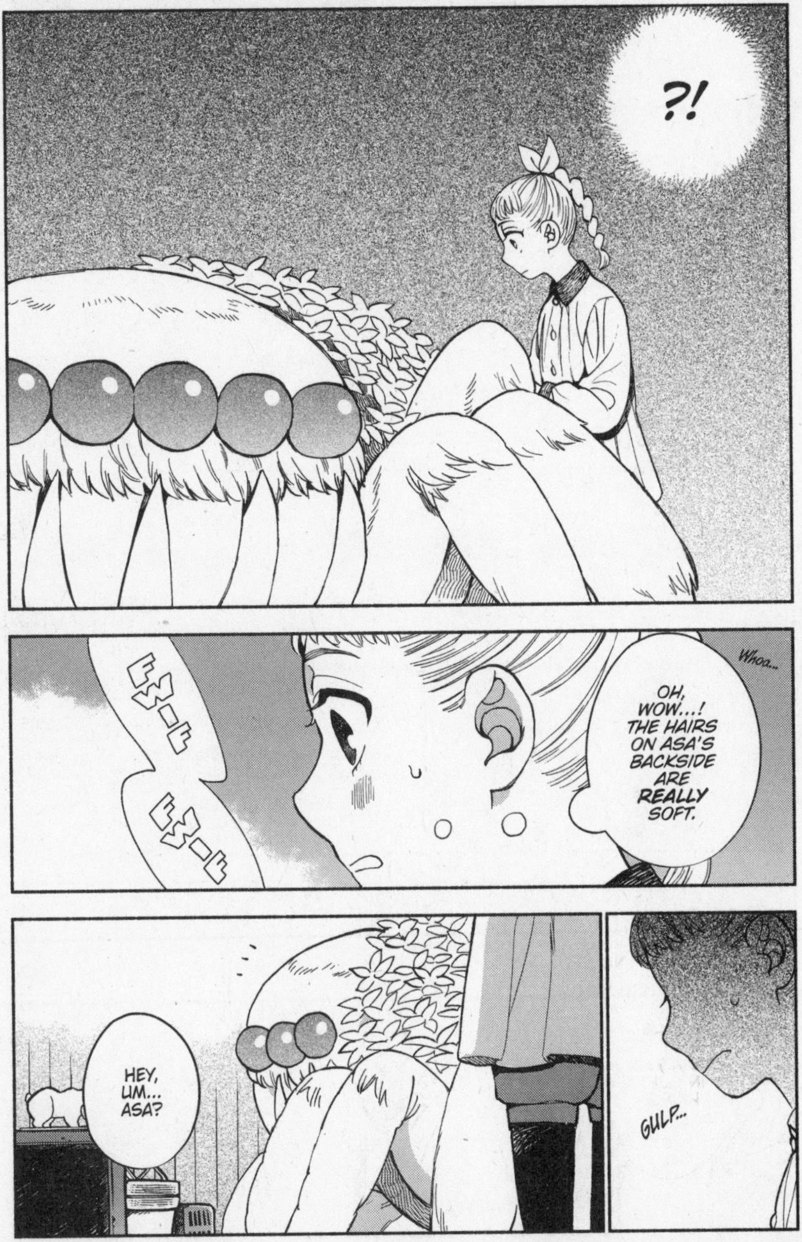
?!
Whoa...
OH, WOW...! THE HAIRS ON ASA'S BACKSIDE ARE **REALLY** SOFT.
FWIF FWIF
GULP...
HEY, UM... ASA?

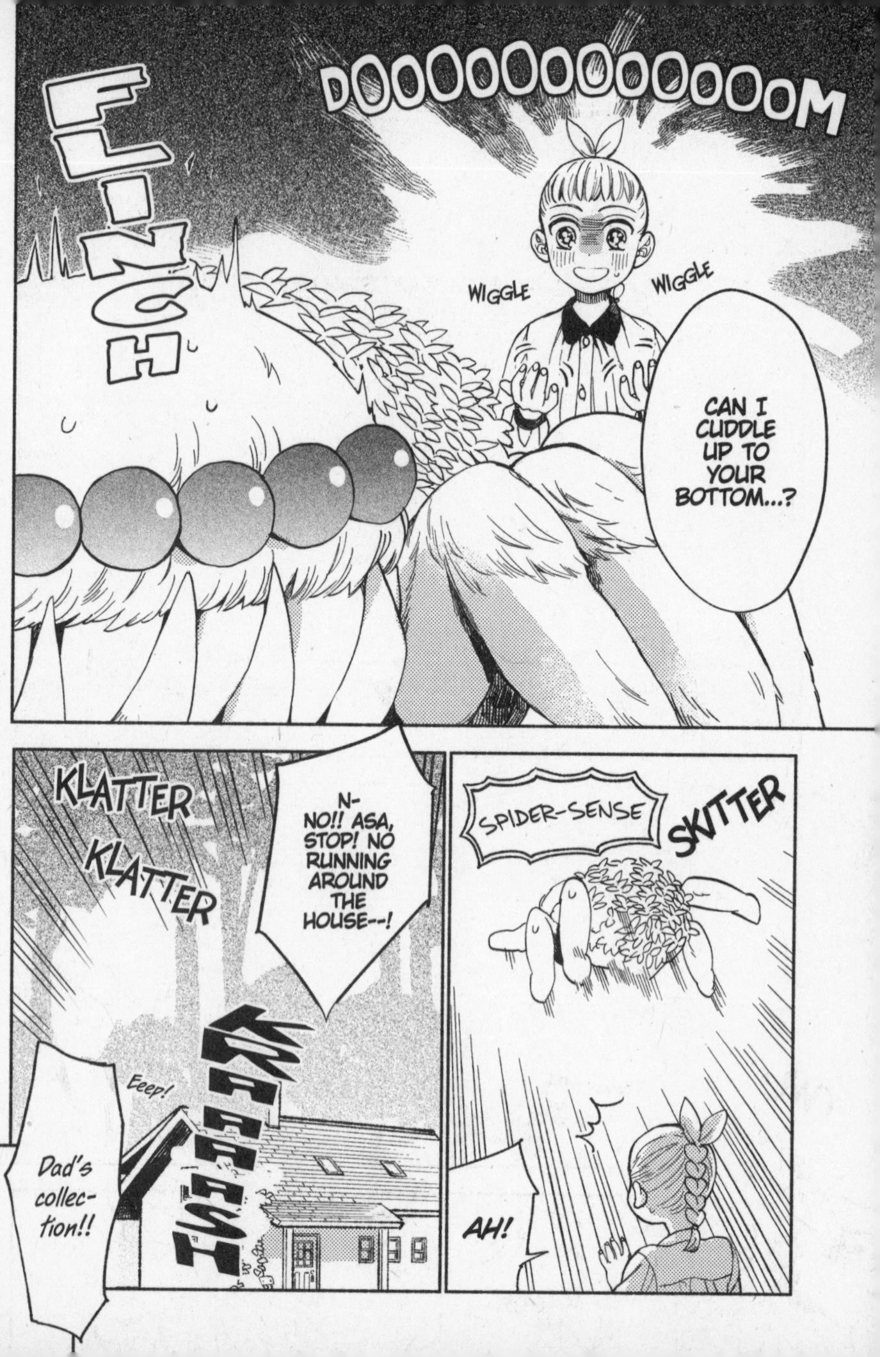
DOOOOOOOOOOOOOM
CAN I CUDDLE UP TO YOUR BOTTOM...?
WIGGLE WIGGLE
FLINCH
SPIDER-SENSE
SKITTER
AH!
N-NO!! ASA, STOP! NO RUNNING AROUND THE HOUSE--!
KLATTER KLATTER
KRASH
Eeep!
Dad's collection!!

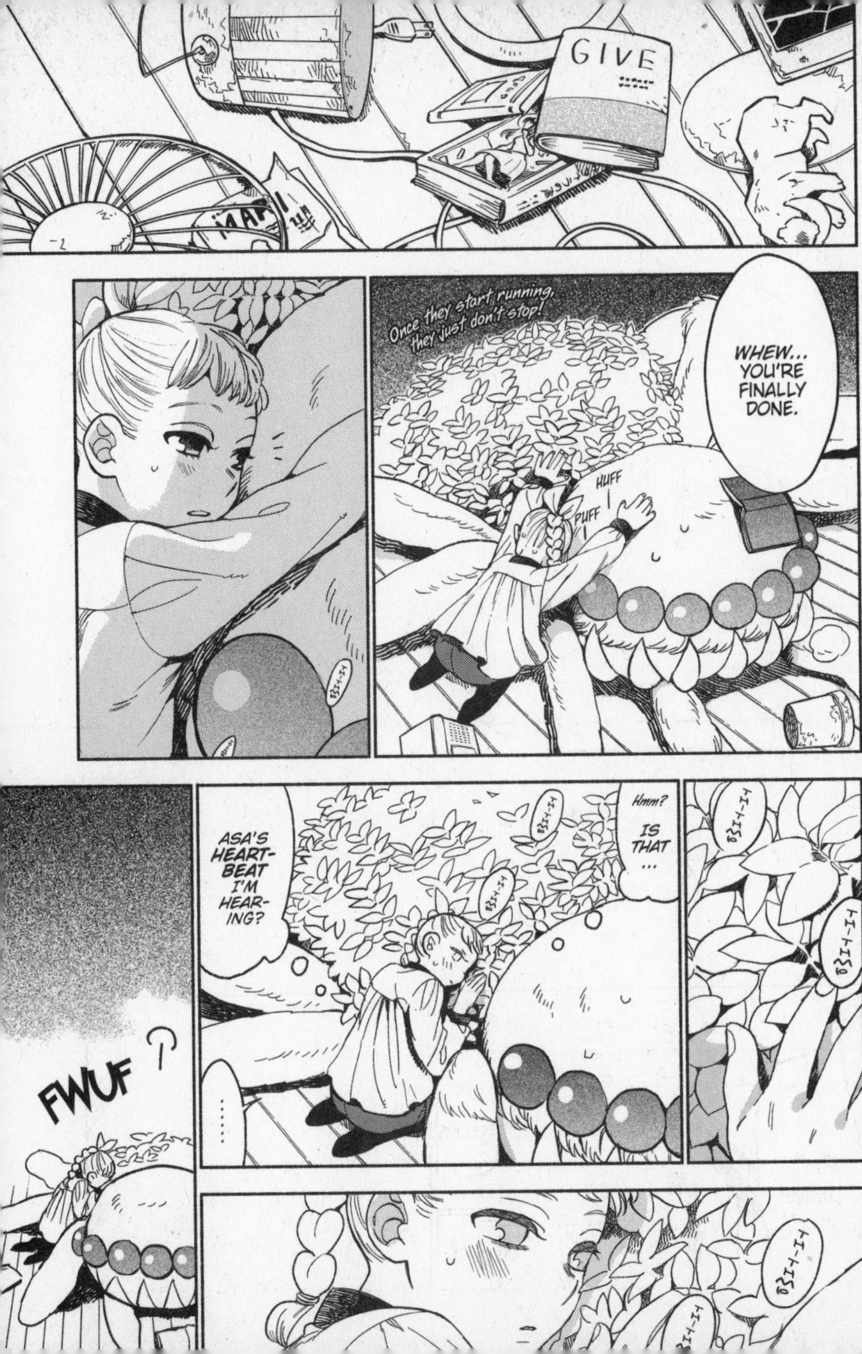
GIVE
Once they start running, they just don't stop!
WHEW... YOU'RE FINALLY DONE.
HUFF PUFF
Hmm? IS THAT ...
ASA'S HEART-BEAT I'M HEAR-ING?
......
FWUF ?

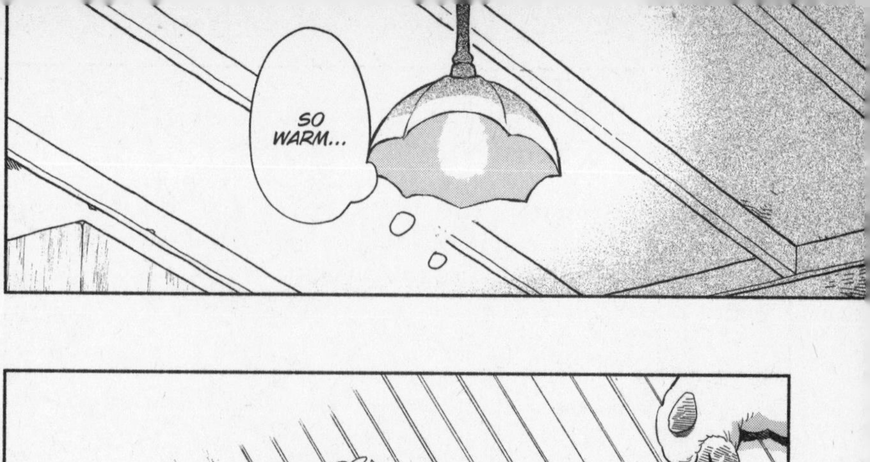
SO WARM...
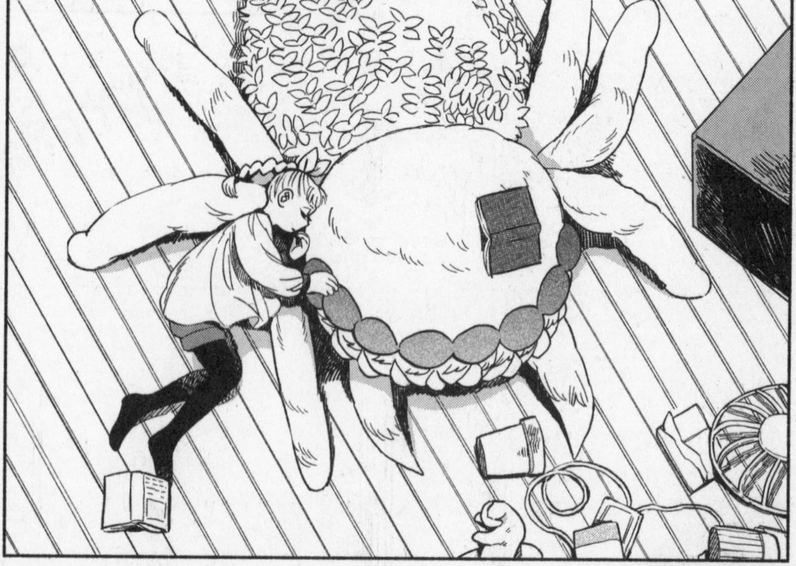
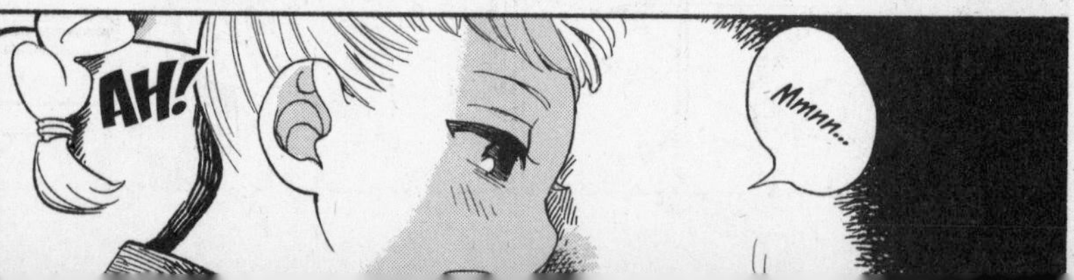
Mmmn...
AH!

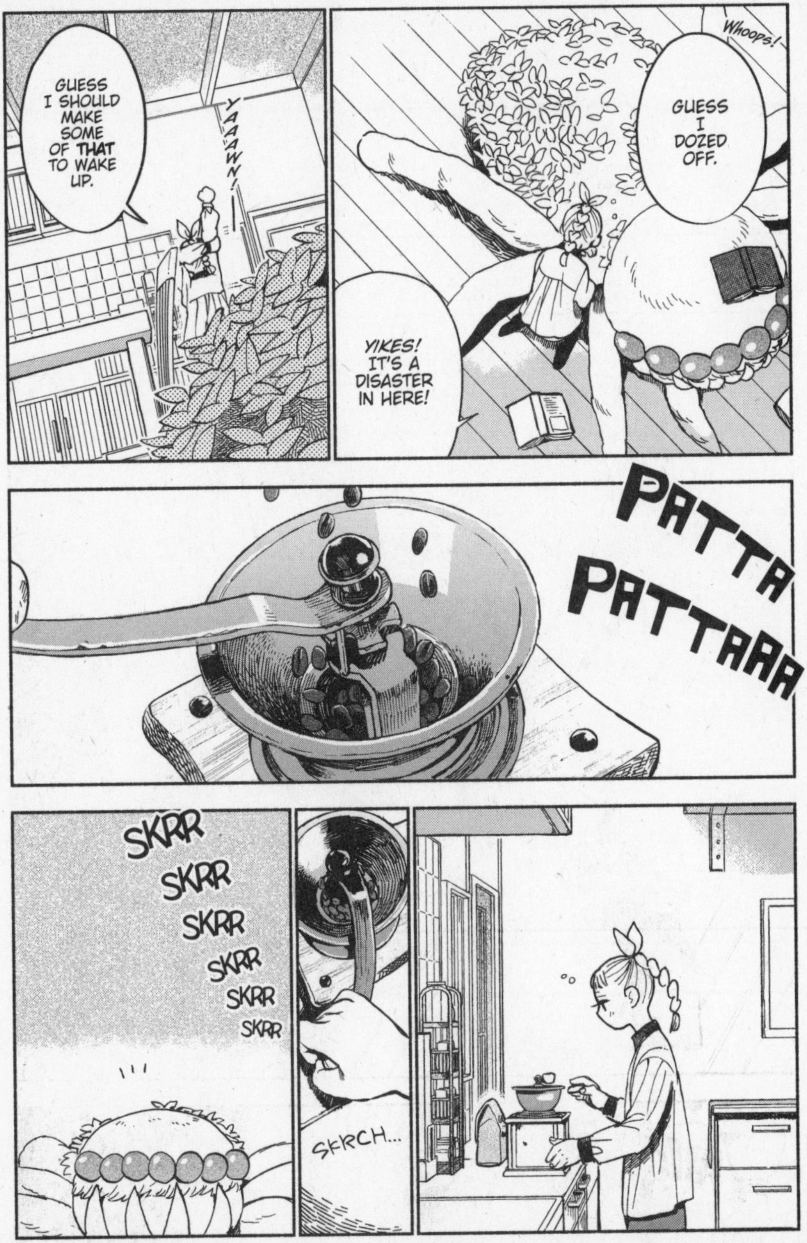
Whoops!
GUESS I DOZED OFF.
YIKES! IT'S A DISASTER IN HERE!
YAAAAWN!
GUESS I SHOULD MAKE SOME OF THAT TO WAKE UP.
PATTA PATTAAA
SKRCH...
SKRR
SKRR
SKRR
SKRR
SKRR
SKRR

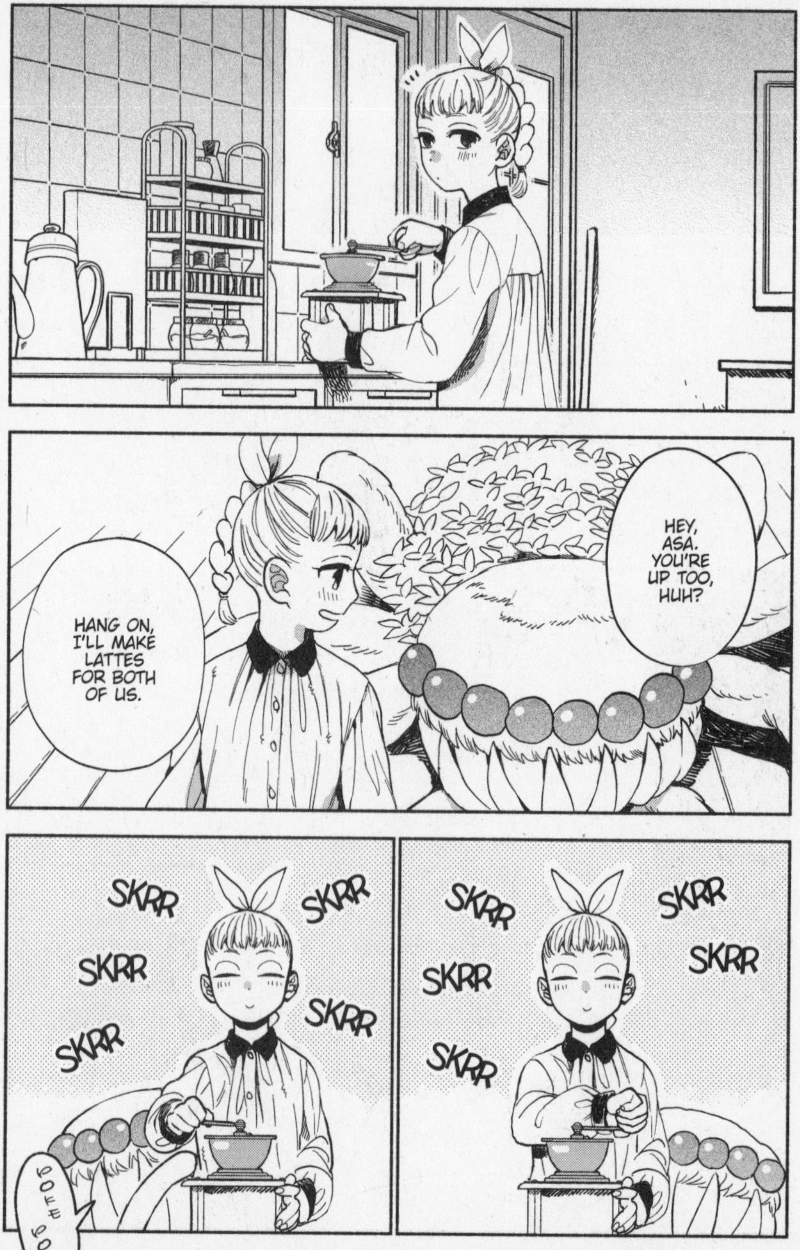
HEY, ASA. YOU'RE UP TOO, HUH?
HANG ON, I'LL MAKE LATTES FOR BOTH OF US.
SKRR
SKRR
SKRR
SKRR
SKRR
SKRR
SKRR
SKRR
SKRR
SKRR
POKE POKE

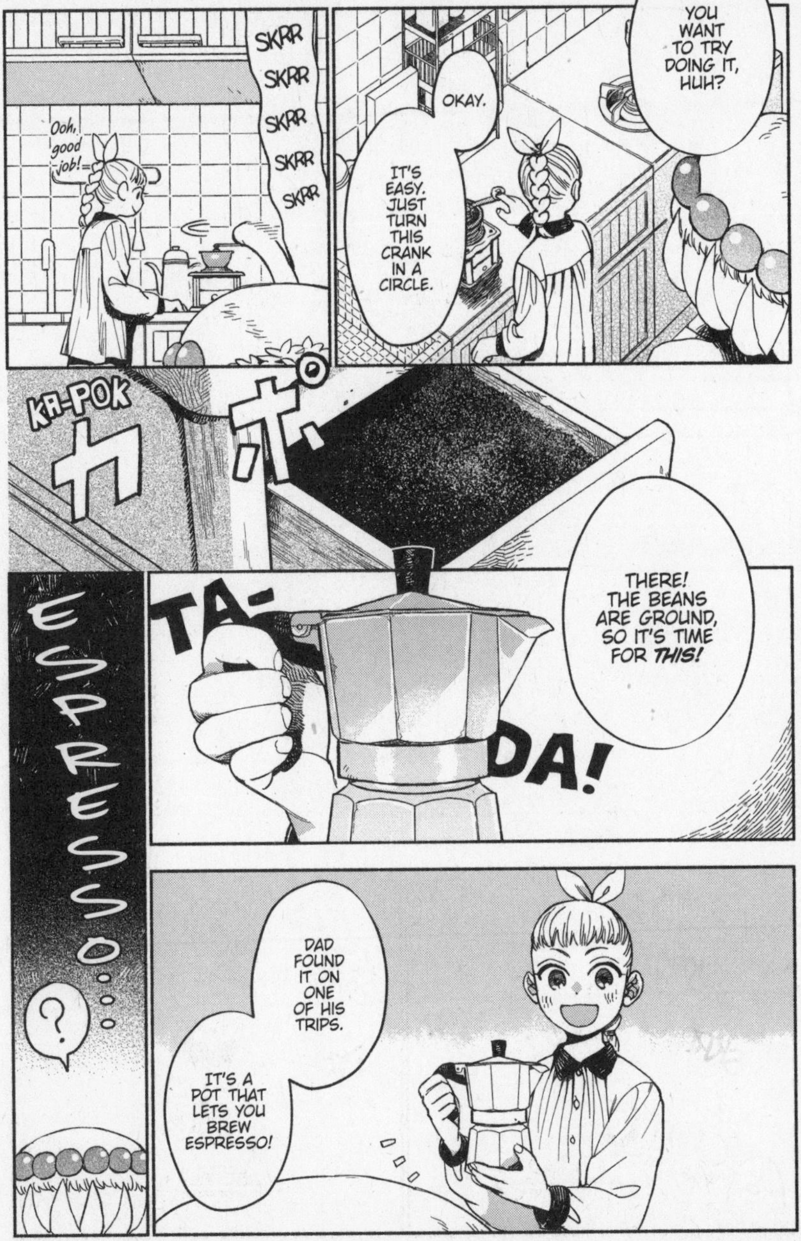
YOU WANT TO TRY DOING IT, HUH?
OKAY.
IT'S EASY. JUST TURN THIS CRANK IN A CIRCLE.
SKRR
SKRR
SKRR
SKRR
SKRR
Ooh, good job!
KA-POK
THERE! THE BEANS ARE GROUND, SO IT'S TIME FOR *THIS!*
TA-DA!
DAD FOUND IT ON ONE OF HIS TRIPS.
IT'S A POT THAT LETS YOU BREW ESPRESSO!
ESPRESSO...
?

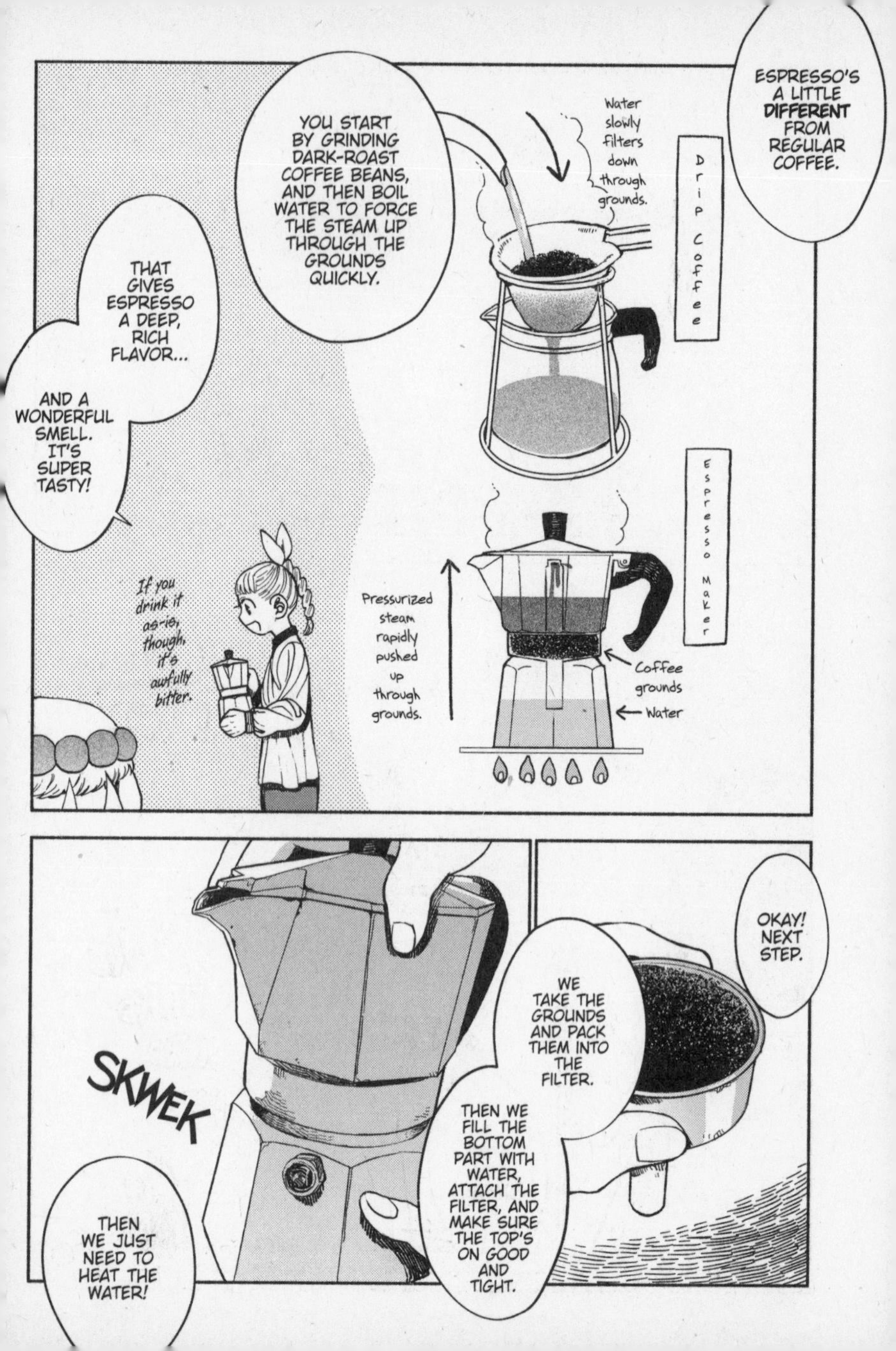
ESPRESSO'S A LITTLE **DIFFERENT** FROM REGULAR COFFEE.
YOU START BY GRINDING DARK-ROAST COFFEE BEANS, AND THEN BOIL WATER TO FORCE THE STEAM UP THROUGH THE GROUNDS QUICKLY.
Drip Coffee
Water slowly filters down through grounds.
Espresso Maker
Pressurized steam rapidly pushed up through grounds.
Coffee grounds
Water
THAT GIVES ESPRESSO A DEEP, RICH FLAVOR...
AND A WONDERFUL SMELL. IT'S SUPER TASTY!
If you drink it as-is, though, it's awfully bitter.
OKAY! NEXT STEP.
WE TAKE THE GROUNDS AND PACK THEM INTO THE FILTER.
THEN WE FILL THE BOTTOM PART WITH WATER, ATTACH THE FILTER, AND MAKE SURE THE TOP'S ON GOOD AND TIGHT.
SKWEK
THEN WE JUST NEED TO HEAT THE WATER!

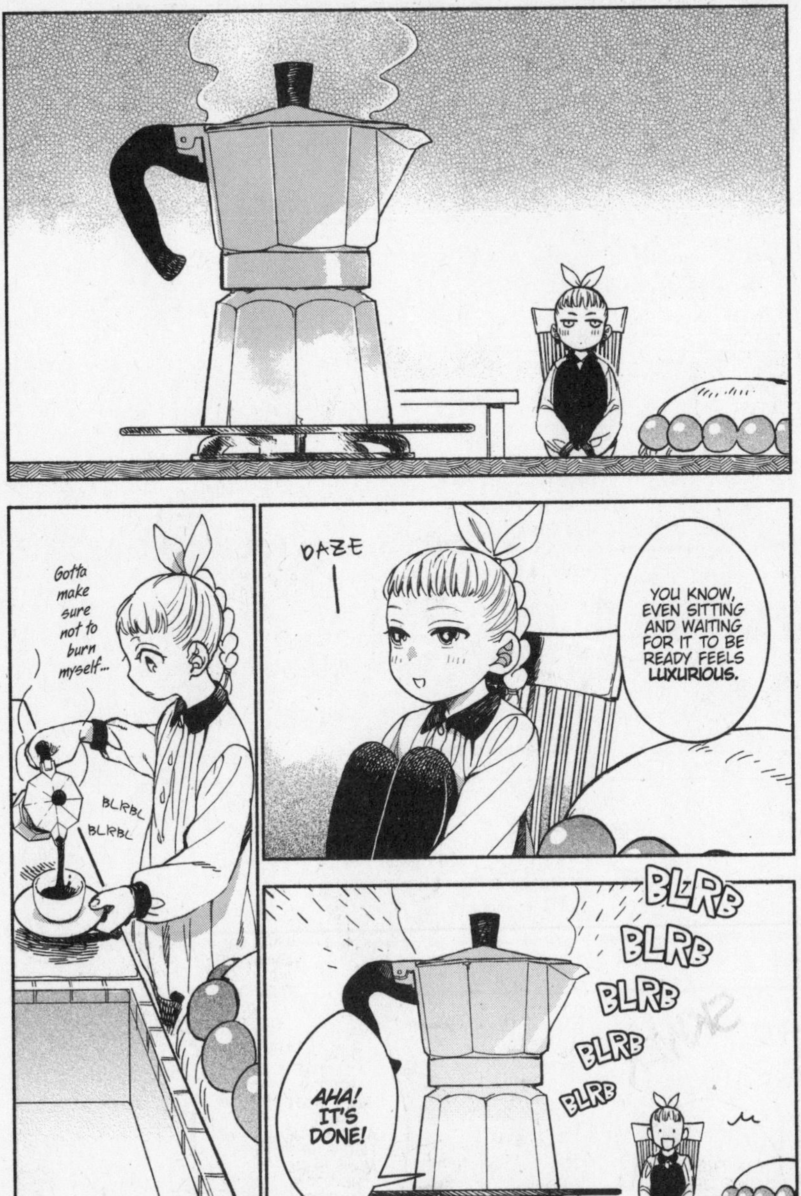
YOU KNOW, EVEN SITTING AND WAITING FOR IT TO BE READY FEELS **LUXURIOUS.**
DAZE
BLRB
BLRB
BLRB
BLRB
BLRB
AHA! IT'S DONE!
Gotta make sure not to burn myself...
BLRBL
BLRBL

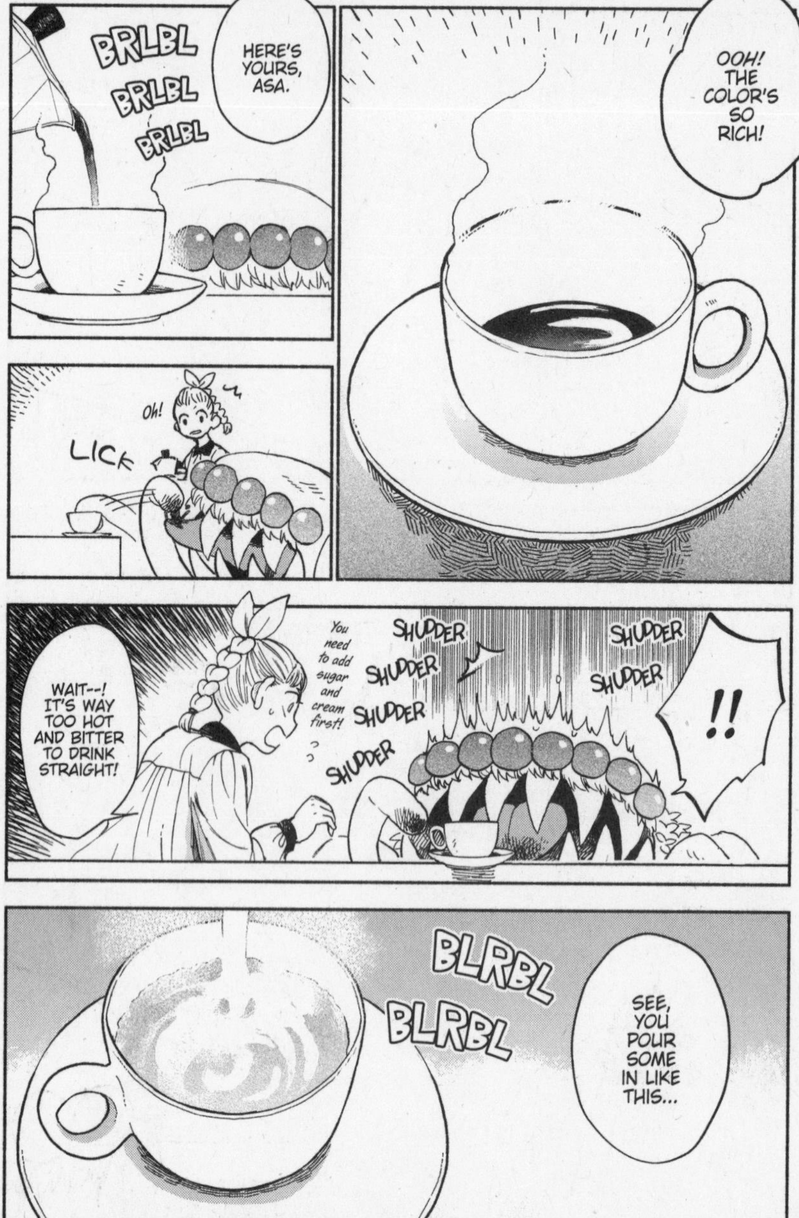
OOH! THE COLOR'S SO RICH!
HERE'S YOURS, ASA.
BRLBL
BRLBL
BRLBL
Oh!
LICK
!!
SHUDDER
SHUDDER
SHUDDER
SHUDDER
SHUDDER
SHUDDER
You need to add sugar and cream first!
WAIT--! IT'S WAY TOO HOT AND BITTER TO DRINK STRAIGHT!
SEE, YOU POUR SOME IN LIKE THIS...
BLRBL
BLRBL

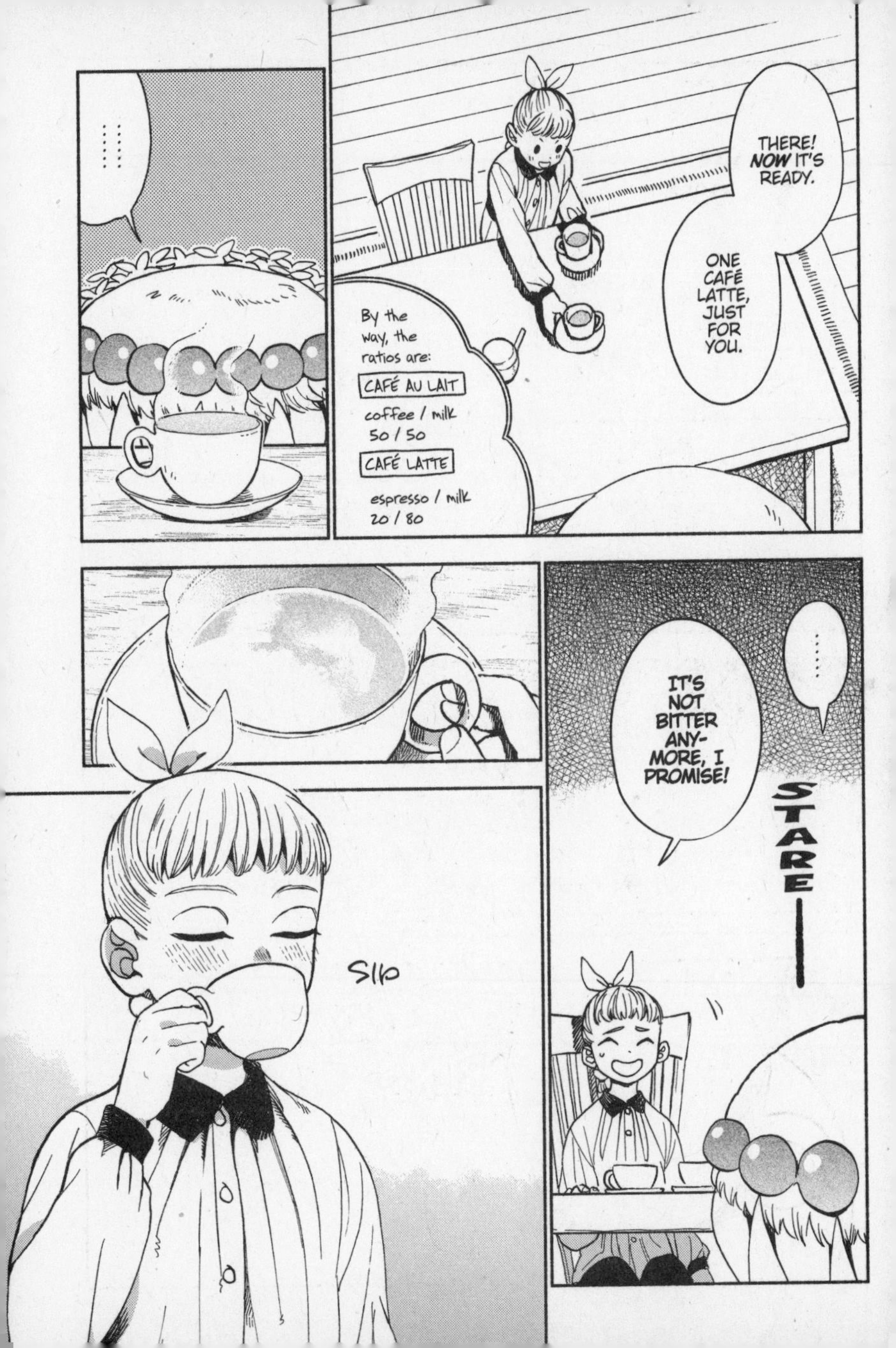
THERE! NOW IT'S READY.
ONE CAFÉ LATTE, JUST FOR YOU.
By the way, the ratios are:
CAFÉ AU LAIT
coffee / milk 50 / 50
CAFÉ LATTE
espresso / milk 20 / 80
......
......
IT'S NOT BITTER ANY-MORE, I PROMISE!
STARE
SIP

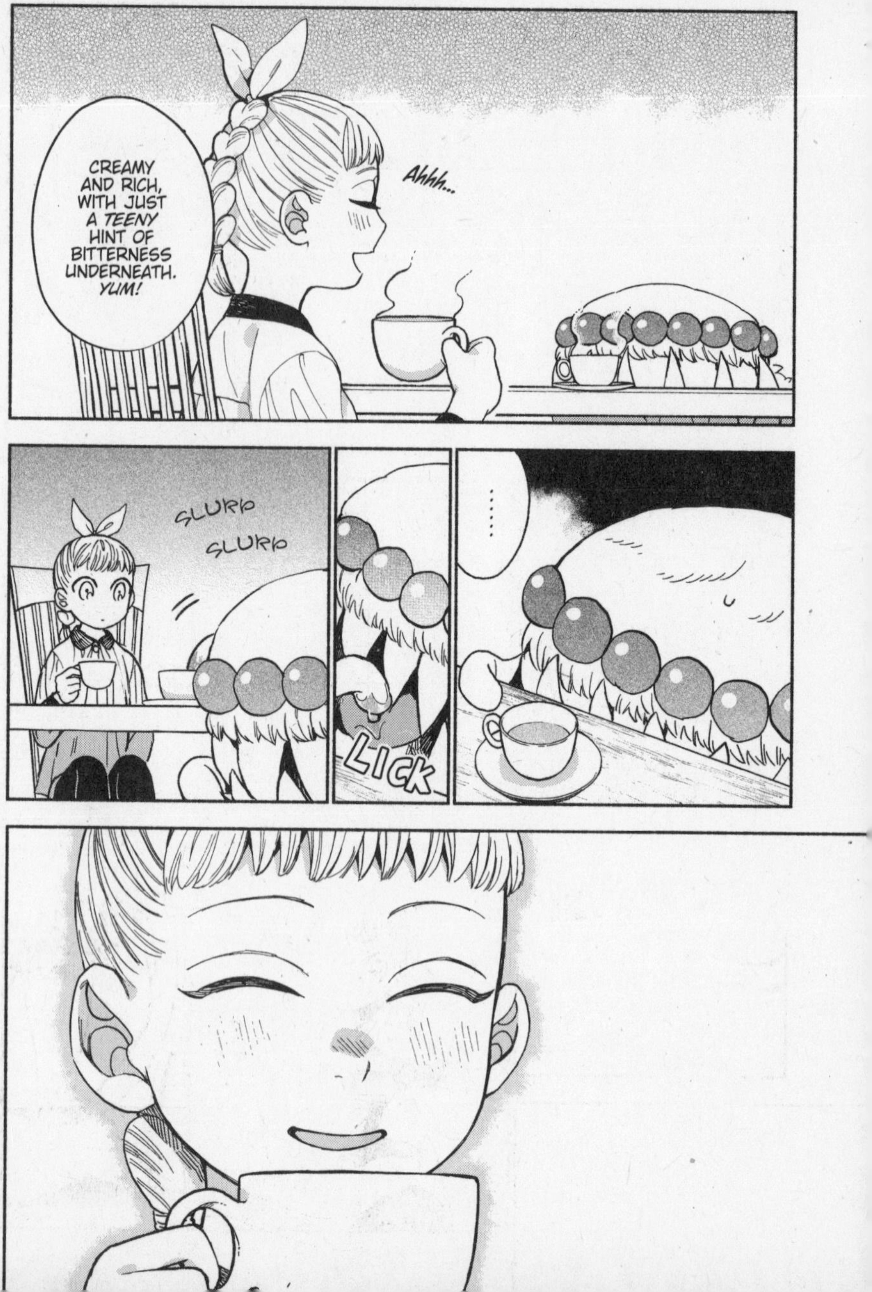
CREAMY AND RICH, WITH JUST A *TEENY* HINT OF BITTERNESS UNDERNEATH. *YUM!*
Ahhh...
......
LICK
SLURP
SLURP

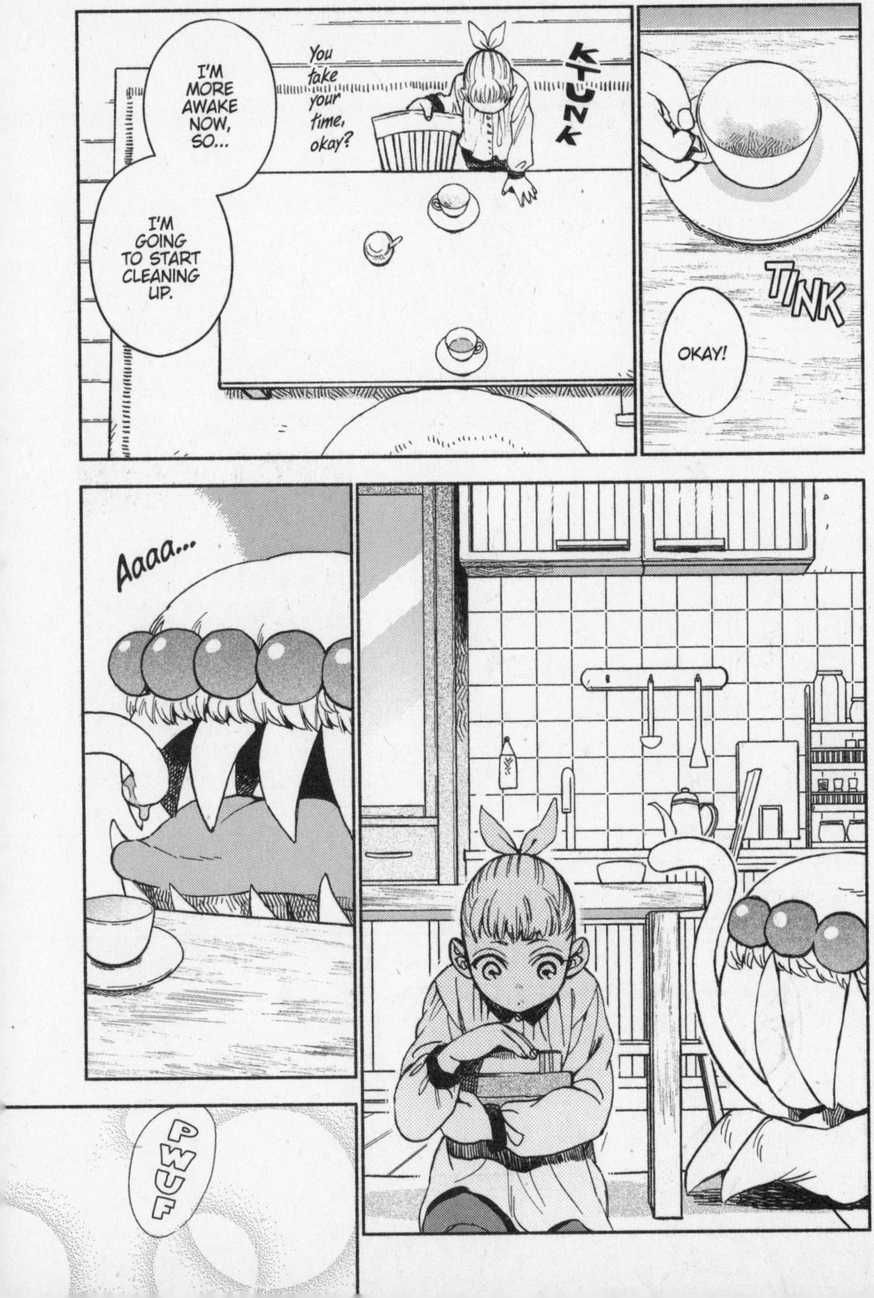
I'M MORE AWAKE NOW, SO...
I'M GOING TO START CLEANING UP.
You take your time, okay?
KTUNK
TINK
OKAY!
Aaaa...
PWUF

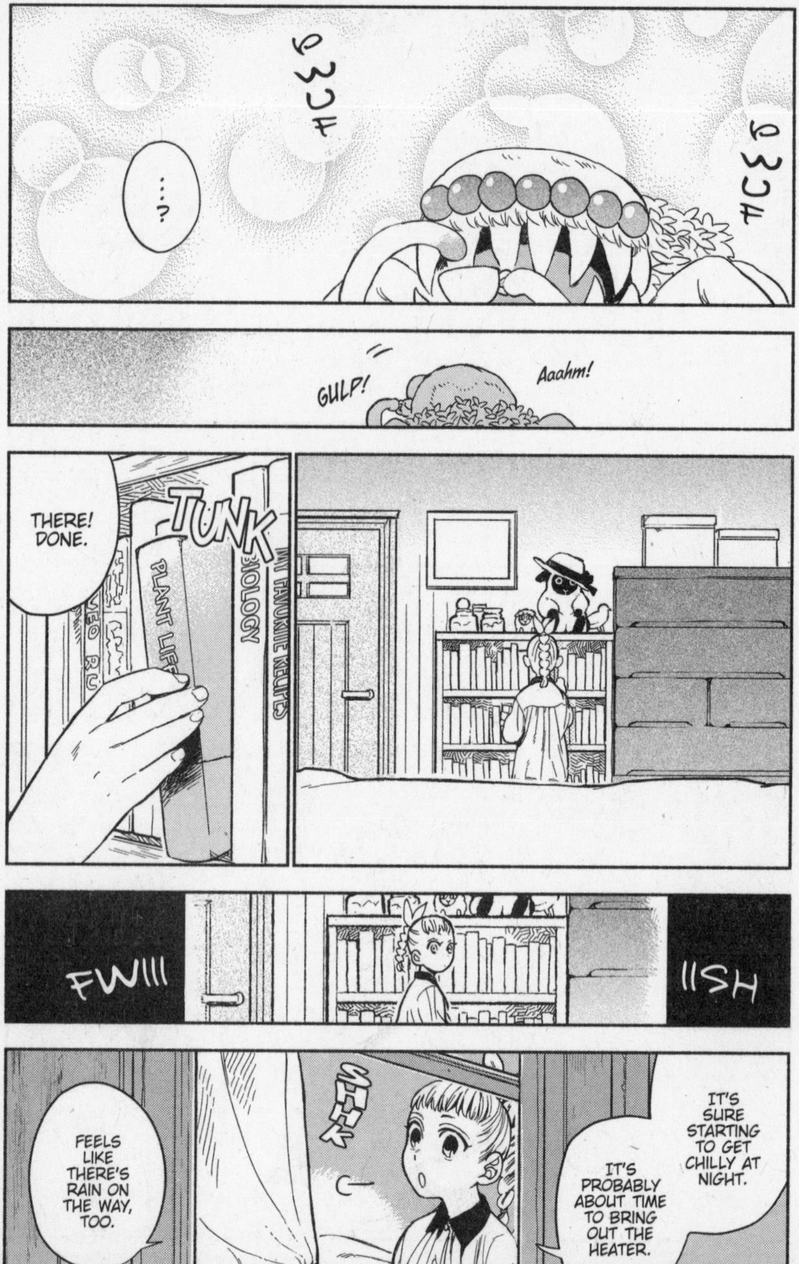
...?
Aaahm!
GULP!
TUNK
THERE! DONE.
MY FAVORITE RECIPES
BIOLOGY
PLANT LIFE
FWIII
IISH
IT'S SURE STARTING TO GET CHILLY AT NIGHT.
IT'S PROBABLY ABOUT TIME TO BRING OUT THE HEATER.
FEELS LIKE THERE'S RAIN ON THE WAY, TOO.

KREE...

BTAM

HMM?

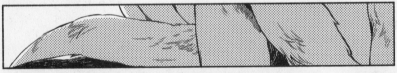

FLOP

UM, ASA? WHAT ARE YOU DOING?

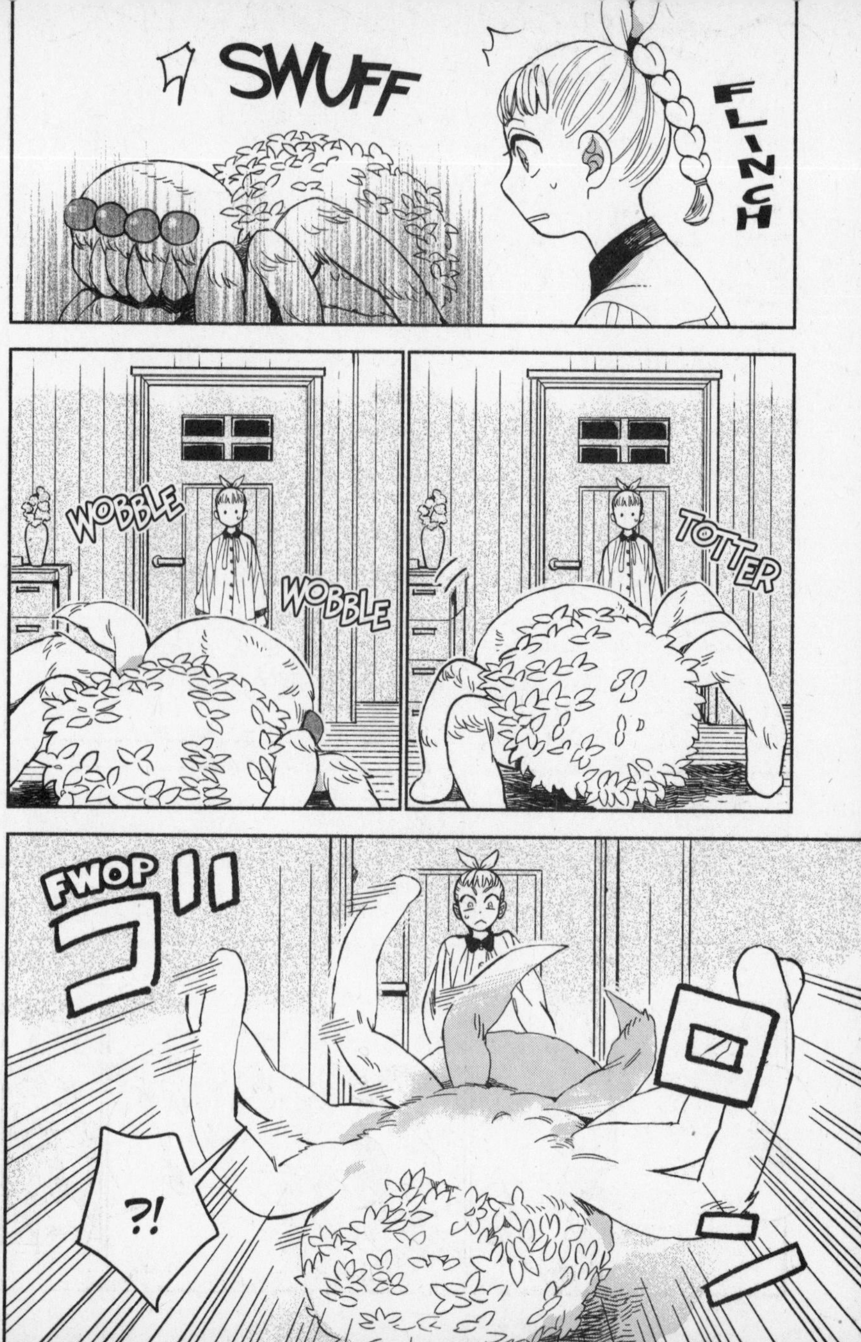
FLINCH
SWUFF
TOTTER
WOBBLE
WOBBLE
FWOP
?!

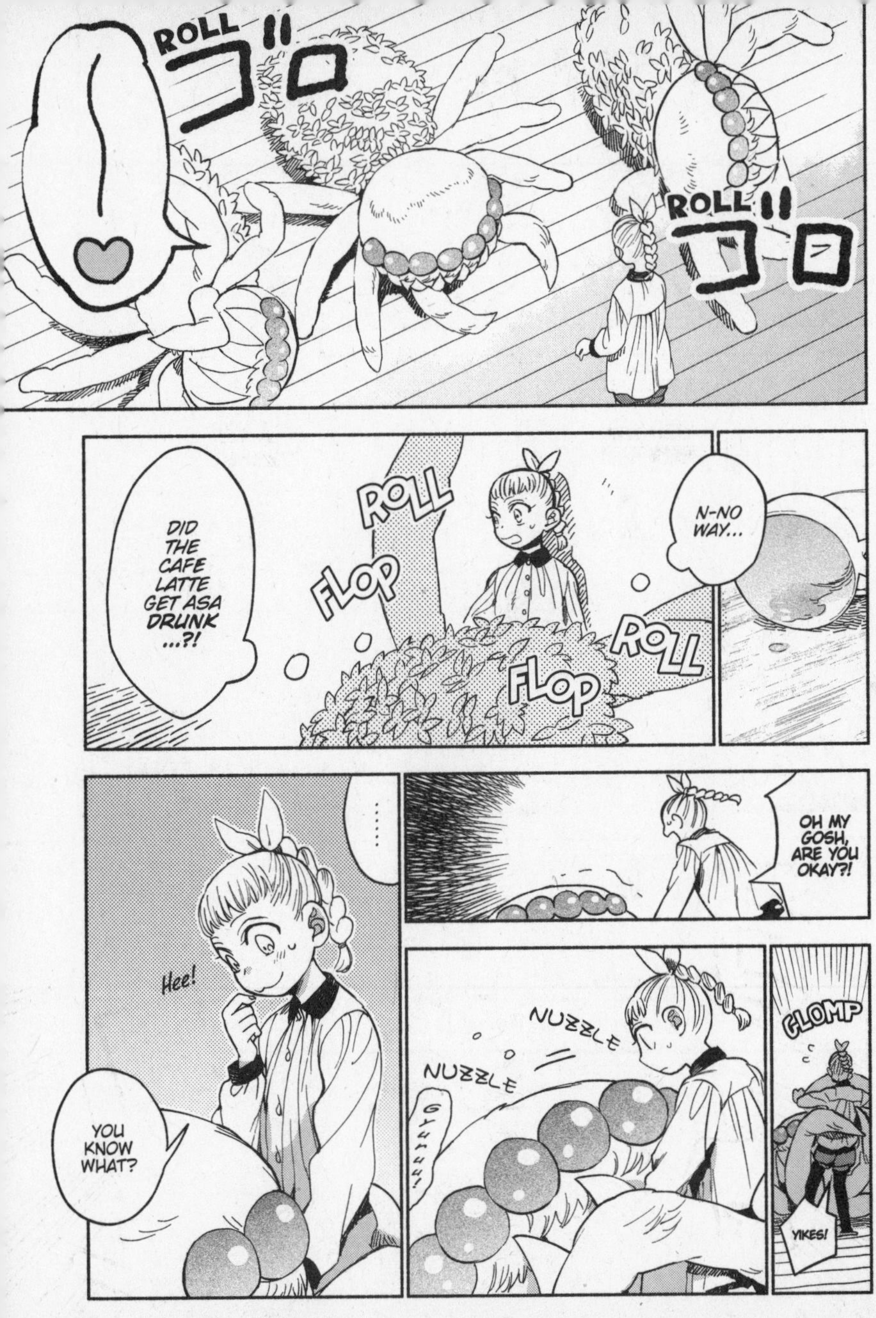
ROLL ゴロ
ROLL ゴロ
N-NO WAY...
ROLL
FLOP
ROLL
FLOP
DID THE CAFE LATTE GET ASA DRUNK ...?!
OH MY GOSH, ARE YOU OKAY?!
GLOMP
YIKES!
NUZZLE
NUZZLE
Gyuruu!
......
Hee!
YOU KNOW WHAT?

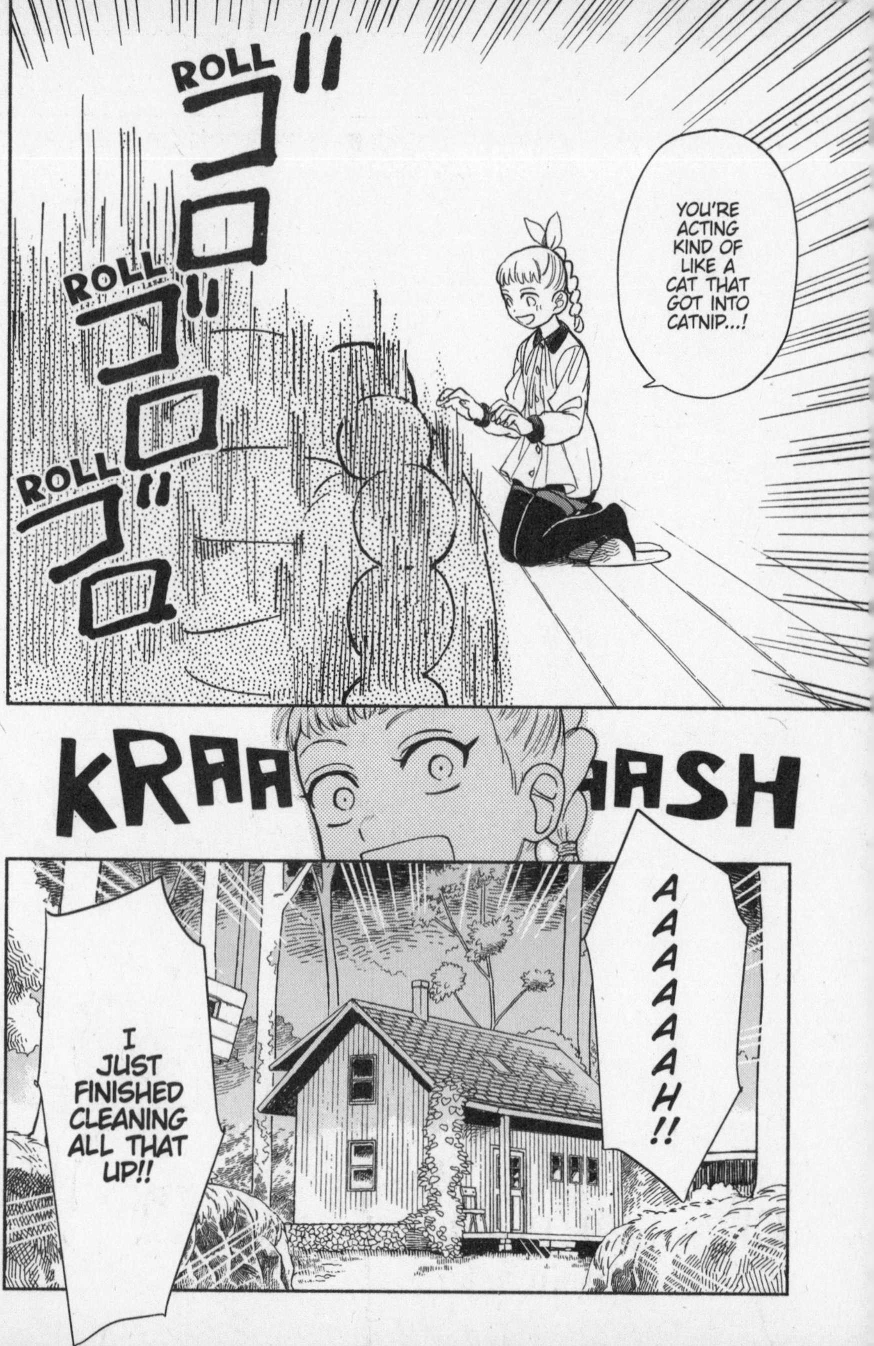
YOU'RE ACTING KIND OF LIKE A CAT THAT GOT INTO CATNIP...!
ROLL
ゴロ
ROLL
ゴロ
ROLL
ゴロ
KRAA
AASH
AAAAAAAH!!
I JUST FINISHED CLEANING ALL THAT UP!!

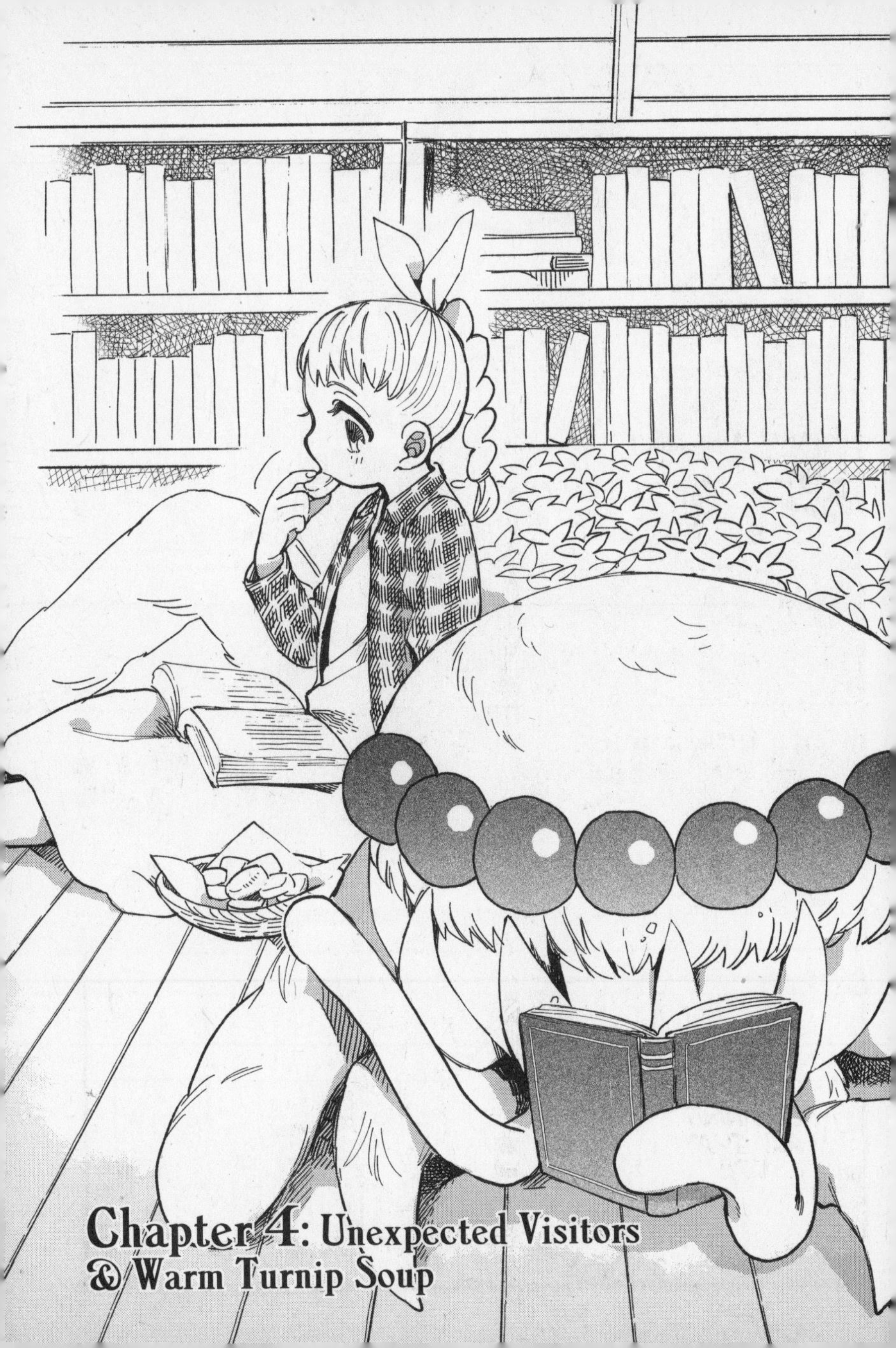

Chapter 4: Unexpected Visitors & Warm Turnip Soup

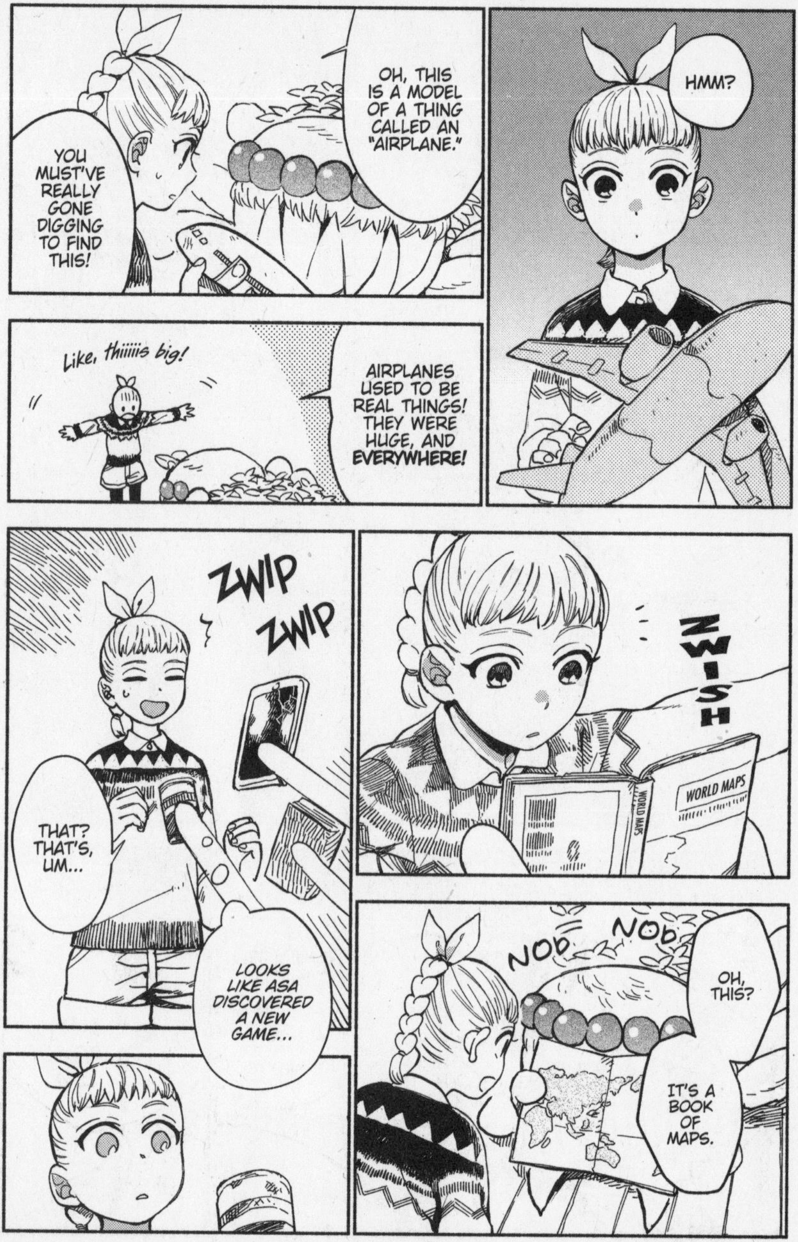
HMM?
OH, THIS IS A MODEL OF A THING CALLED AN "AIRPLANE."
YOU MUST'VE REALLY GONE DIGGING TO FIND THIS!
AIRPLANES USED TO BE REAL THINGS! THEY WERE HUGE, AND EVERYWHERE!
Like, thiiiis big!
ZWISH
WORLD MAPS
WORLD MAPS
NOD NOD
OH, THIS?
IT'S A BOOK OF MAPS.
ZWIP
ZWIP
THAT? THAT'S, UM...
LOOKS LIKE ASA DISCOVERED A NEW GAME...

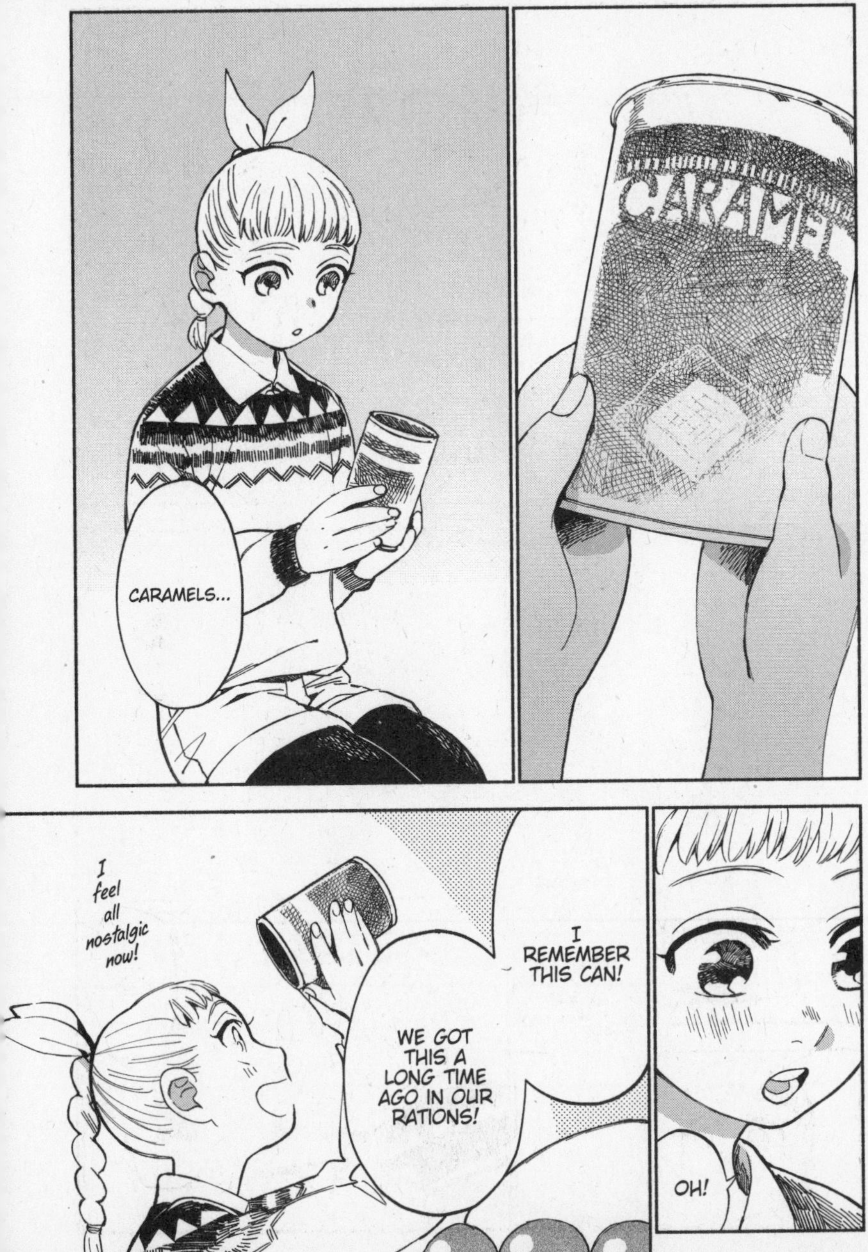
CARAMELS...
OH!
I REMEMBER THIS CAN!
WE GOT THIS A LONG TIME AGO IN OUR RATIONS!
I feel all nostalgic now!

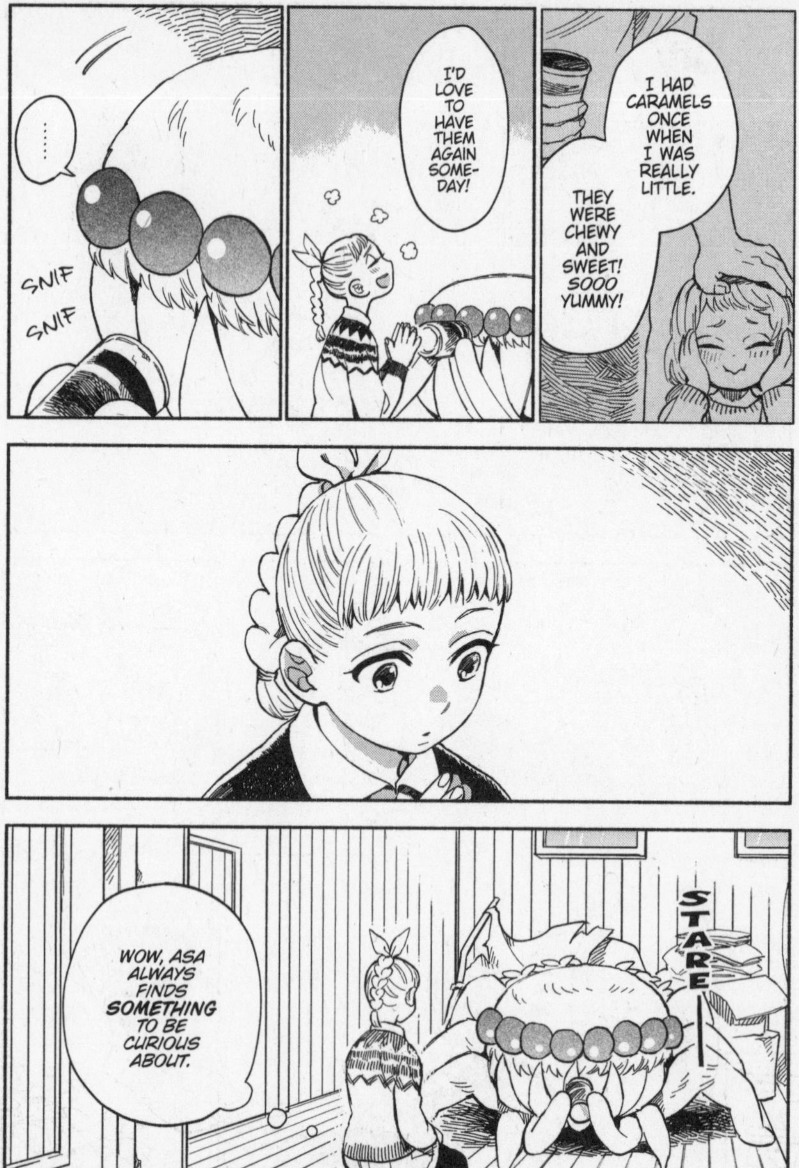
I HAD CARAMELS ONCE WHEN I WAS REALLY LITTLE.
THEY WERE CHEWY AND SWEET! SOOO YUMMY!
I'D LOVE TO HAVE THEM AGAIN SOME-DAY!
......
SNIF
SNIF
STARE
WOW, ASA ALWAYS FINDS SOMETHING TO BE CURIOUS ABOUT.

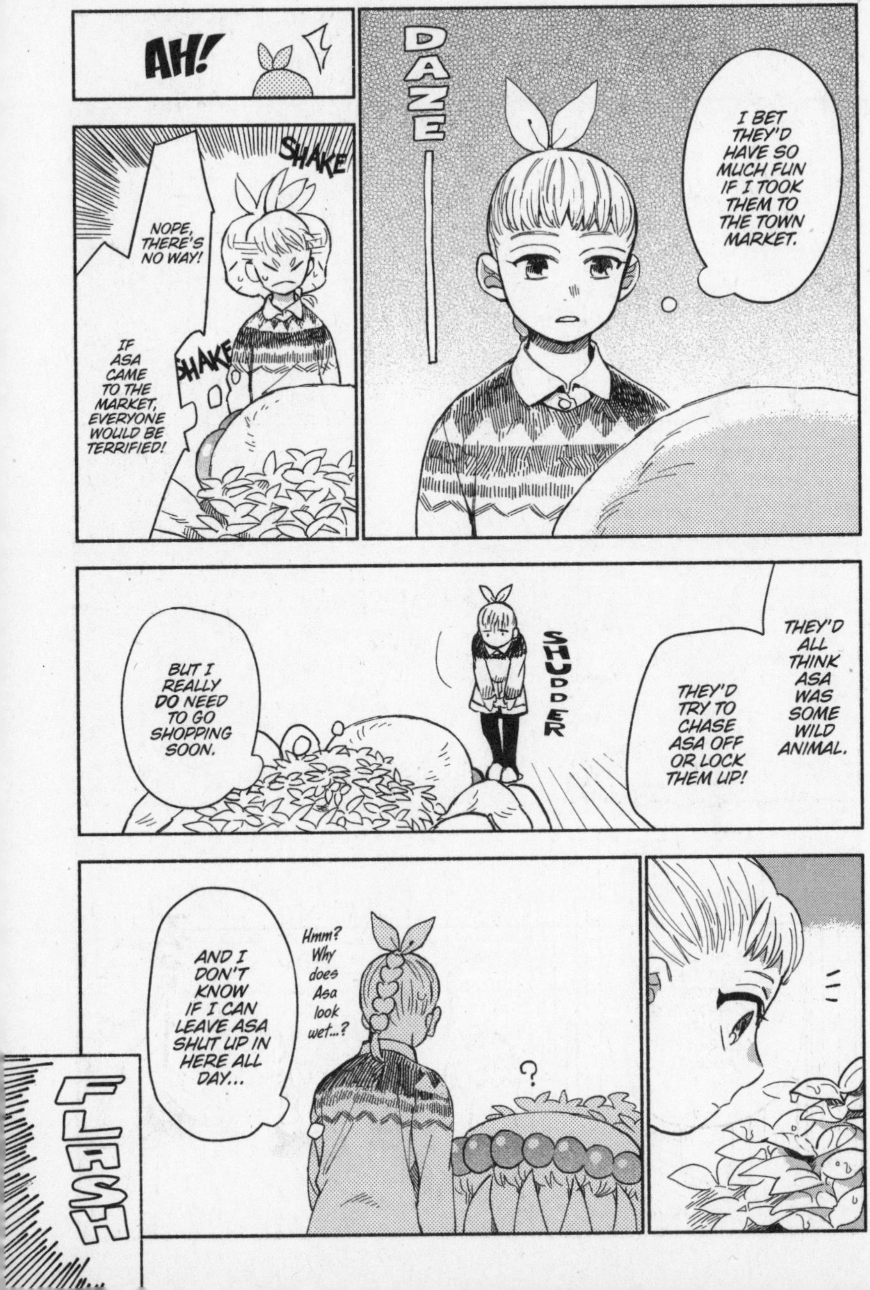
DAZE
I BET THEY'D HAVE SO MUCH FUN IF I TOOK THEM TO THE TOWN MARKET.
AH!
SHAKE
NOPE, THERE'S NO WAY!
SHAKE
IF ASA CAME TO THE MARKET, EVERYONE WOULD BE TERRIFIED!
THEY'D ALL THINK ASA WAS SOME WILD ANIMAL.
THEY'D TRY TO CHASE ASA OFF OR LOCK THEM UP!
SHUDDER
BUT I REALLY DO NEED TO GO SHOPPING SOON.
AND I DON'T KNOW IF I CAN LEAVE ASA SHUT UP IN HERE ALL DAY...
Hmm? Why does Asa look wet...?
?
FLASH

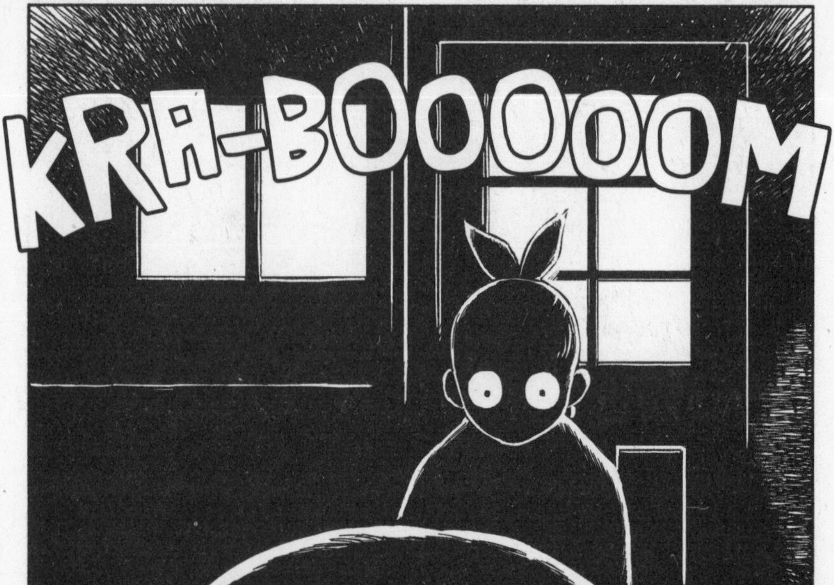
KRA-BOOOOOM
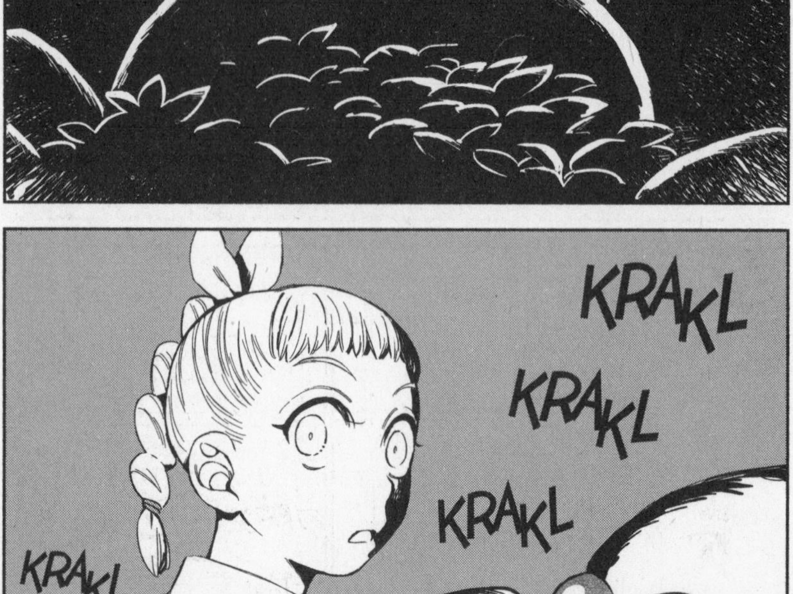
KRAKL
KRAKL
KRAKL
KRAKL

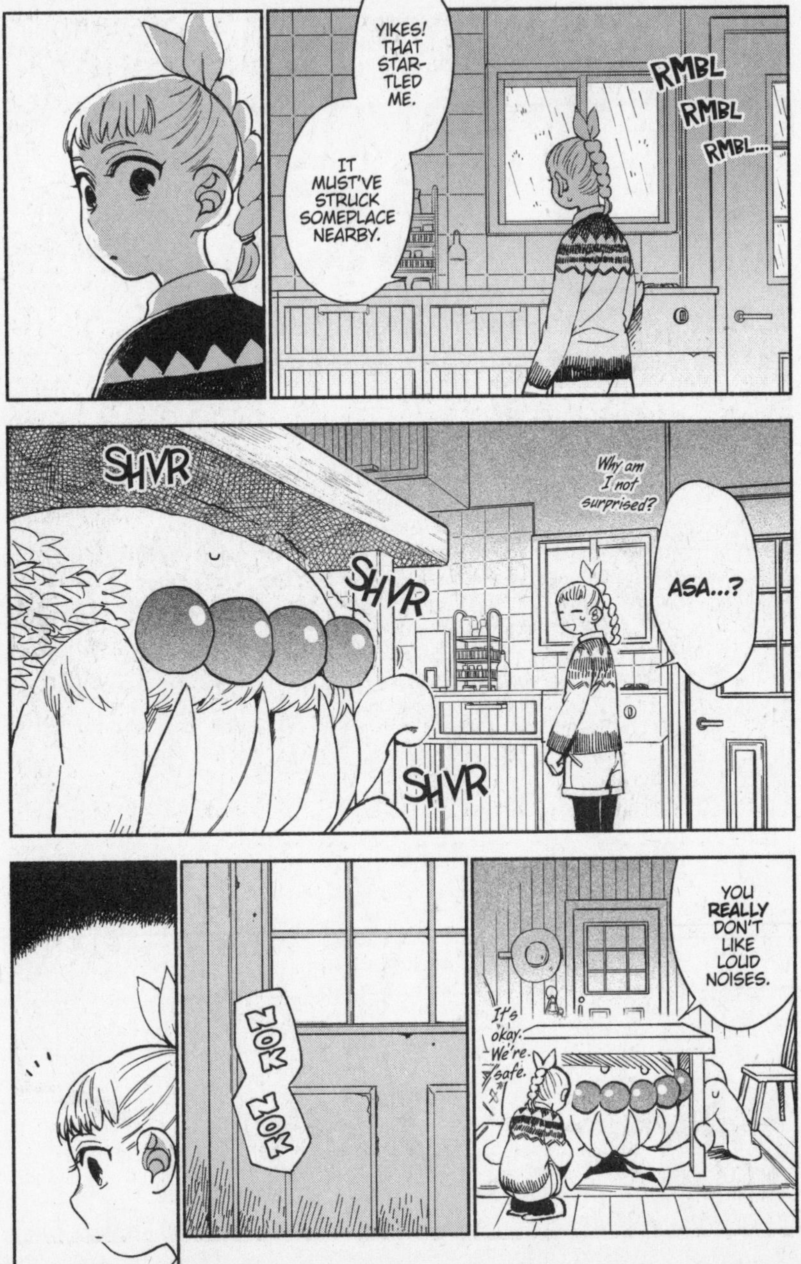
RMBL RMBL RMBL...
YIKES! THAT STAR-TLED ME.
IT MUST'VE STRUCK SOMEPLACE NEARBY.
ASA...?
Why am I not surprised?
SHVR
SHVR
SHVR
YOU REALLY DON'T LIKE LOUD NOISES.
It's okay. We're safe.
NOK NOK NOK

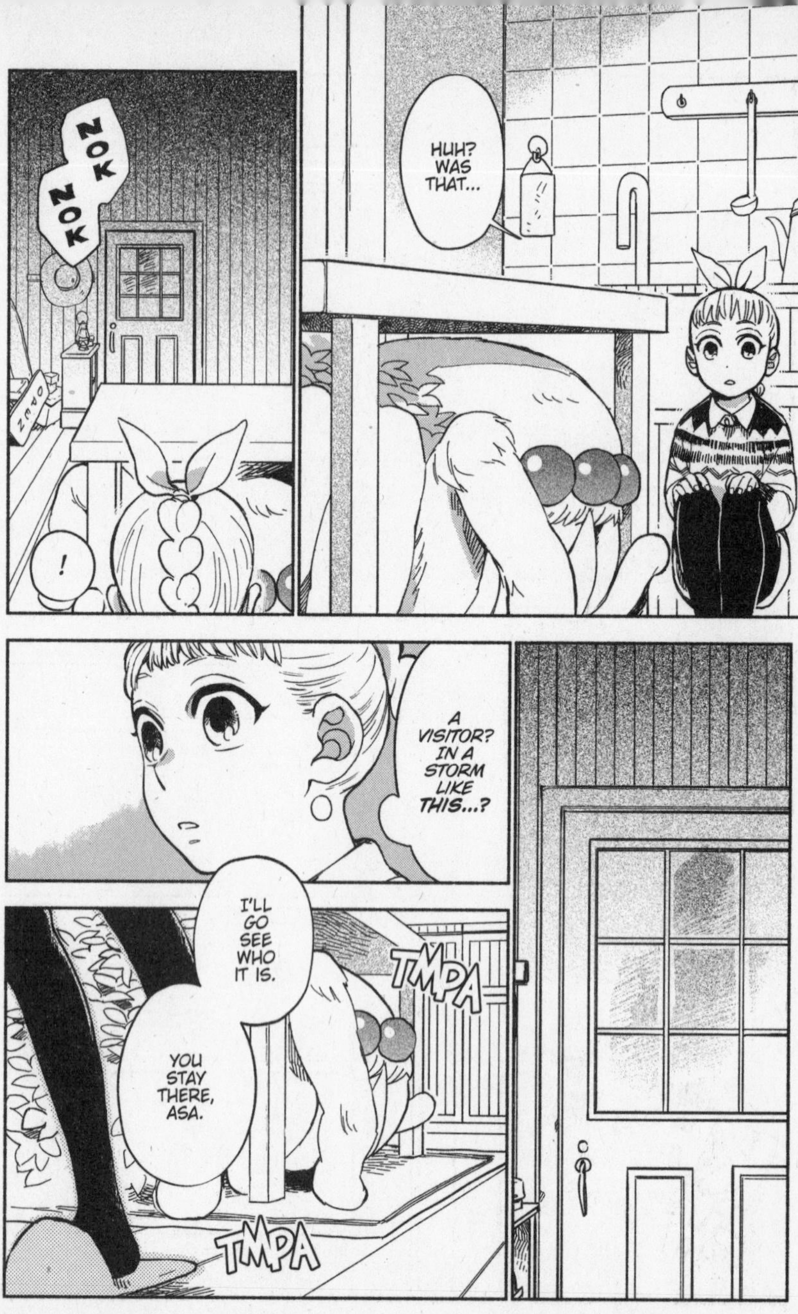
HUH? WAS THAT...
NOK NOK
!
A VISITOR? IN A STORM LIKE THIS...?
I'LL GO SEE WHO IT IS.
YOU STAY THERE, ASA.
TMPA
TMPA

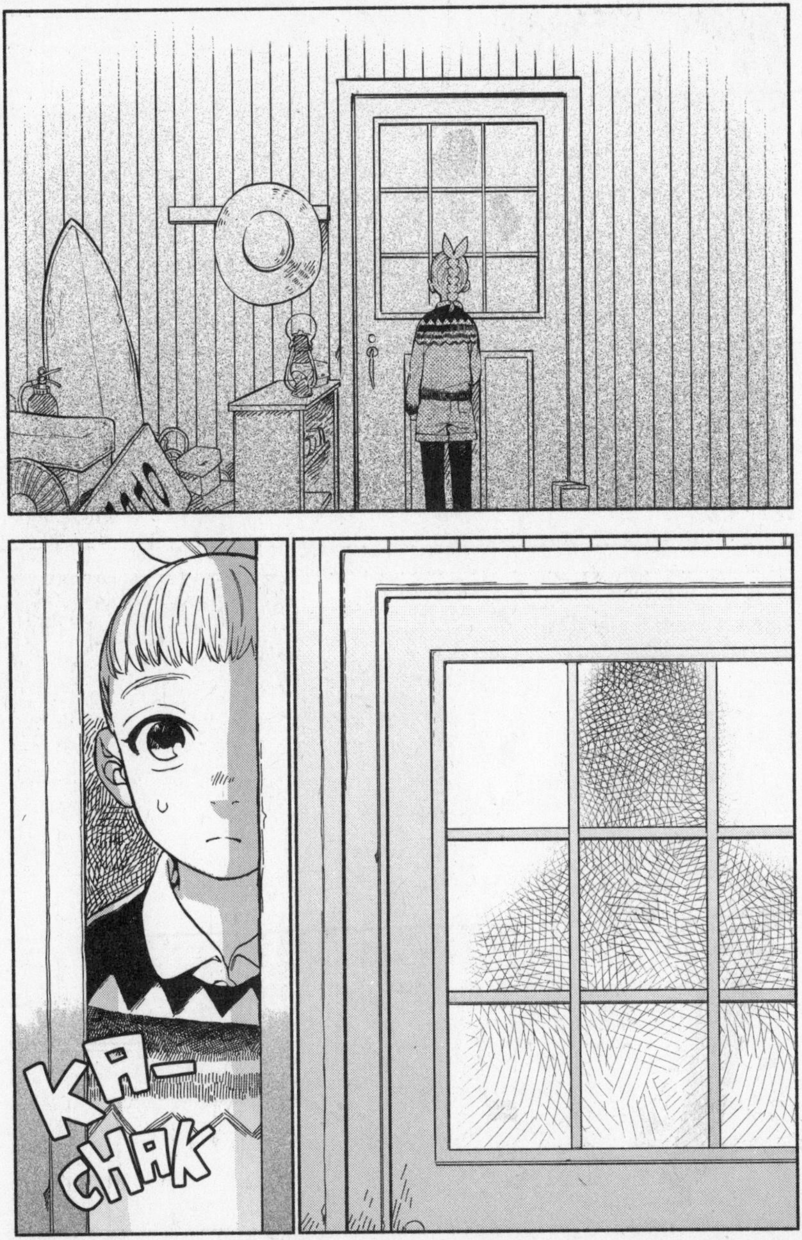
KA-CHAK

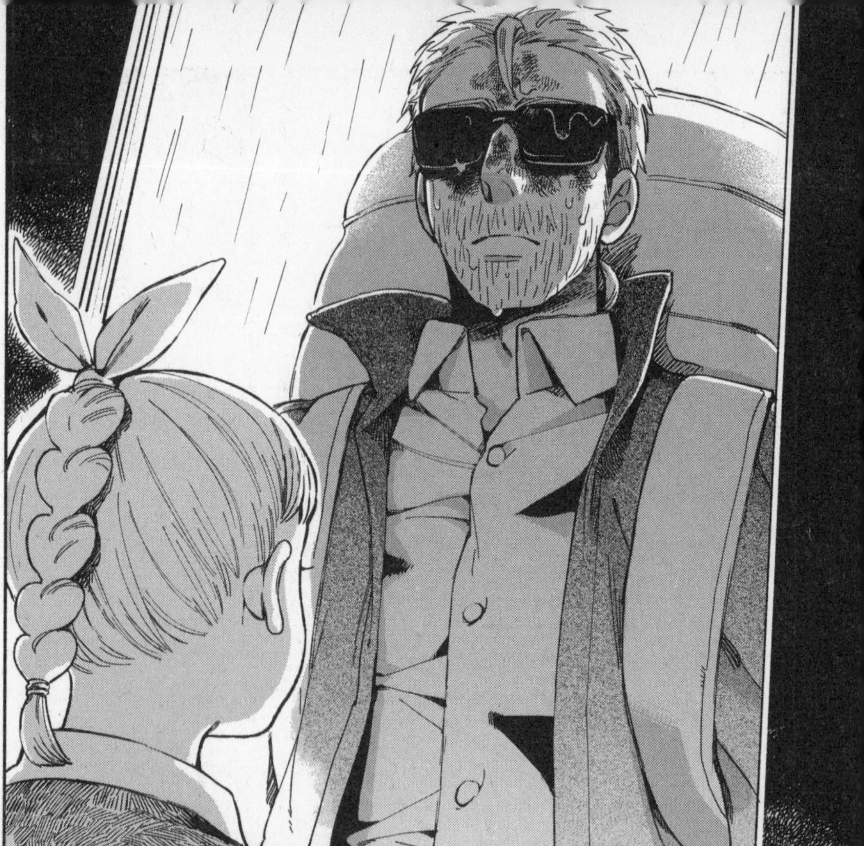

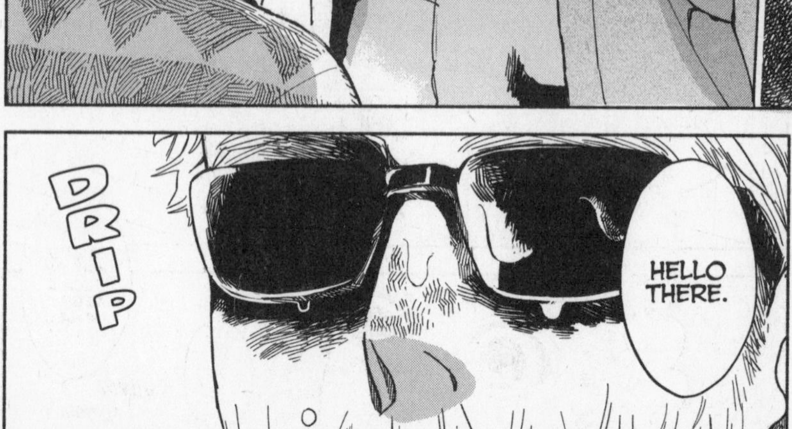
HELLO THERE.
DRIP

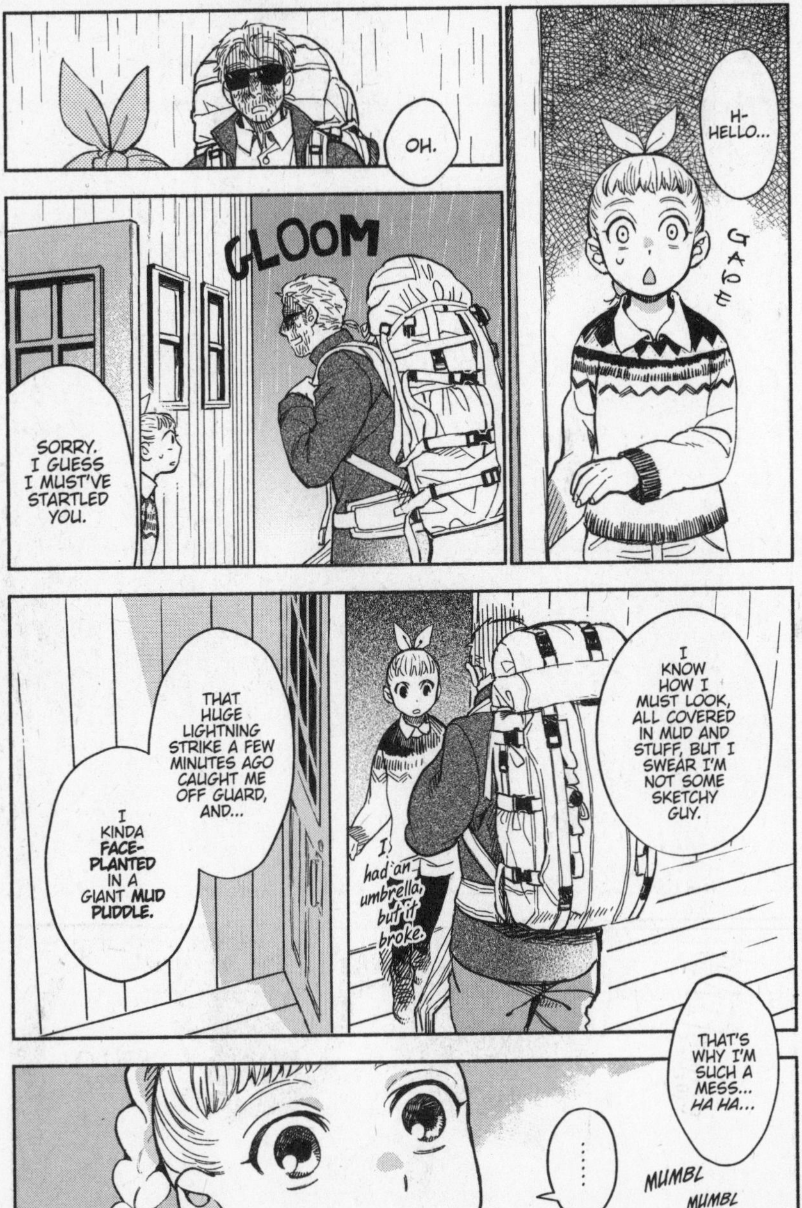
H- HELLO...
GAPE
OH.
GLOOM
SORRY. I GUESS I MUST'VE STARTLED YOU.
I KNOW HOW I MUST LOOK, ALL COVERED IN MUD AND STUFF, BUT I SWEAR I'M NOT SOME SKETCHY GUY.
I had an umbrella, but it broke.
THAT HUGE LIGHTNING STRIKE A FEW MINUTES AGO CAUGHT ME OFF GUARD, AND...
I KINDA FACE-PLANTED IN A GIANT MUD PUDDLE.
THAT'S WHY I'M SUCH A MESS... HA HA...
MUMBL MUMBL
......

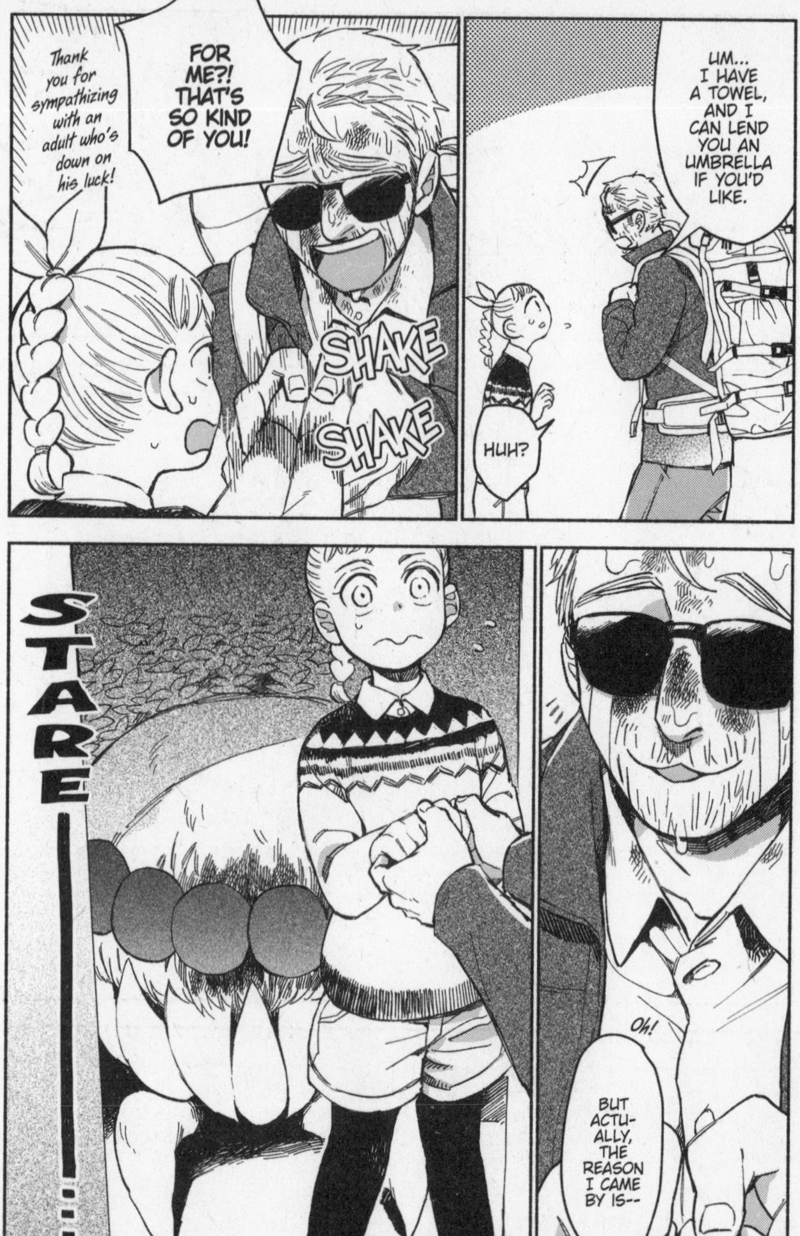
UM... I HAVE A TOWEL, AND I CAN LEND YOU AN UMBRELLA IF YOU'D LIKE.
HUH?
FOR ME?! THAT'S SO KIND OF YOU!
Thank you for sympathizing with an adult who's down on his luck!
SHAKE
SHAKE
Oh!
BUT ACTU-ALLY, THE REASON I CAME BY IS--
STARE.....

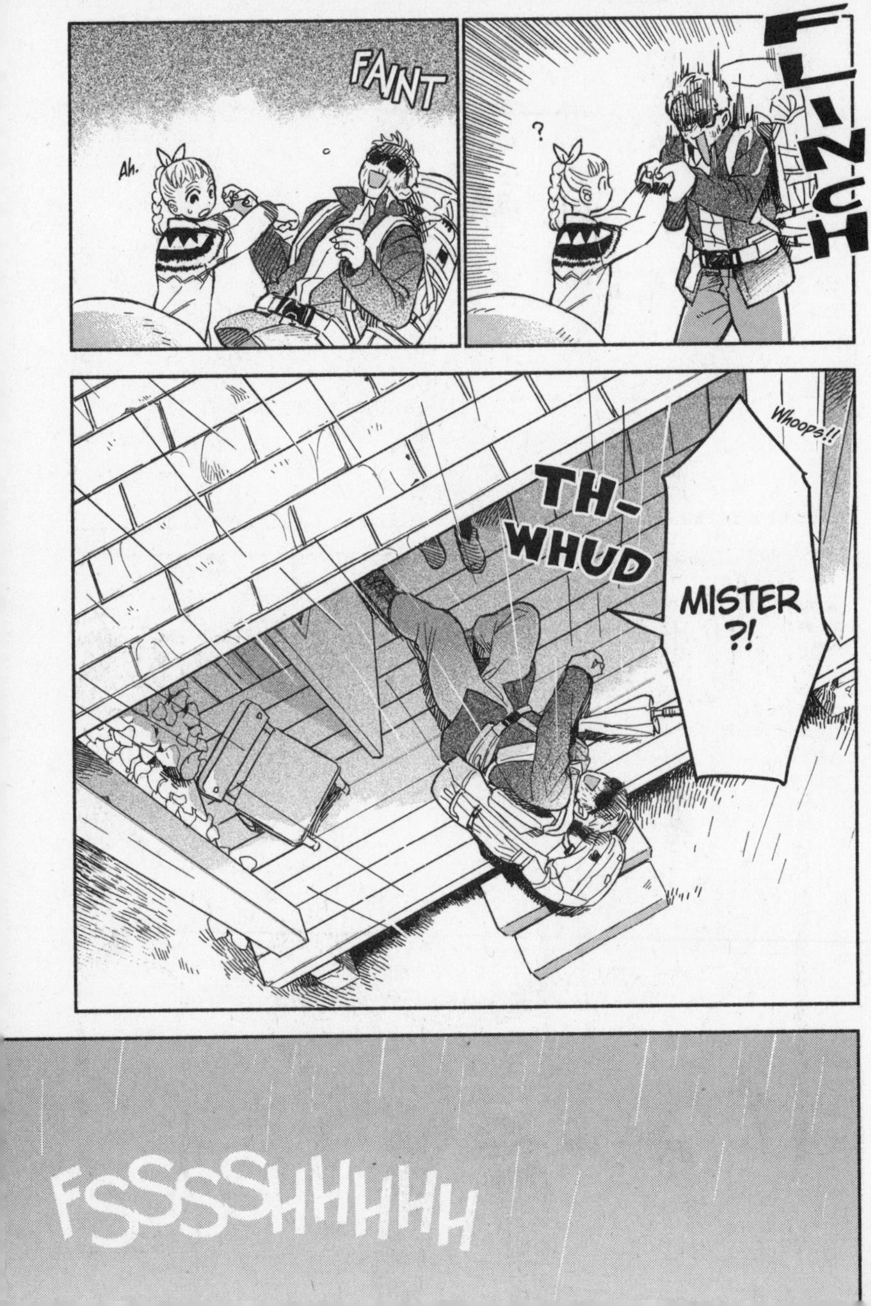
FLINCH
?
FAINT
Ah.
Whoops!!
TH-WHUD
MISTER ?!
FSSSSHHHHHH

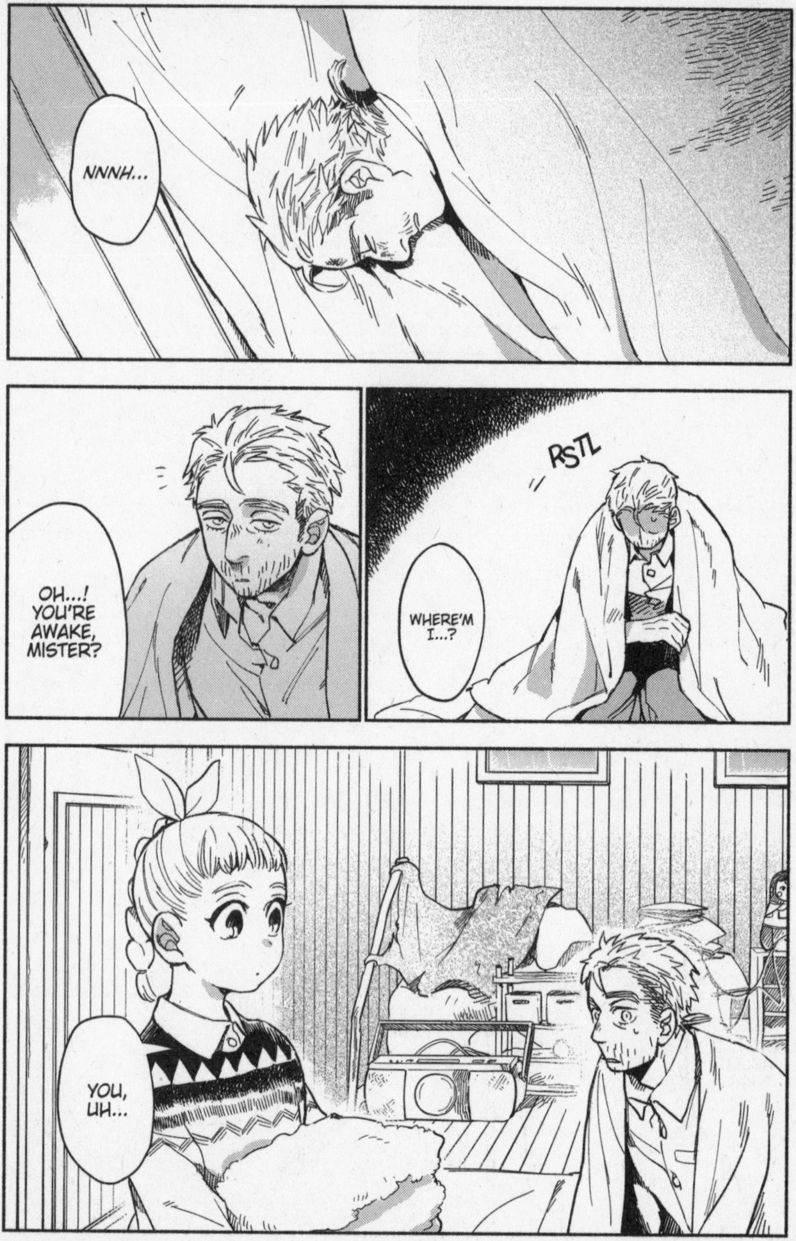
NNNH...
RSTL
WHERE'M I...?
OH...! YOU'RE AWAKE, MISTER?
YOU, UH...

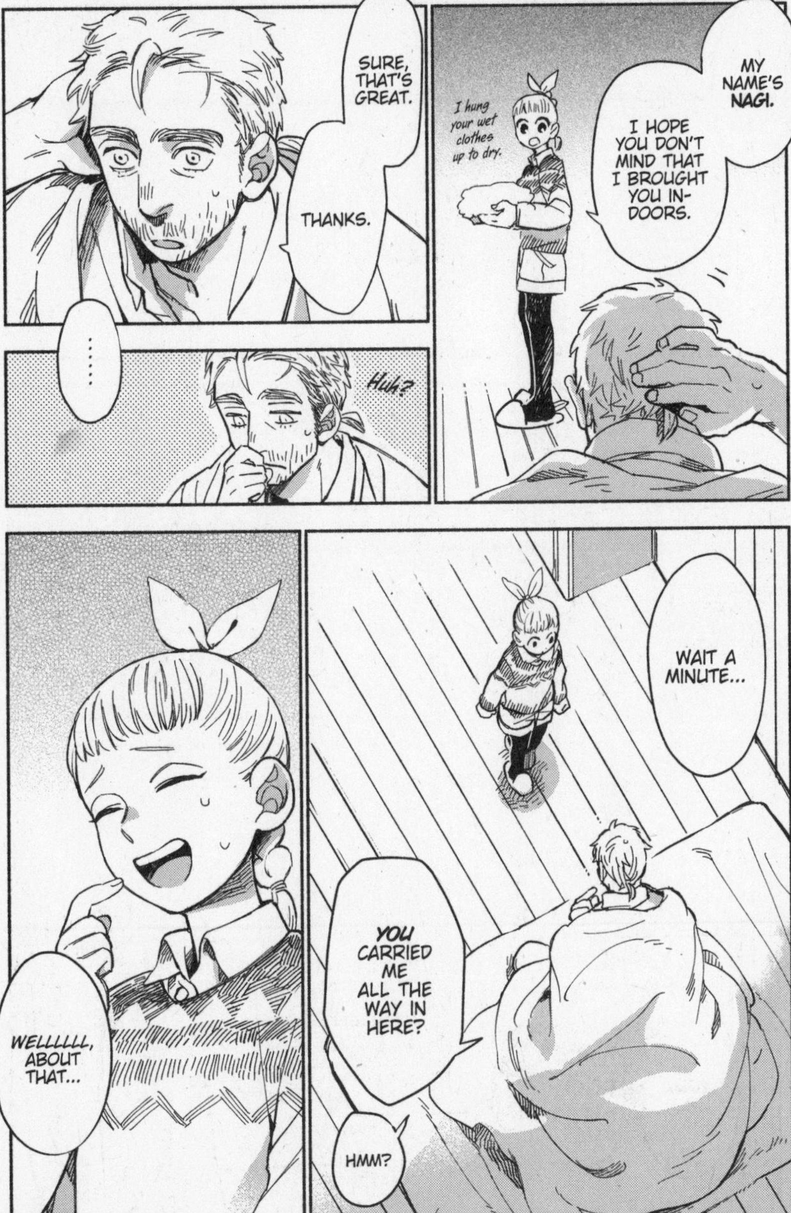
MY NAME'S NAGI.
I HOPE YOU DON'T MIND THAT I BROUGHT YOU IN-DOORS.
I hung your wet clothes up to dry.
SURE, THAT'S GREAT.
THANKS.
......
Huh?
WAIT A MINUTE...
YOU CARRIED ME ALL THE WAY IN HERE?
HMM?
WELLLLLLL, ABOUT THAT...

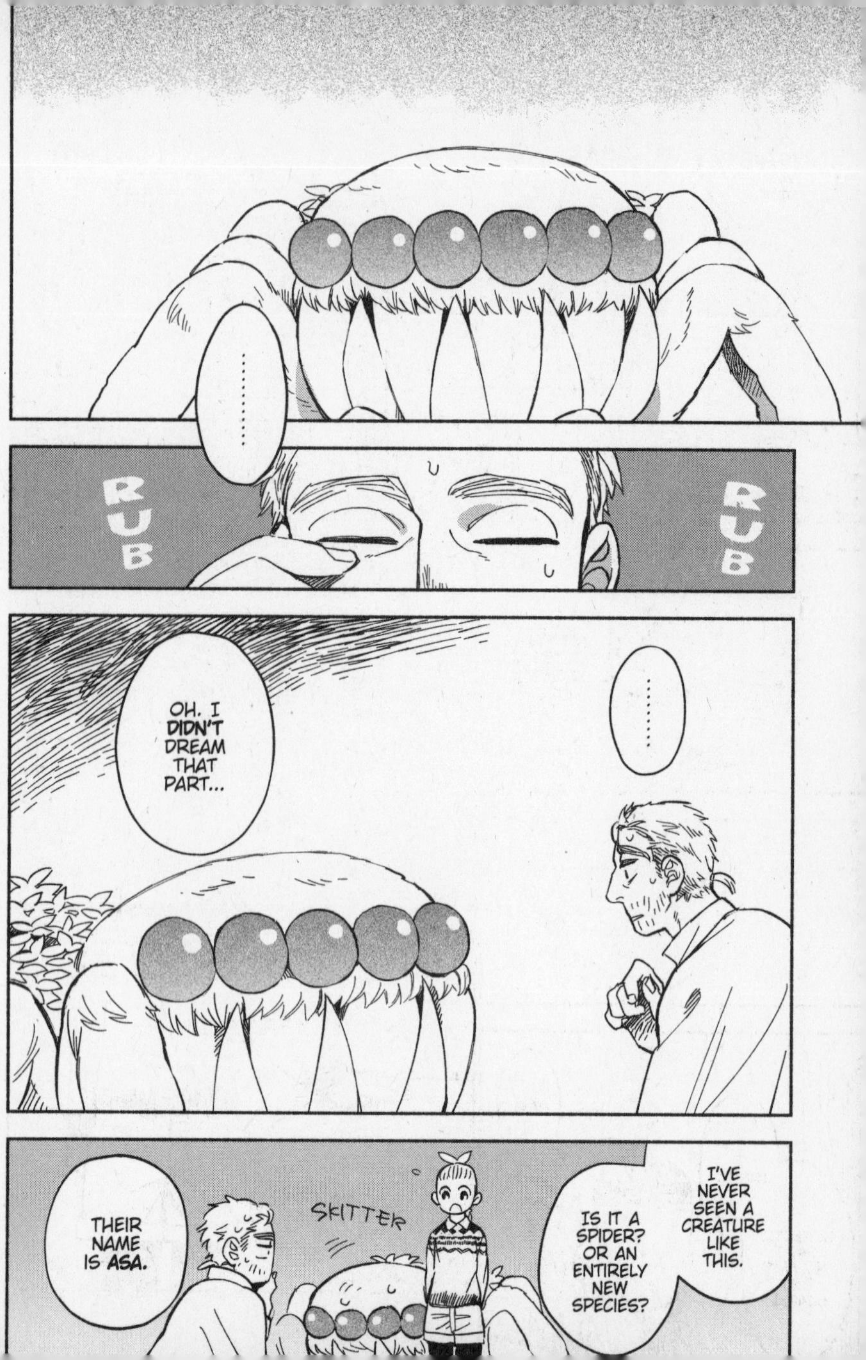
......
RUB
RUB
......
OH. I DIDN'T DREAM THAT PART...
I'VE NEVER SEEN A CREATURE LIKE THIS.
IS IT A SPIDER? OR AN ENTIRELY NEW SPECIES?
SKITTER
THEIR NAME IS ASA.

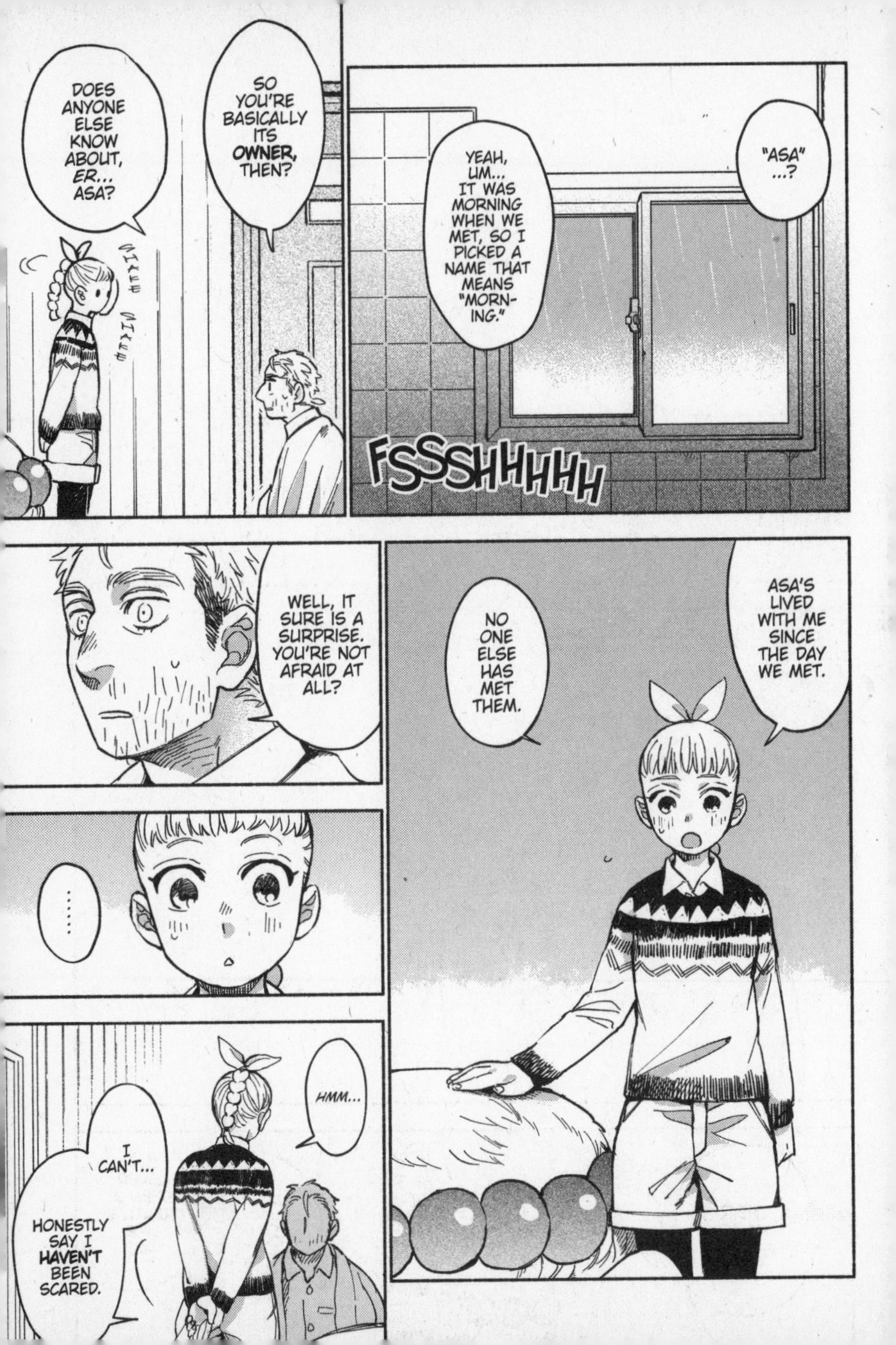
"ASA" ...?
YEAH, UM... IT WAS MORNING WHEN WE MET, SO I PICKED A NAME THAT MEANS "MORNING."
FSSSHHHHH
SO YOU'RE BASICALLY ITS OWNER, THEN?
DOES ANYONE ELSE KNOW ABOUT, ER... ASA?
SHAKE SHAKE
ASA'S LIVED WITH ME SINCE THE DAY WE MET.
NO ONE ELSE HAS MET THEM.
WELL, IT SURE IS A SURPRISE. YOU'RE NOT AFRAID AT ALL?
......
HMM...
I CAN'T...
HONESTLY SAY I HAVEN'T BEEN SCARED.

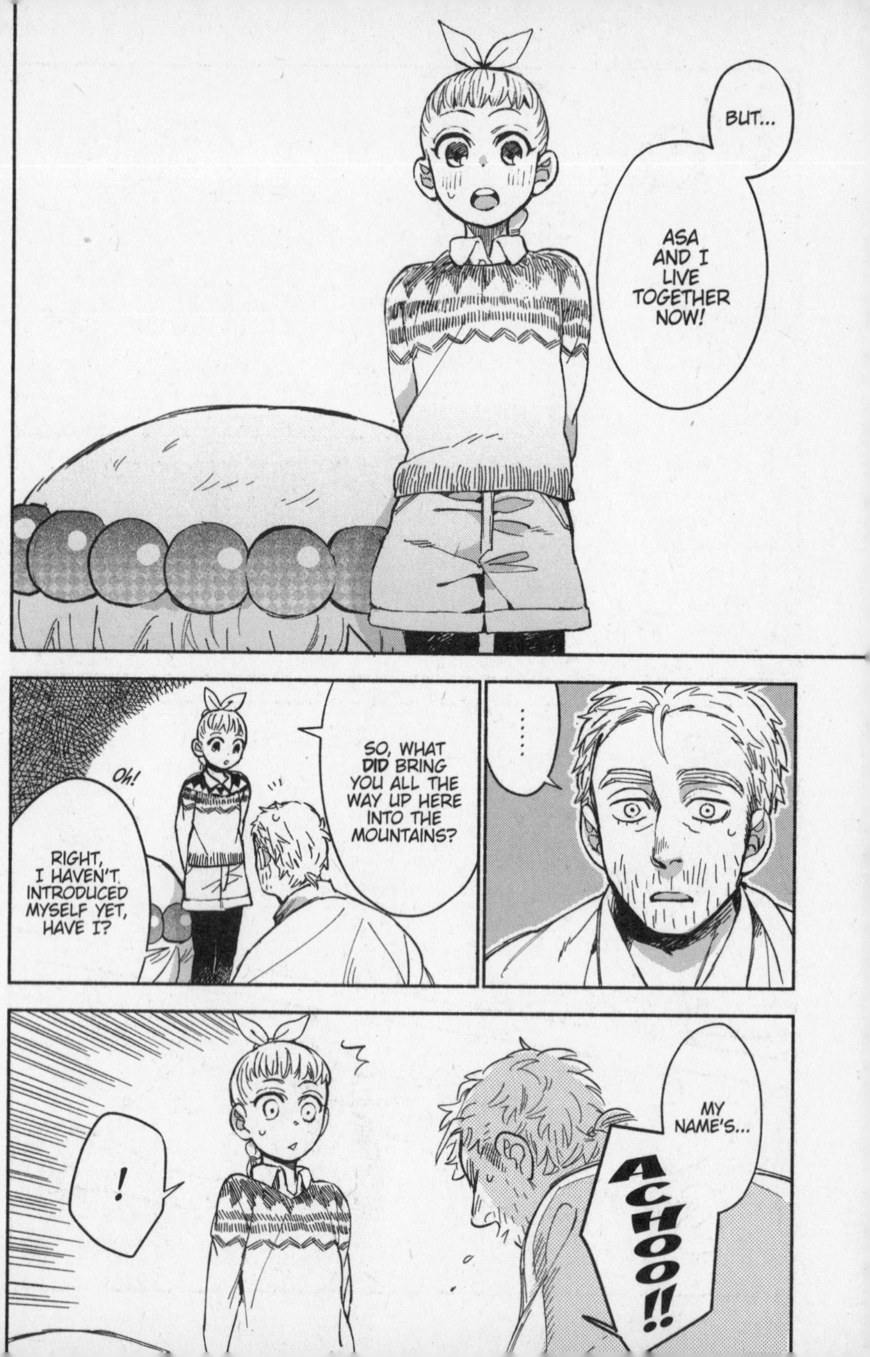
BUT...
ASA AND I LIVE TOGETHER NOW!
......
SO, WHAT DID BRING YOU ALL THE WAY UP HERE INTO THE MOUNTAINS?
Oh!
RIGHT, I HAVEN'T INTRODUCED MYSELF YET, HAVE I?
MY NAME'S...
ACHOO!!
!

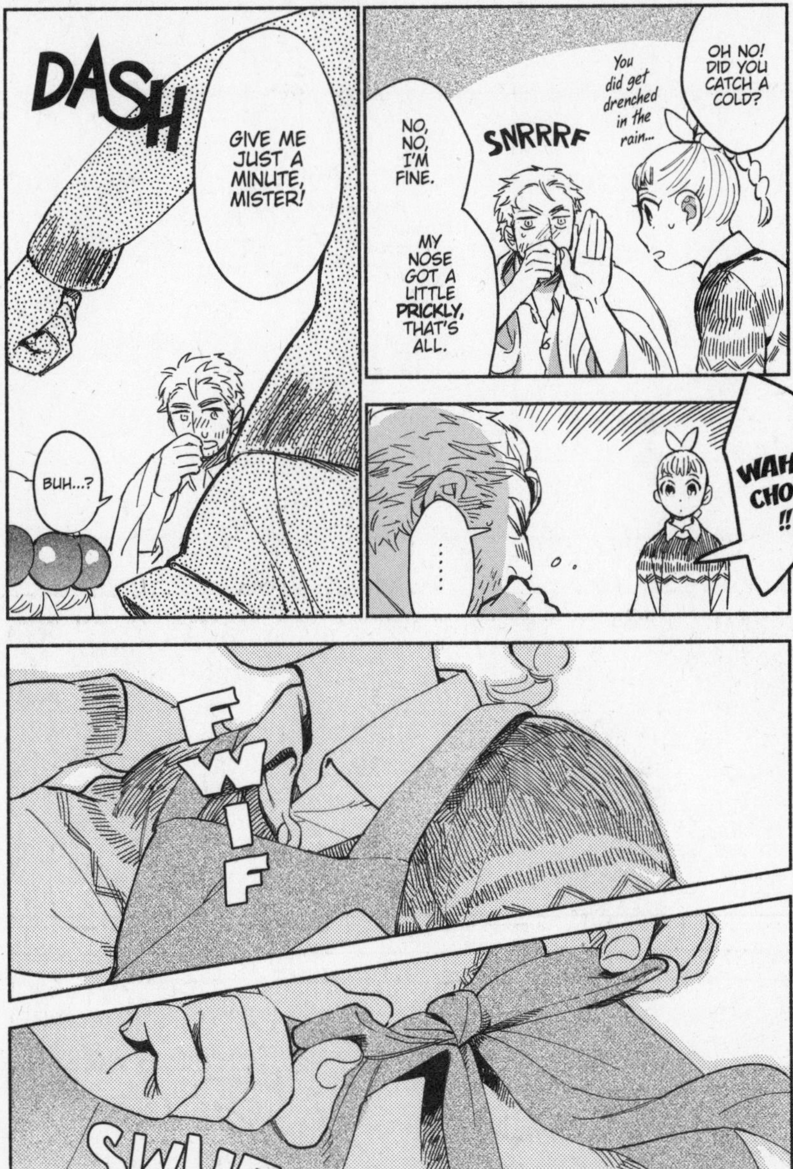
OH NO! DID YOU CATCH A COLD?
You did get drenched in the rain...
SNRRRF
NO, NO, I'M FINE.
MY NOSE GOT A LITTLE PRICKLY, THAT'S ALL.
WAH-CHOO!!
......
DASH
GIVE ME JUST A MINUTE, MISTER!
BUH...?
FWIF
SWUFF

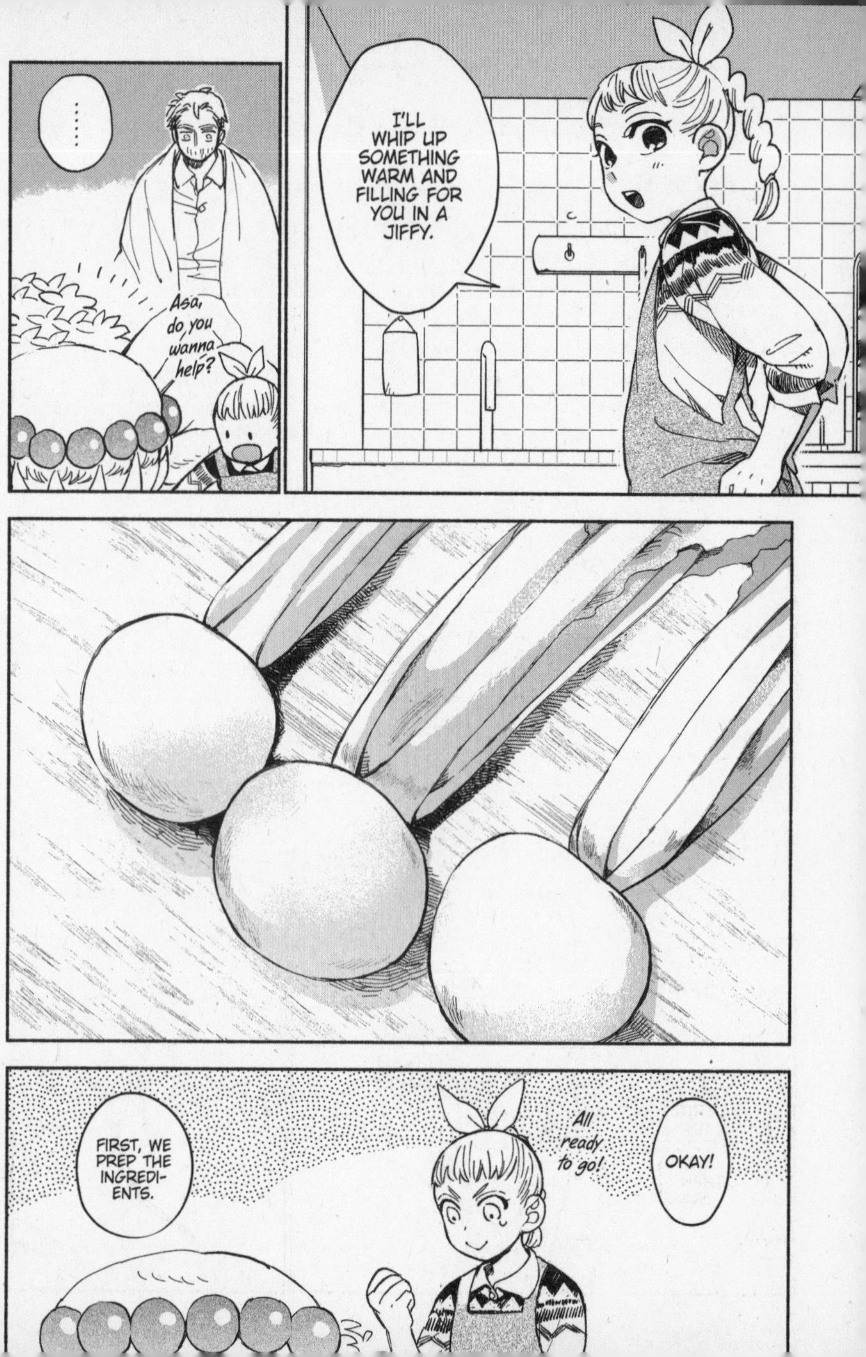
I'LL WHIP UP SOMETHING WARM AND FILLING FOR YOU IN A JIFFY.
......
Asa, do you wanna help?
OKAY!
All ready to go!
FIRST, WE PREP THE INGREDI-ENTS.

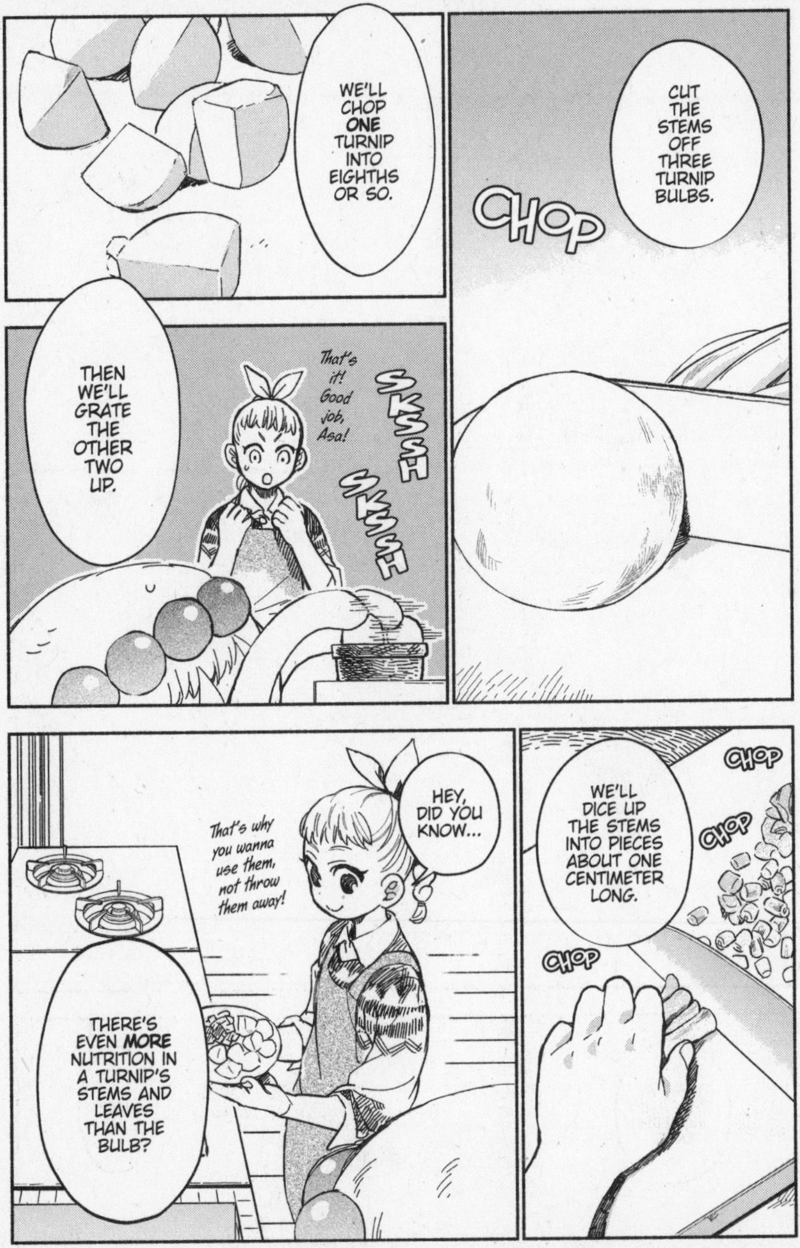
CUT THE STEMS OFF THREE TURNIP BULBS.
CHOP
WE'LL CHOP ONE TURNIP INTO EIGHTHS OR SO.
THEN WE'LL GRATE THE OTHER TWO UP.
SKSSH
SKSSH
That's it! Good job, Asa!
WE'LL DICE UP THE STEMS INTO PIECES ABOUT ONE CENTIMETER LONG.
CHOP
CHOP
CHOP
HEY, DID YOU KNOW...
THERE'S EVEN MORE NUTRITION IN A TURNIP'S STEMS AND LEAVES THAN THE BULB?
That's why you wanna use them, not throw them away!

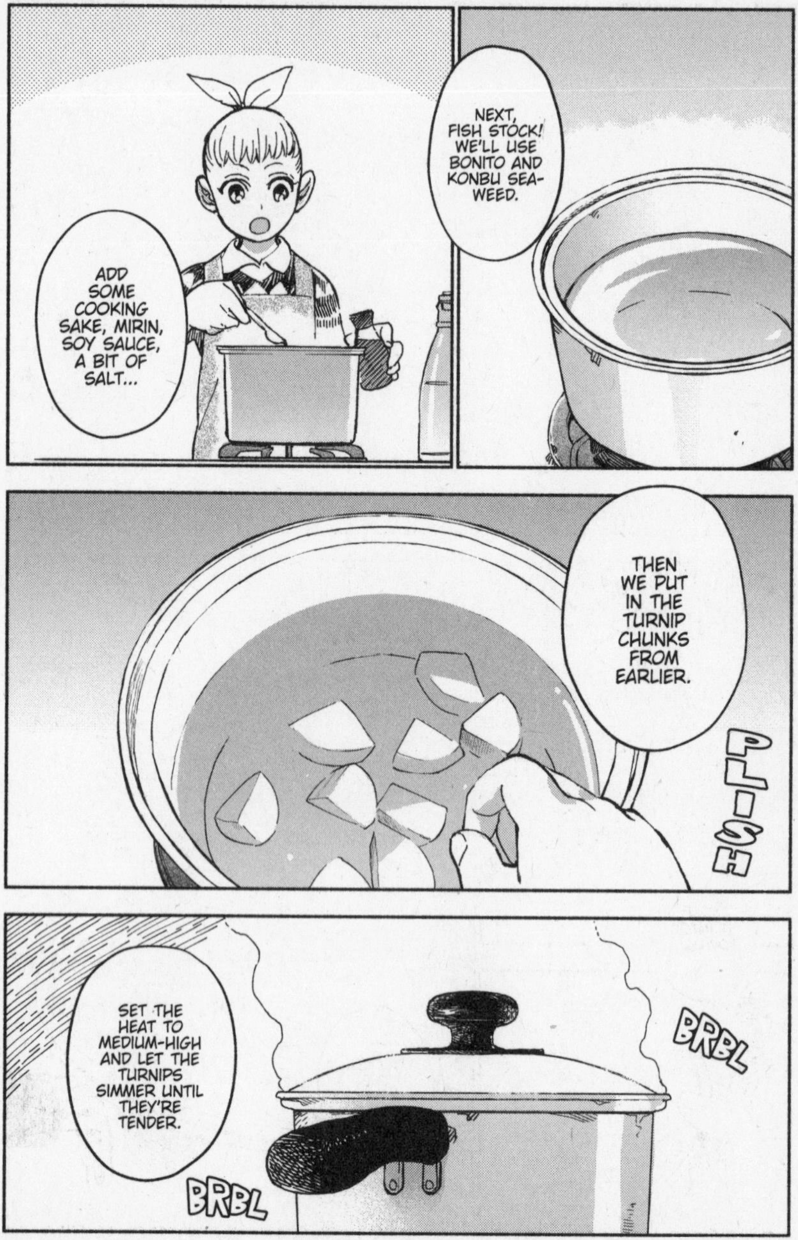
NEXT, FISH STOCK! WE'LL USE BONITO AND KONBU SEA-WEED.
ADD SOME COOKING SAKE, MIRIN, SOY SAUCE, A BIT OF SALT...
THEN WE PUT IN THE TURNIP CHUNKS FROM EARLIER.
PLISH
SET THE HEAT TO MEDIUM-HIGH AND LET THE TURNIPS SIMMER UNTIL THEY'RE TENDER.
BRBL
BRBL

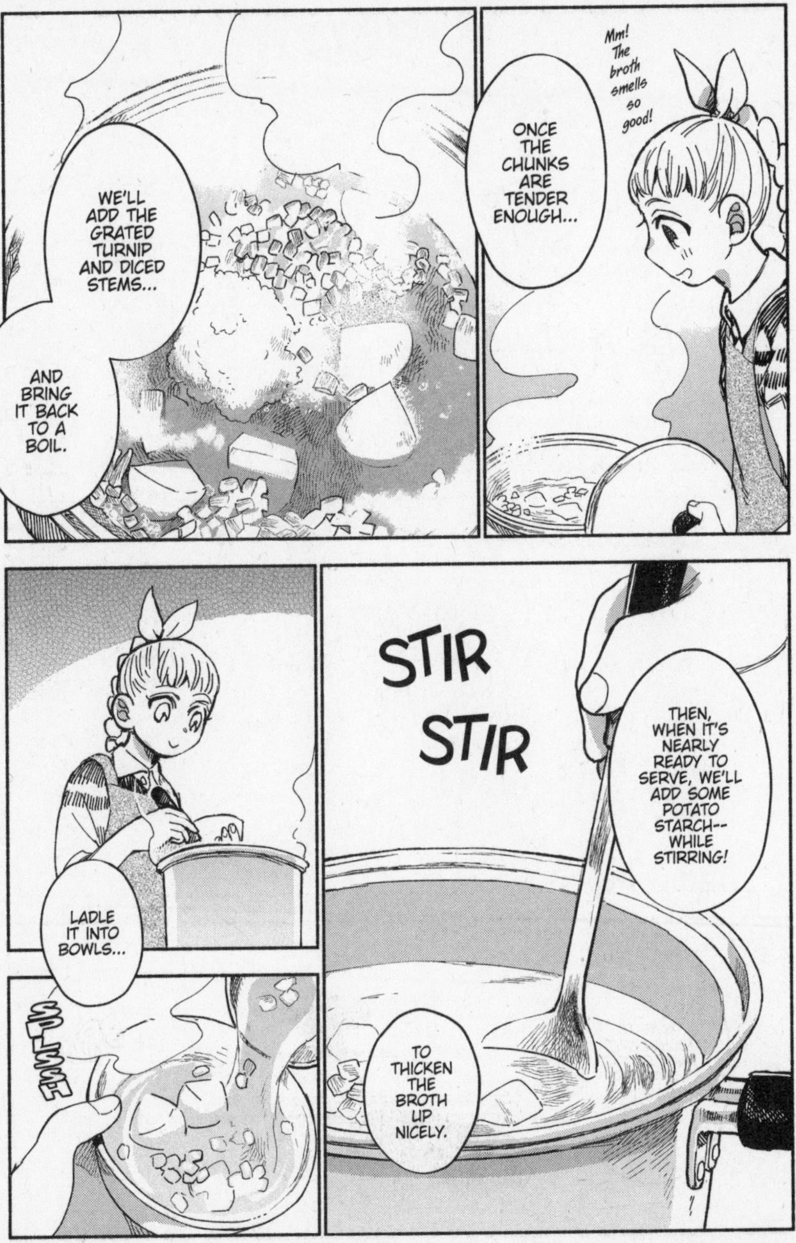
Mm! The broth smells so good!
ONCE THE CHUNKS ARE TENDER ENOUGH...
WE'LL ADD THE GRATED TURNIP AND DICED STEMS...
AND BRING IT BACK TO A BOIL.
STIR STIR
THEN, WHEN IT'S NEARLY READY TO SERVE, WE'LL ADD SOME POTATO STARCH-- WHILE STIRRING!
TO THICKEN THE BROTH UP NICELY.
LADLE IT INTO BOWLS...

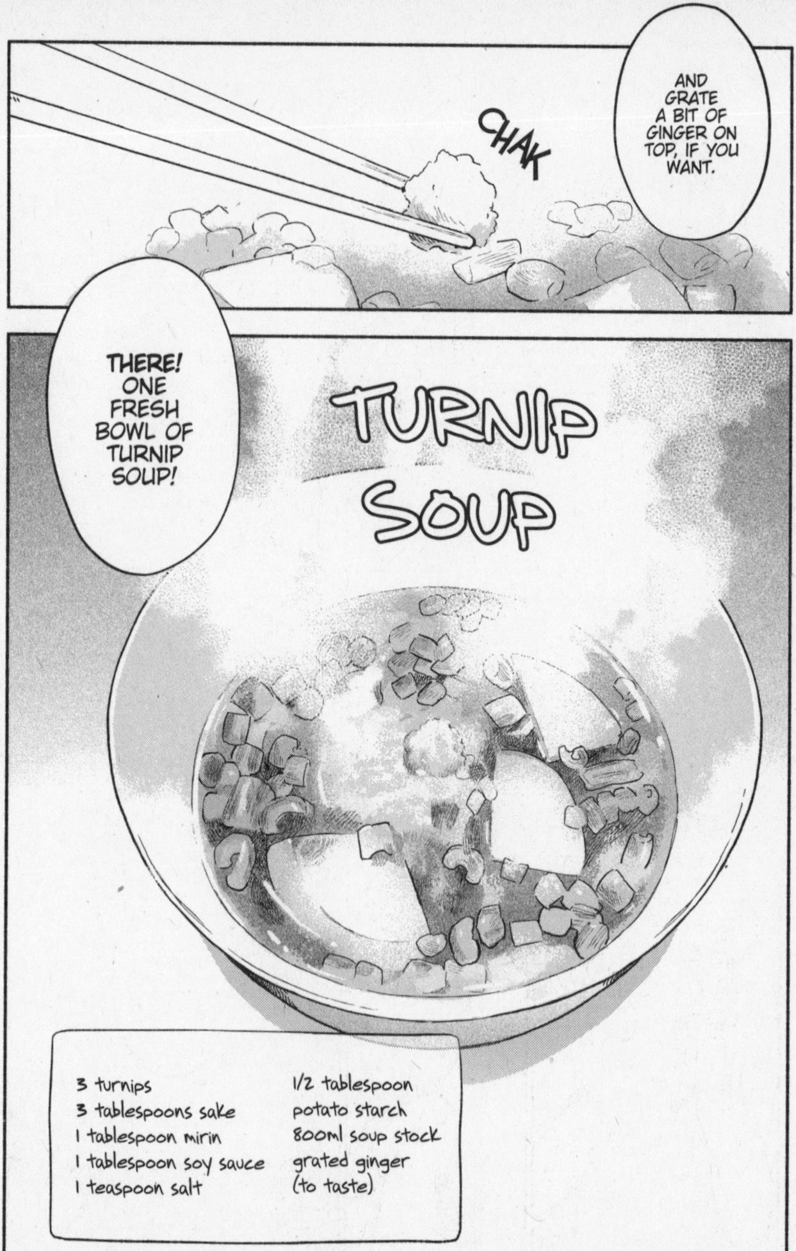
AND GRATE A BIT OF GINGER ON TOP, IF YOU WANT.
CHAK
THERE! ONE FRESH BOWL OF TURNIP SOUP!
TURNIP SOUP
3 turnips
3 tablespoons sake
1 tablespoon mirin
1 tablespoon soy sauce
1 teaspoon salt
1/2 tablespoon potato starch
800ml soup stock
grated ginger (to taste)

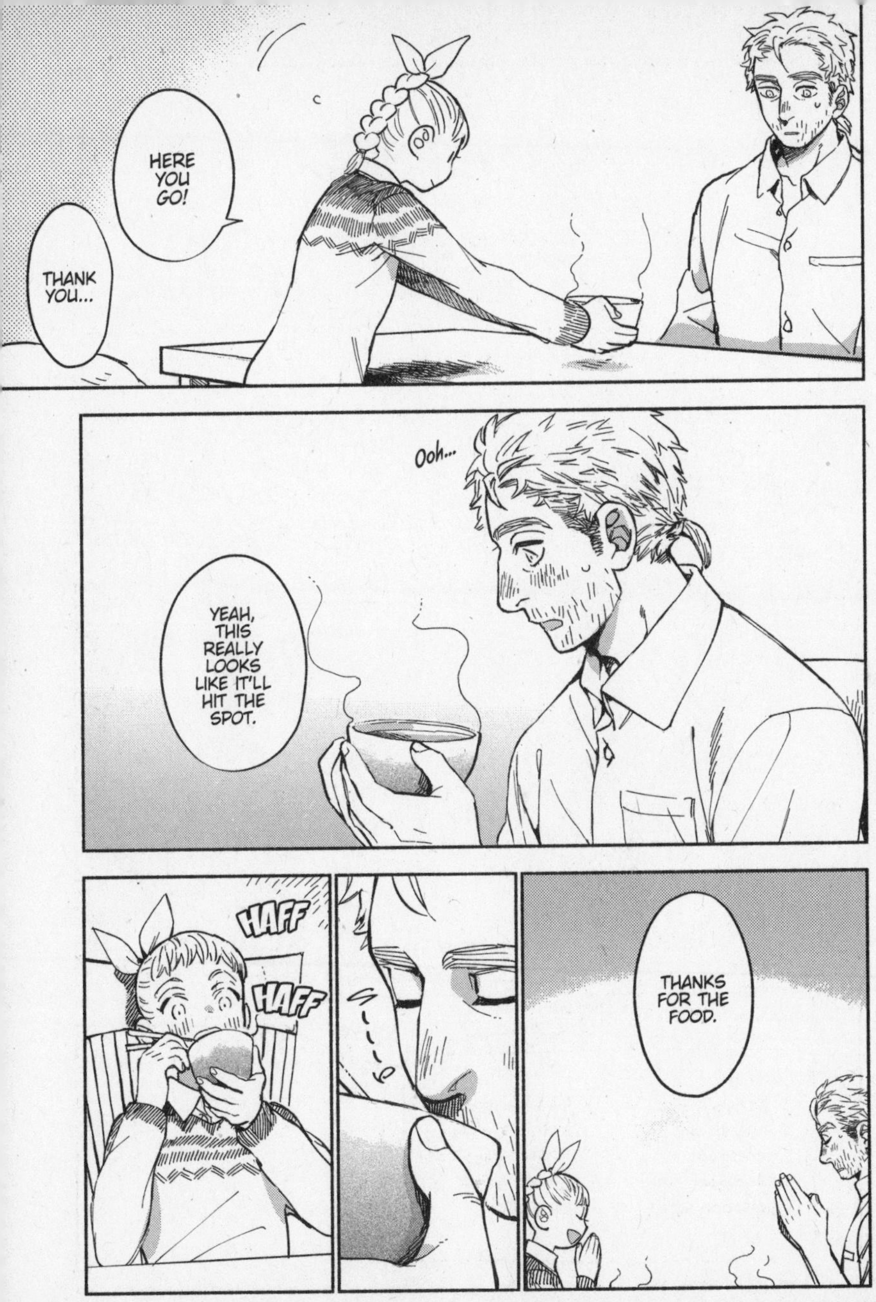
HERE YOU GO!
THANK YOU...
Ooh...
YEAH, THIS REALLY LOOKS LIKE IT'LL HIT THE SPOT.
THANKS FOR THE FOOD.
HAFF
HAFF

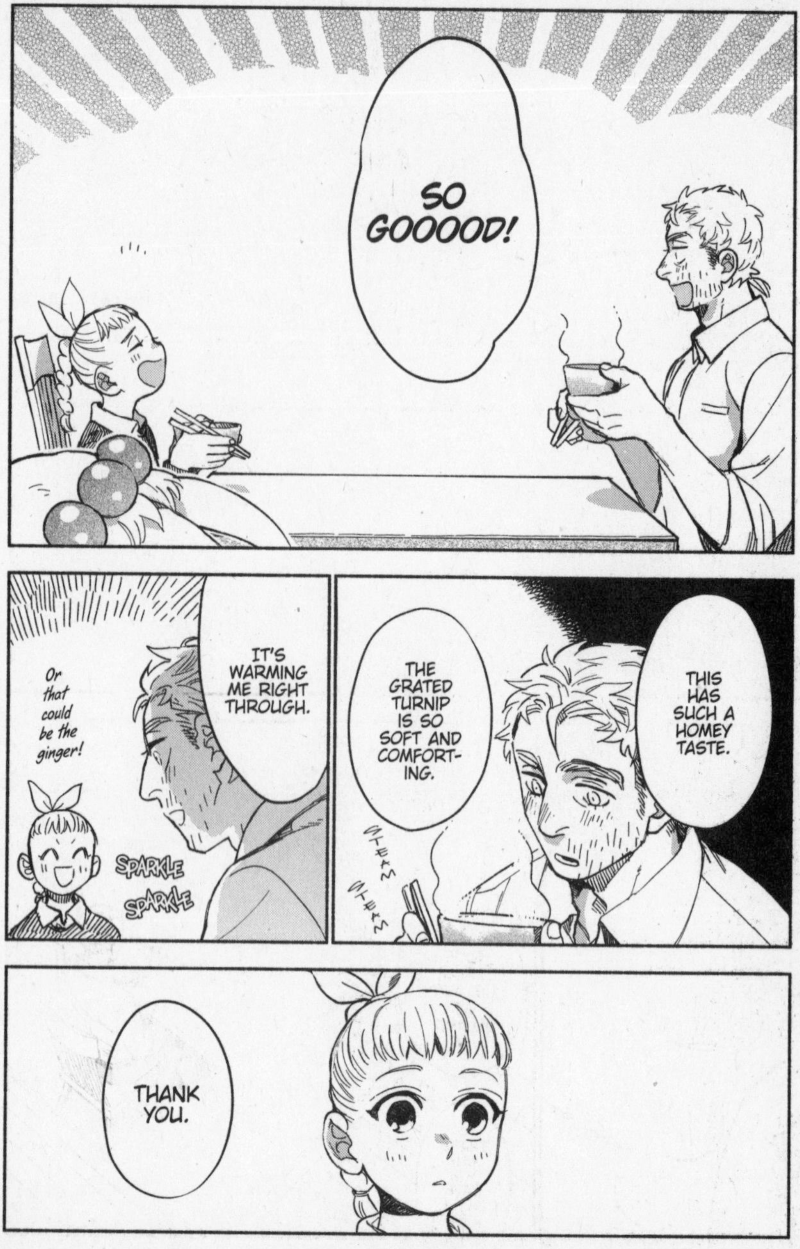
SO GOOOOD!
THIS HAS SUCH A HOMEY TASTE.
THE GRATED TURNIP IS SO SOFT AND COMFORT-ING.
STEAM
STEAM
IT'S WARMING ME RIGHT THROUGH.
Or that could be the ginger!
SPARKLE
SPARKLE
THANK YOU.

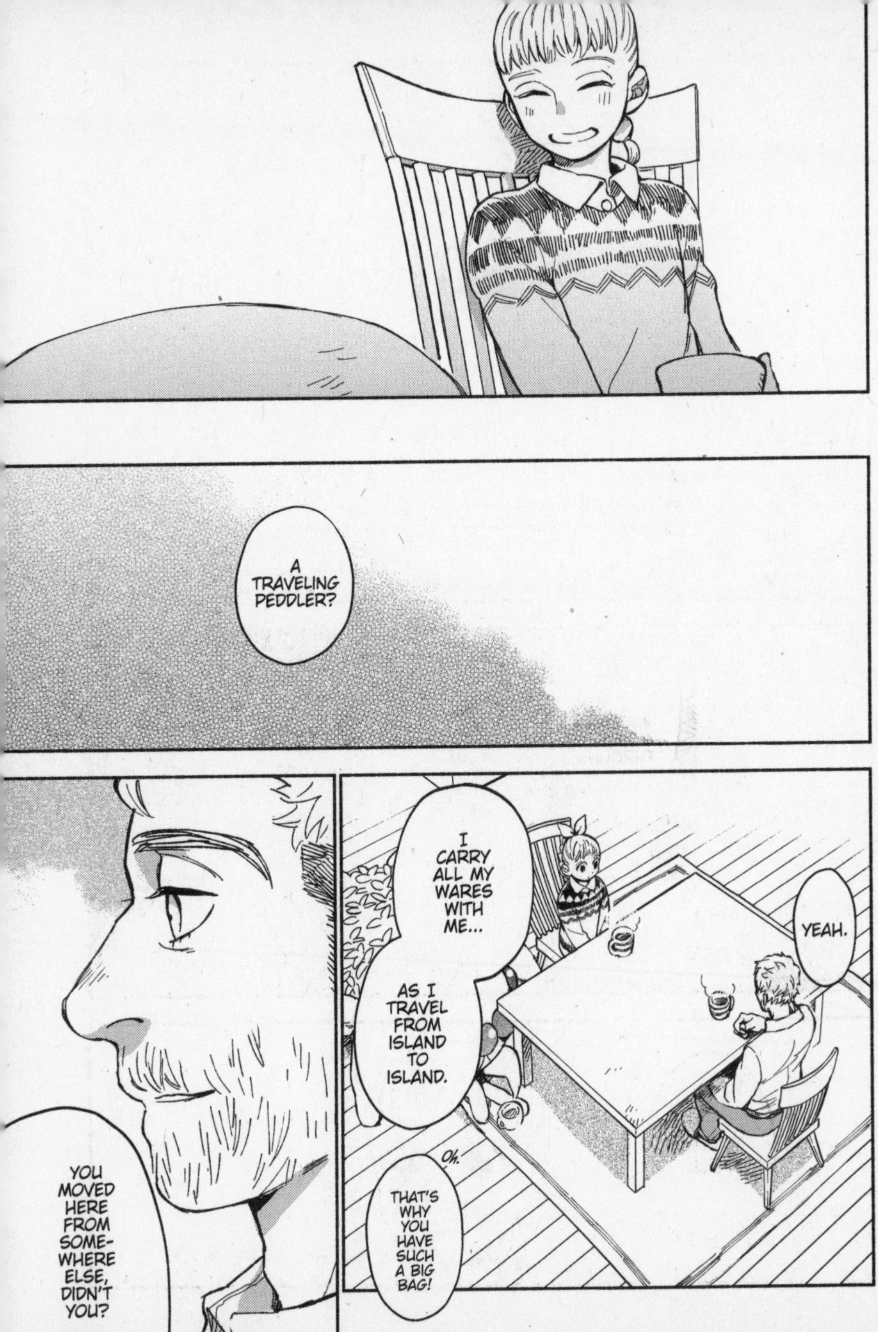
A TRAVELING PEDDLER?
YEAH.
I CARRY ALL MY WARES WITH ME...
AS I TRAVEL FROM ISLAND TO ISLAND.
Oh.
THAT'S WHY YOU HAVE SUCH A BIG BAG!
YOU MOVED HERE FROM SOME-WHERE ELSE, DIDN'T YOU?

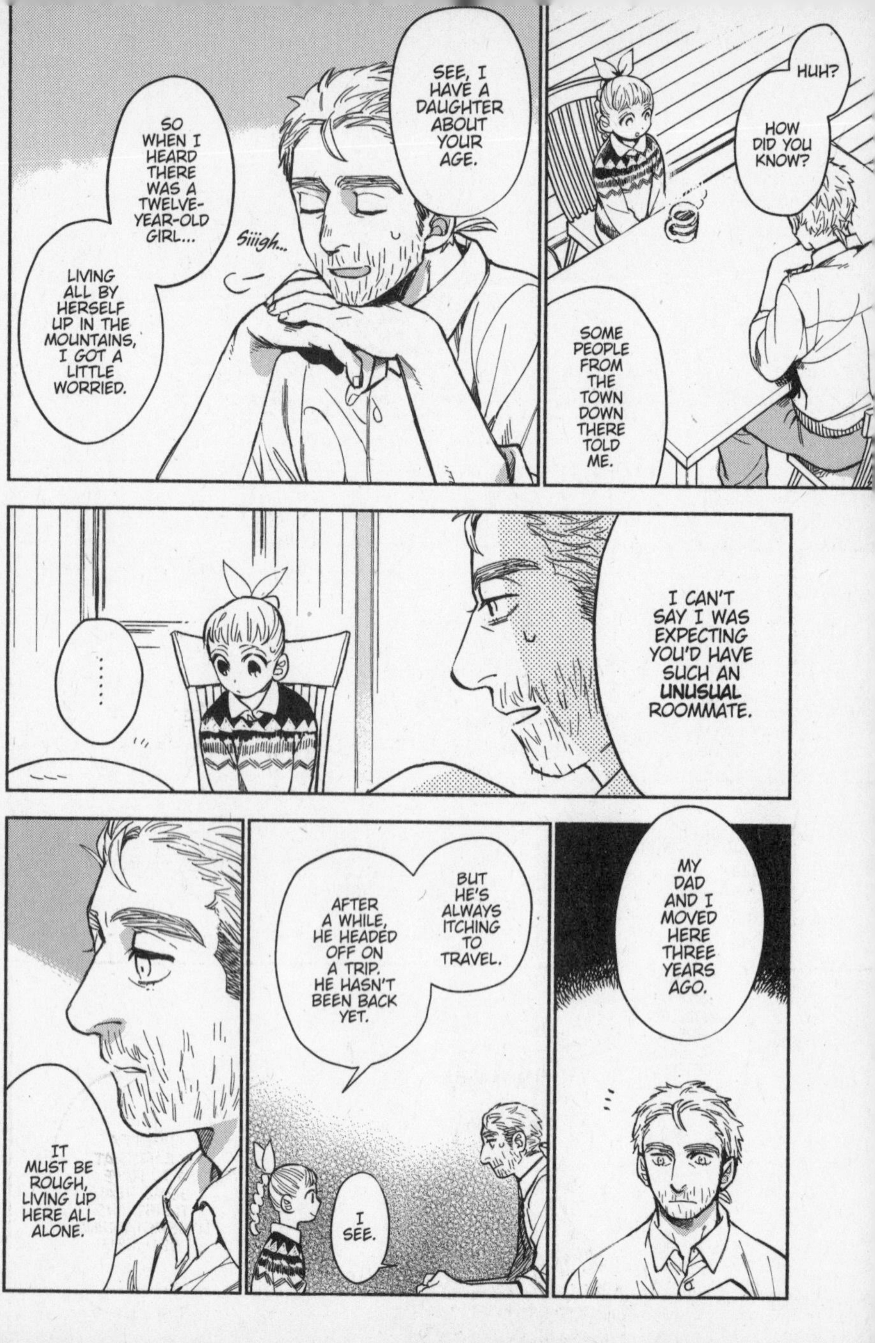
HUH? HOW DID YOU KNOW?
SOME PEOPLE FROM THE TOWN DOWN THERE TOLD ME.
SEE, I HAVE A DAUGHTER ABOUT YOUR AGE.
SO WHEN I HEARD THERE WAS A TWELVE-YEAR-OLD GIRL...
Siiigh...
LIVING ALL BY HERSELF UP IN THE MOUNTAINS, I GOT A LITTLE WORRIED.
I CAN'T SAY I WAS EXPECTING YOU'D HAVE SUCH AN **UNUSUAL** ROOMMATE.
......
MY DAD AND I MOVED HERE THREE YEARS AGO.
BUT HE'S ALWAYS ITCHING TO TRAVEL.
AFTER A WHILE, HE HEADED OFF ON A TRIP. HE HASN'T BEEN BACK YET.
I SEE.
IT MUST BE ROUGH, LIVING UP HERE ALL ALONE.

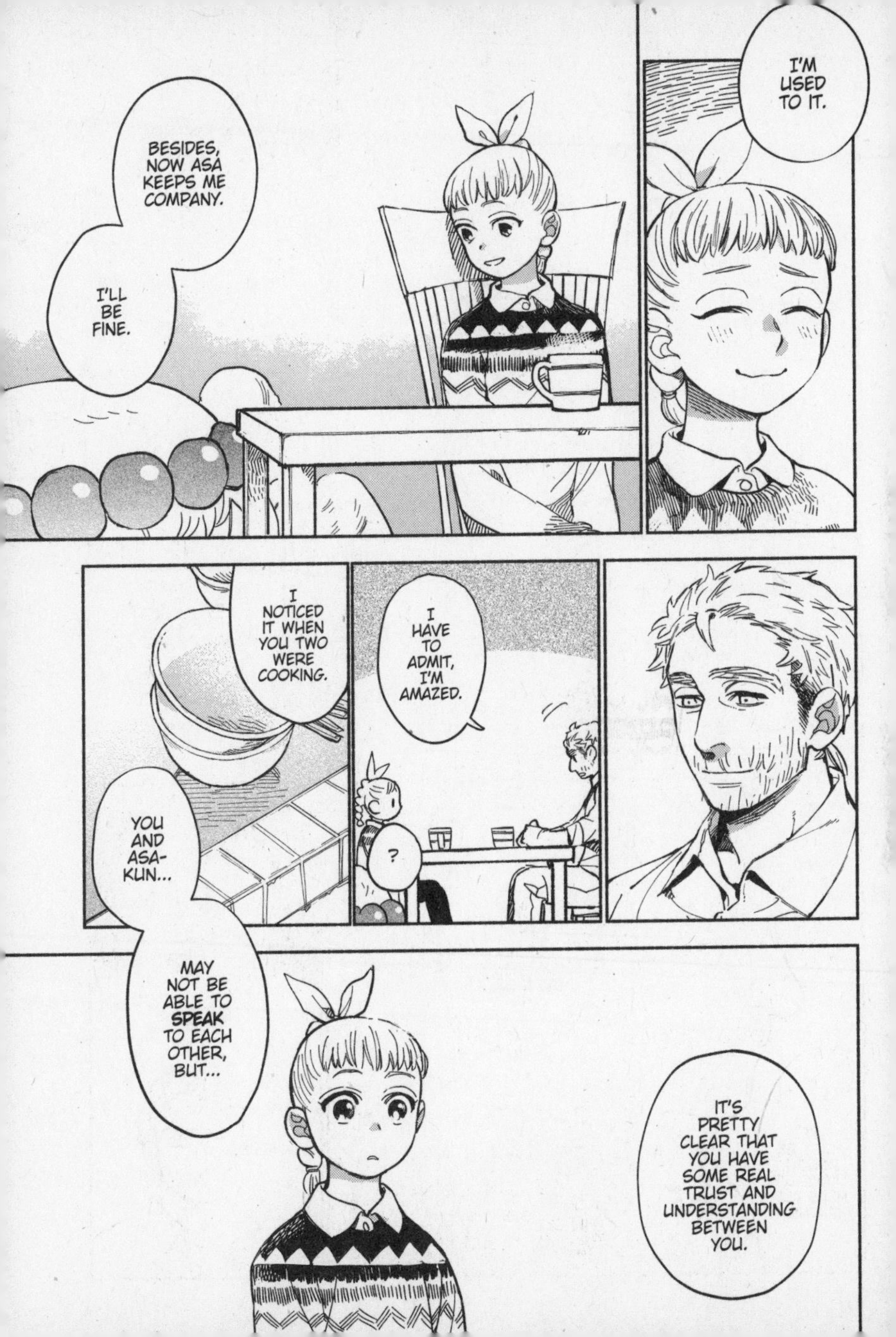
I'M USED TO IT.
BESIDES, NOW ASA KEEPS ME COMPANY.
I'LL BE FINE.
I HAVE TO ADMIT, I'M AMAZED.
?
I NOTICED IT WHEN YOU TWO WERE COOKING.
YOU AND ASA-KUN...
MAY NOT BE ABLE TO SPEAK TO EACH OTHER, BUT...
IT'S PRETTY CLEAR THAT YOU HAVE SOME REAL TRUST AND UNDERSTANDING BETWEEN YOU.

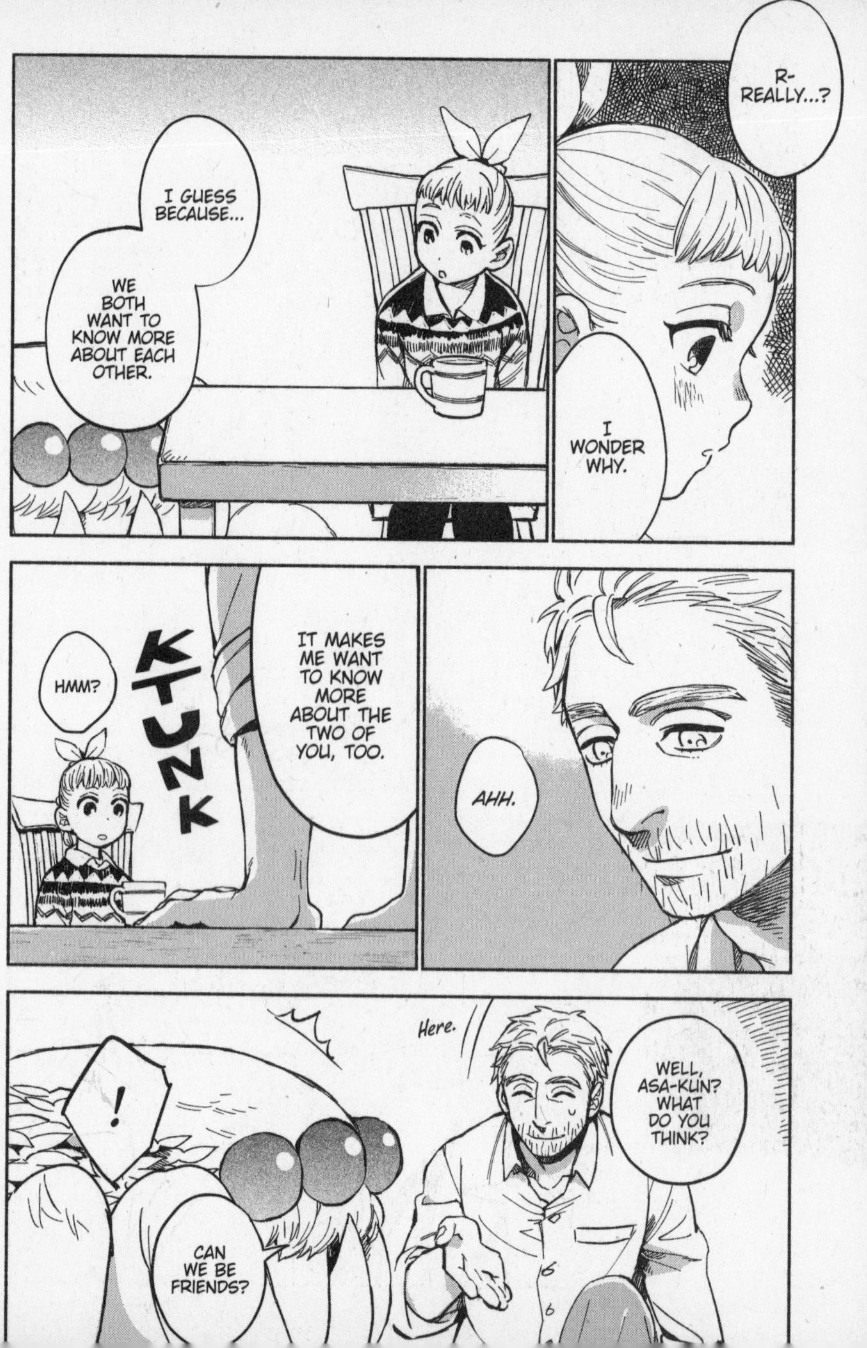
R- REALLY...?
I WONDER WHY.
I GUESS BECAUSE...
WE BOTH WANT TO KNOW MORE ABOUT EACH OTHER.
AHH.
IT MAKES ME WANT TO KNOW MORE ABOUT THE TWO OF YOU, TOO.
KTUNK
HMM?
Here.
WELL, ASA-KUN? WHAT DO YOU THINK?
!
CAN WE BE FRIENDS?

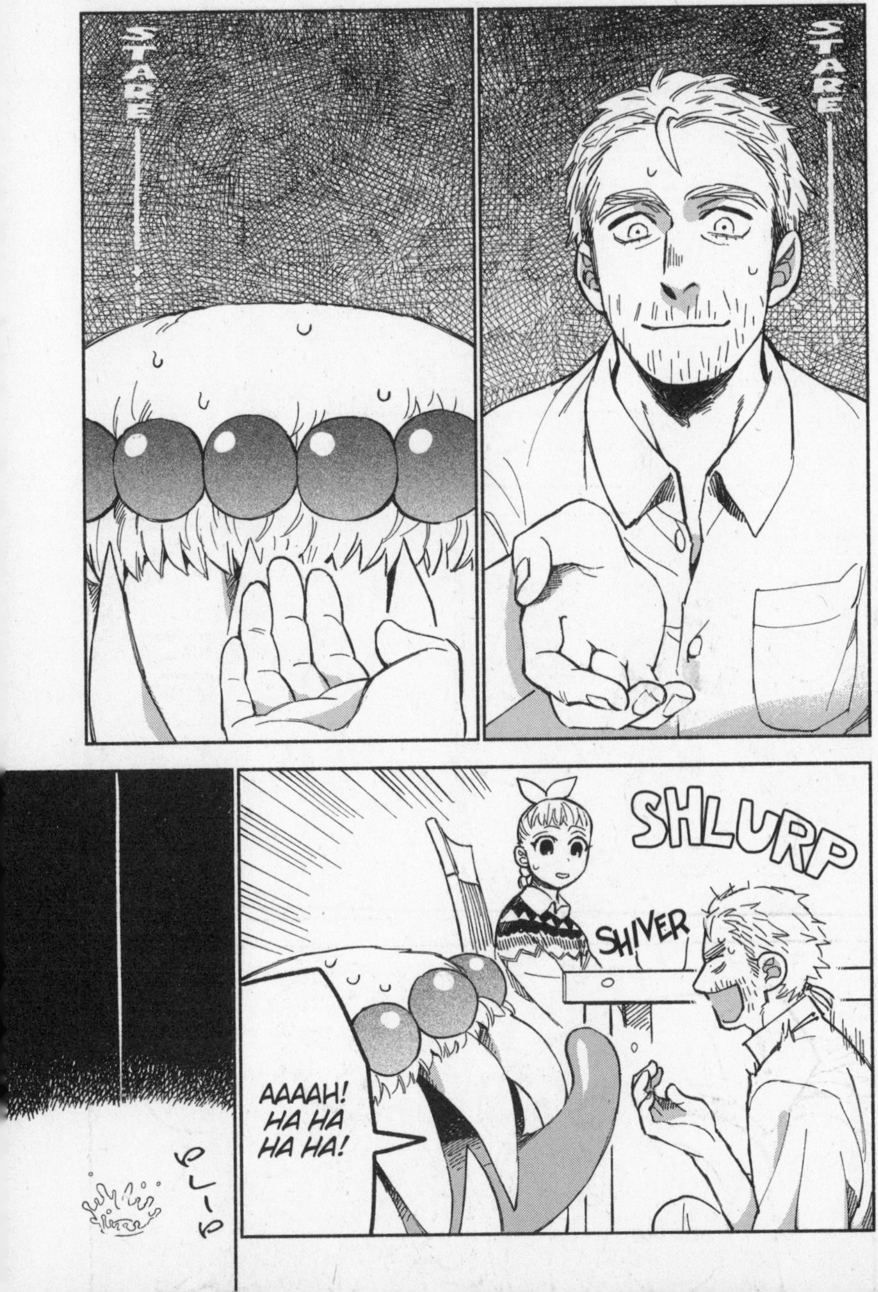
STARE
STARE
SHLURP
SHIVER
AAAAH! HA HA HA HA!

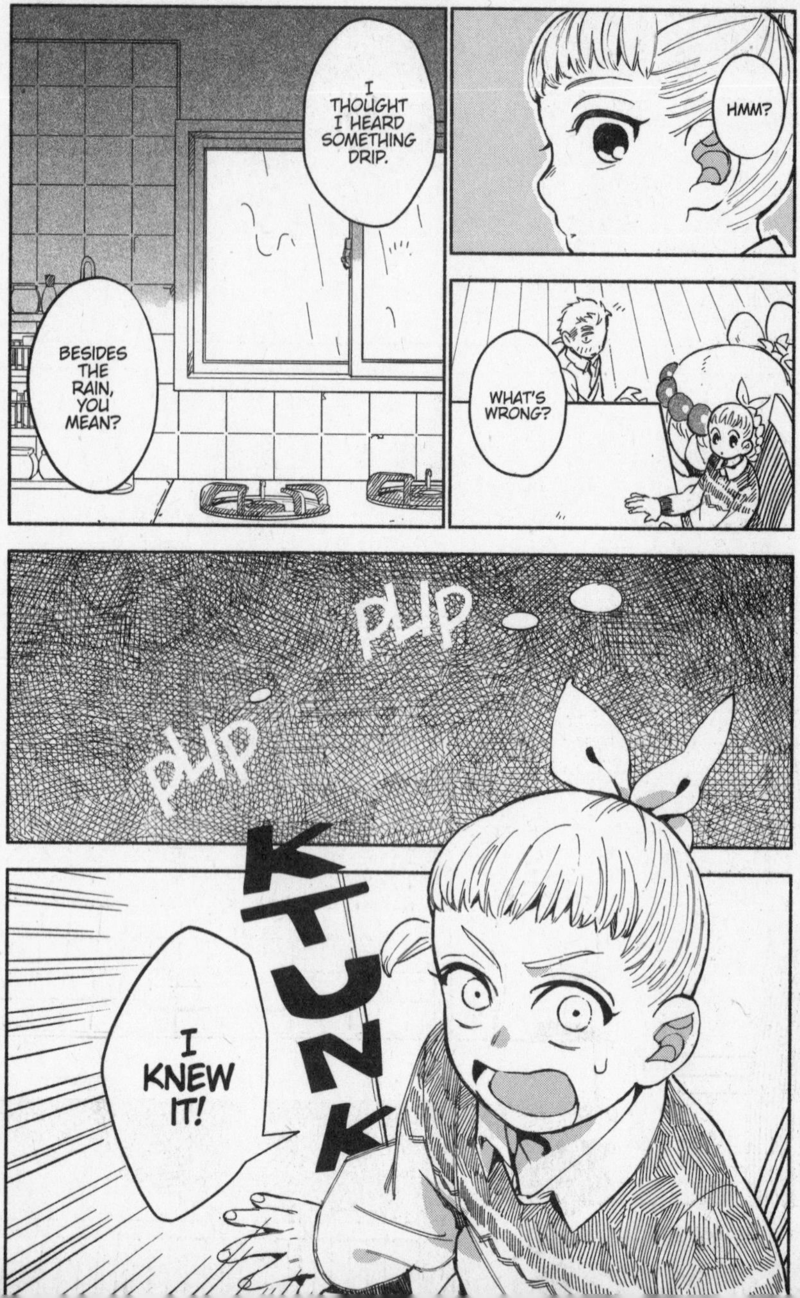
HMM?
WHAT'S WRONG?
I THOUGHT I HEARD SOMETHING DRIP.
BESIDES THE RAIN, YOU MEAN?
PLIP
PLIP
KTUNK
I KNEW IT!

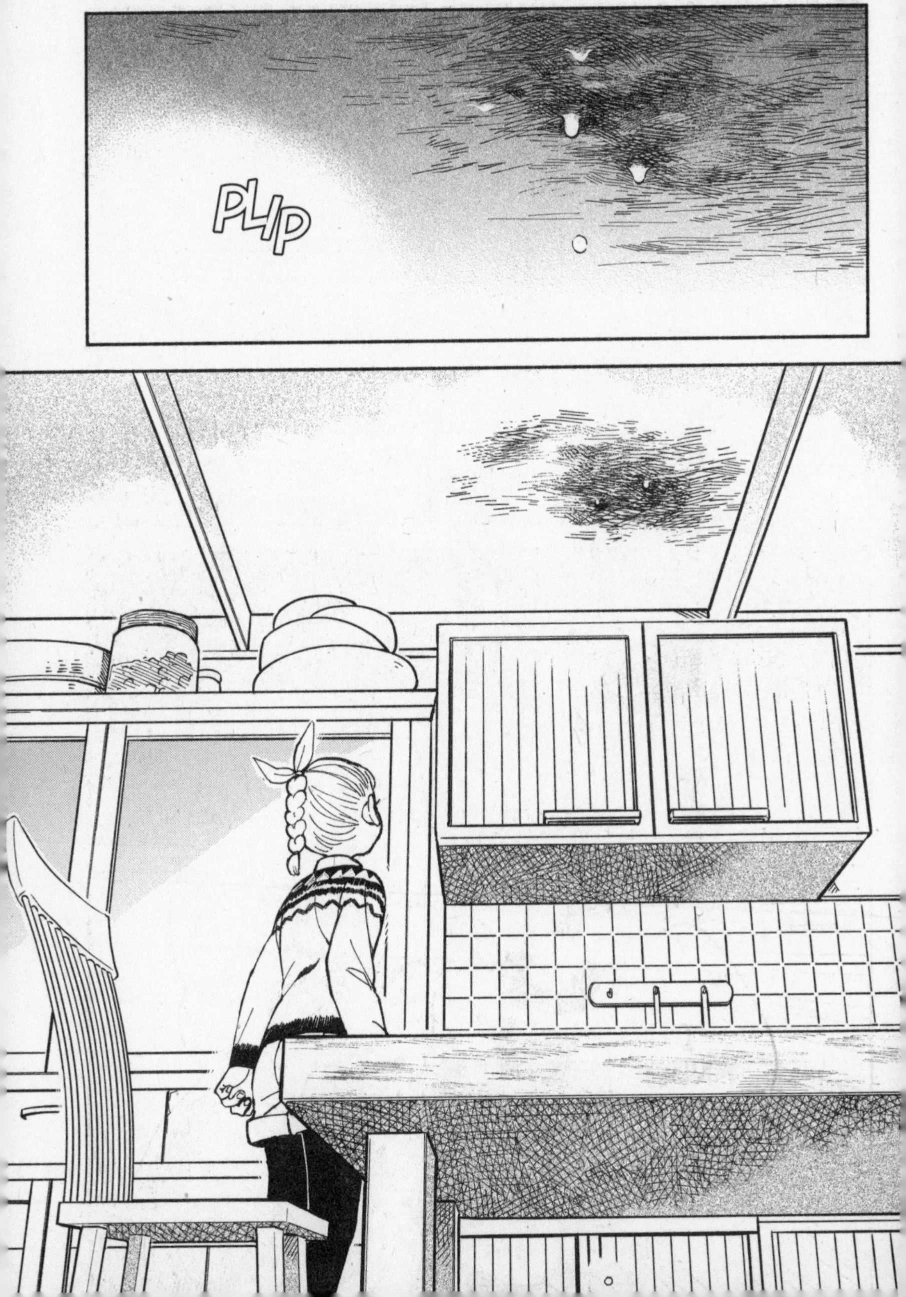
PLIP

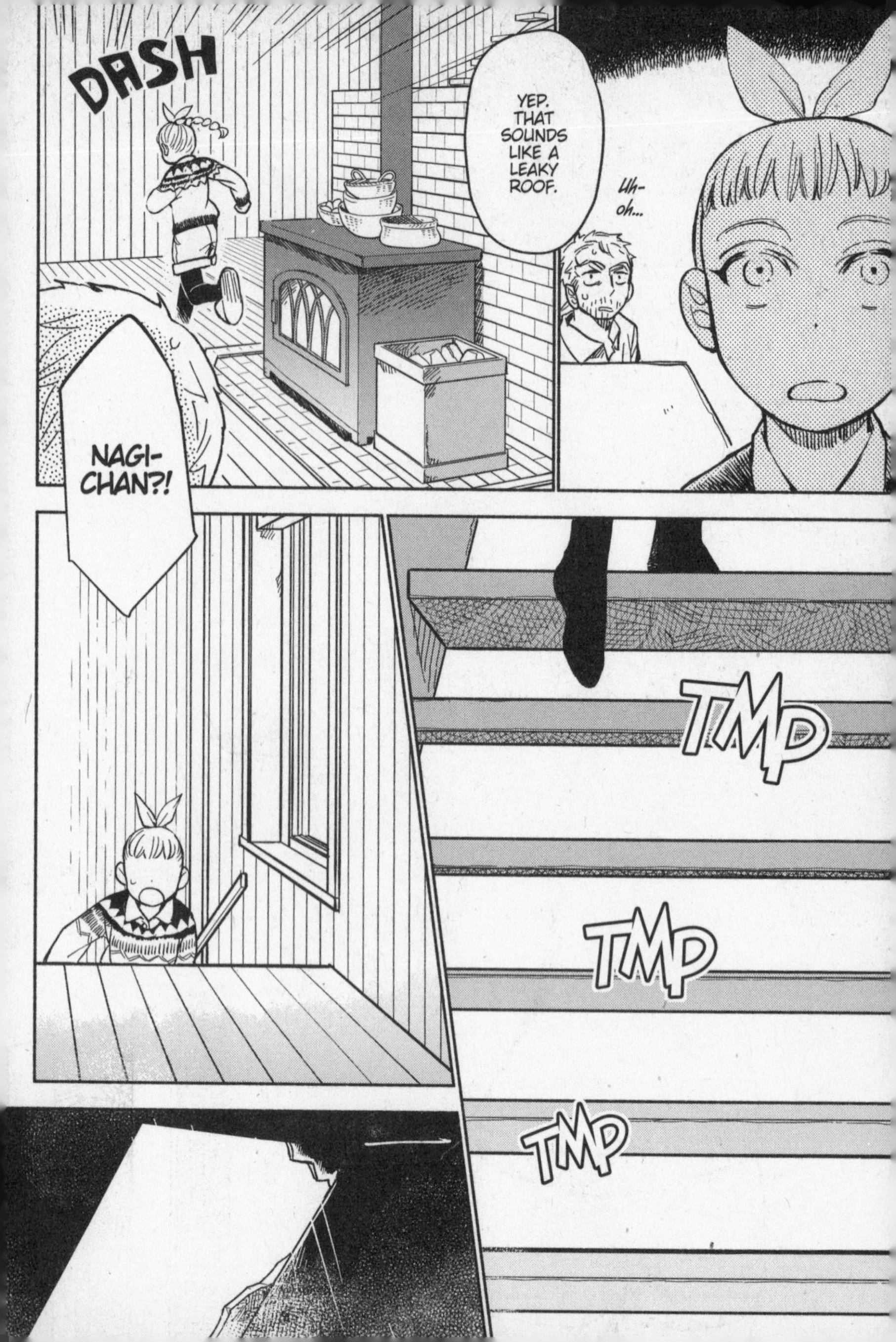
YEP. THAT SOUNDS LIKE A LEAKY ROOF.
Uh-oh...
DASH
NAGI-CHAN?!
TMP
TMP
TMP

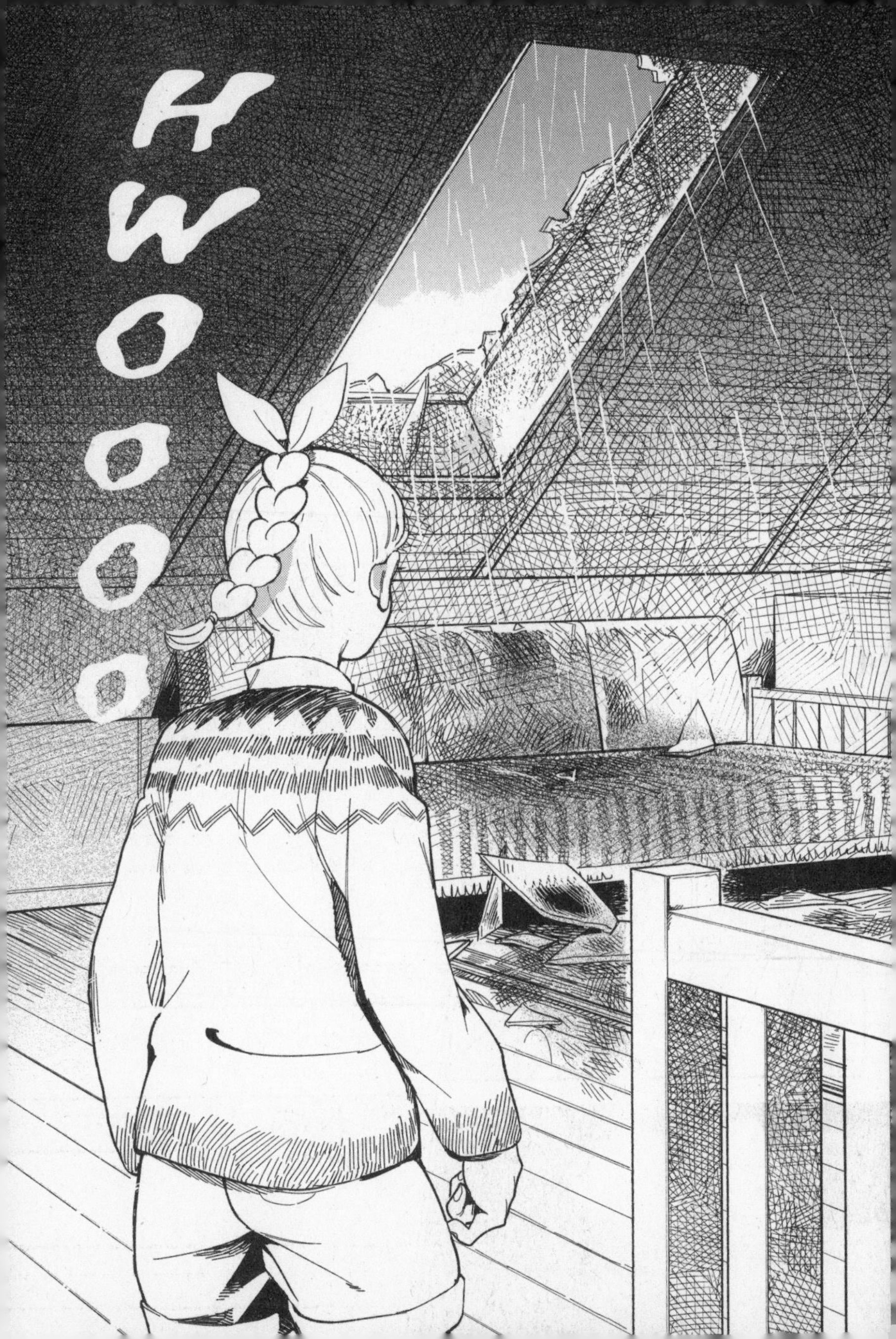
HWOOOO

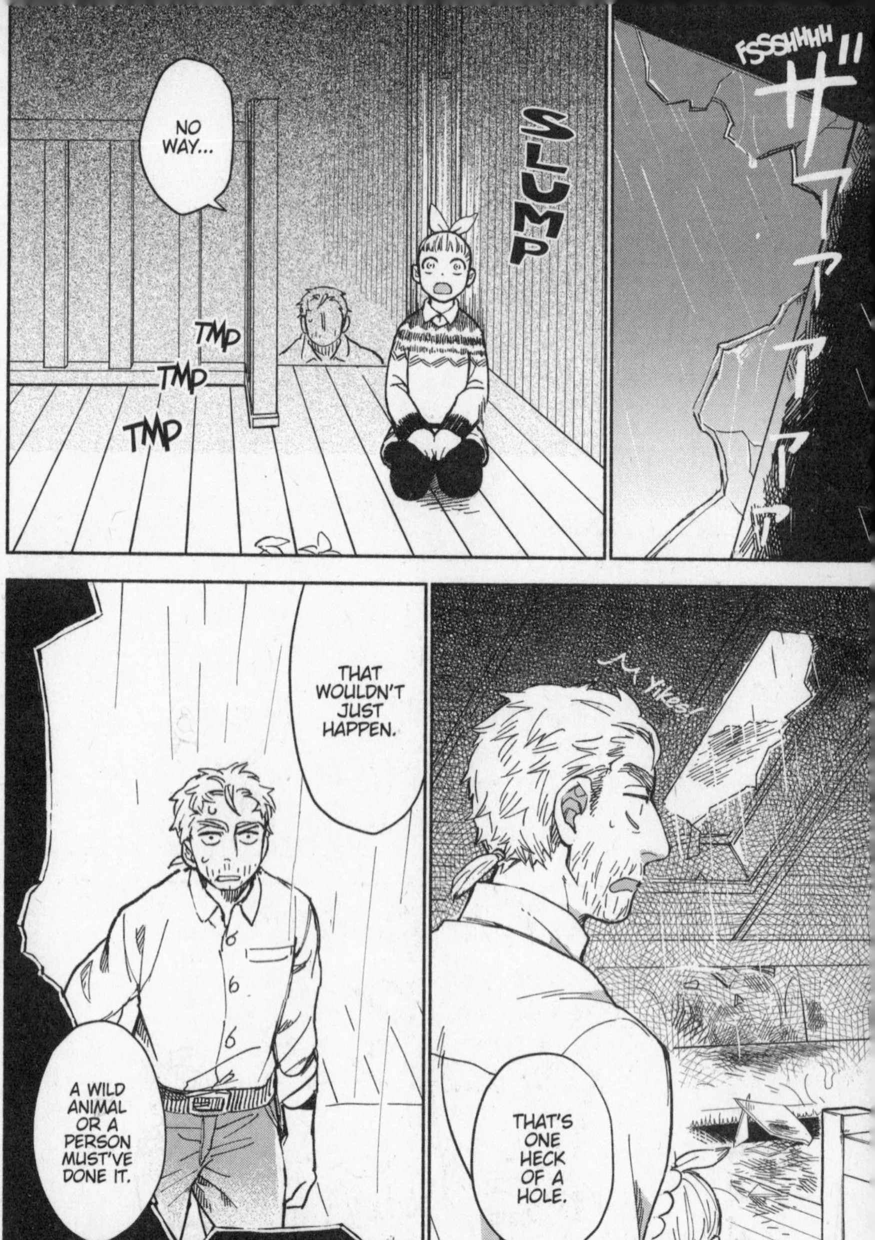
FSSSHHHH
SLUMP
NO WAY...
TMP
TMP
TMP
Yikes!
THAT'S ONE HECK OF A HOLE.
THAT WOULDN'T JUST HAPPEN.
A WILD ANIMAL OR A PERSON MUST'VE DONE IT.

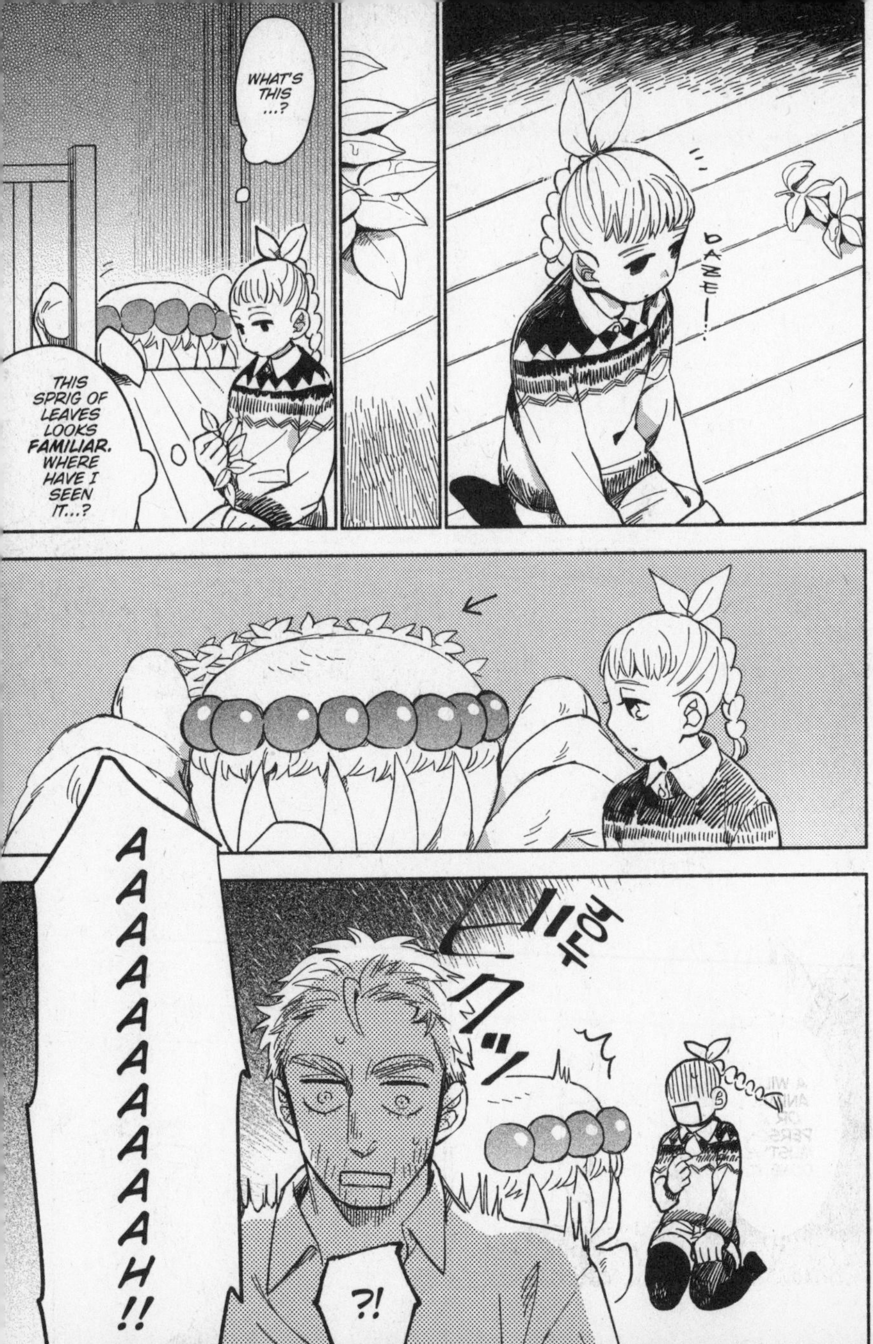
DAZE...
WHAT'S THIS ...?
THIS SPRIG OF LEAVES LOOKS FAMILIAR. WHERE HAVE I SEEN IT...?
AAAAAAAAAAAAAH!!
?!

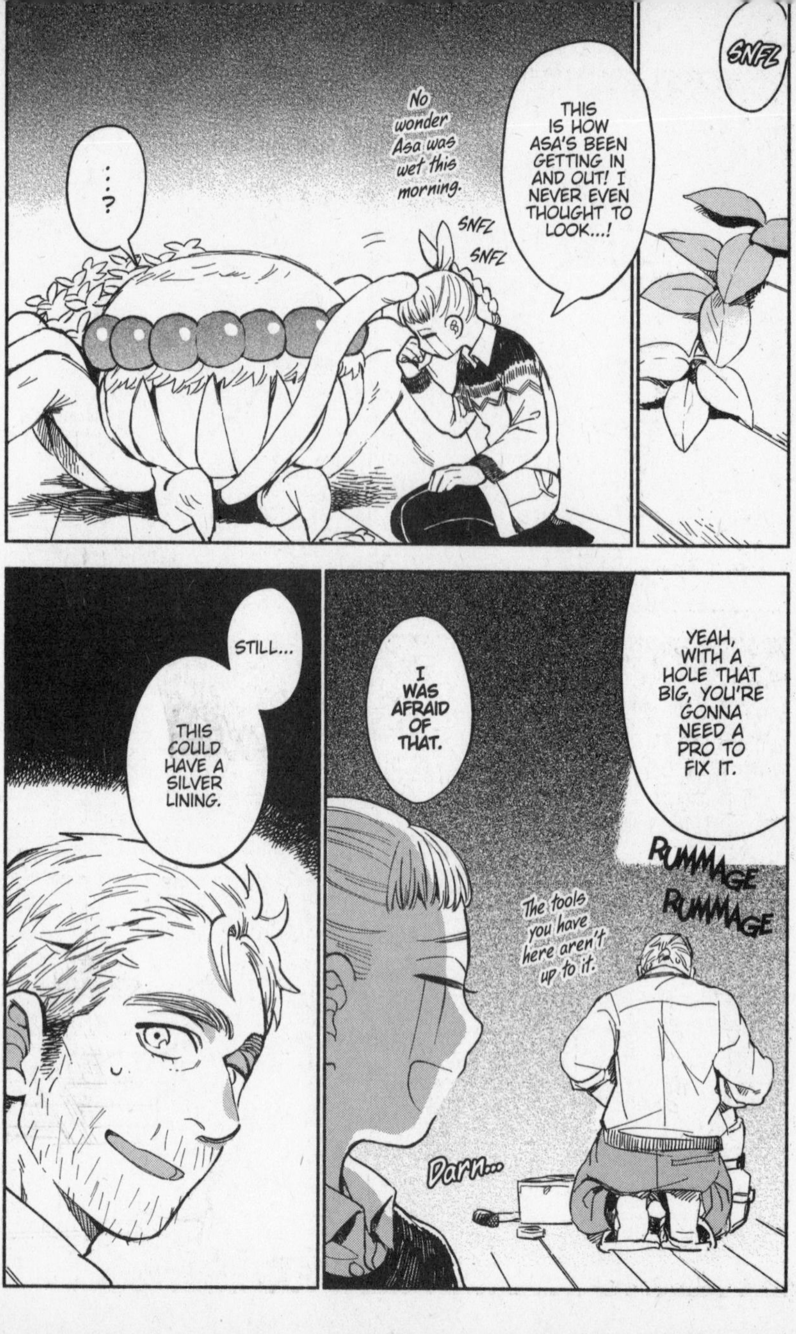
SNFL
THIS IS HOW ASA'S BEEN GETTING IN AND OUT! I NEVER EVEN THOUGHT TO LOOK...!
No wonder Asa was wet this morning.
SNFL
SNFL
...?
YEAH, WITH A HOLE THAT BIG, YOU'RE GONNA NEED A PRO TO FIX IT.
I WAS AFRAID OF THAT.
RUMMAGE
RUMMAGE
The tools you have here aren't up to it.
Darn...
STILL...
THIS COULD HAVE A SILVER LINING.

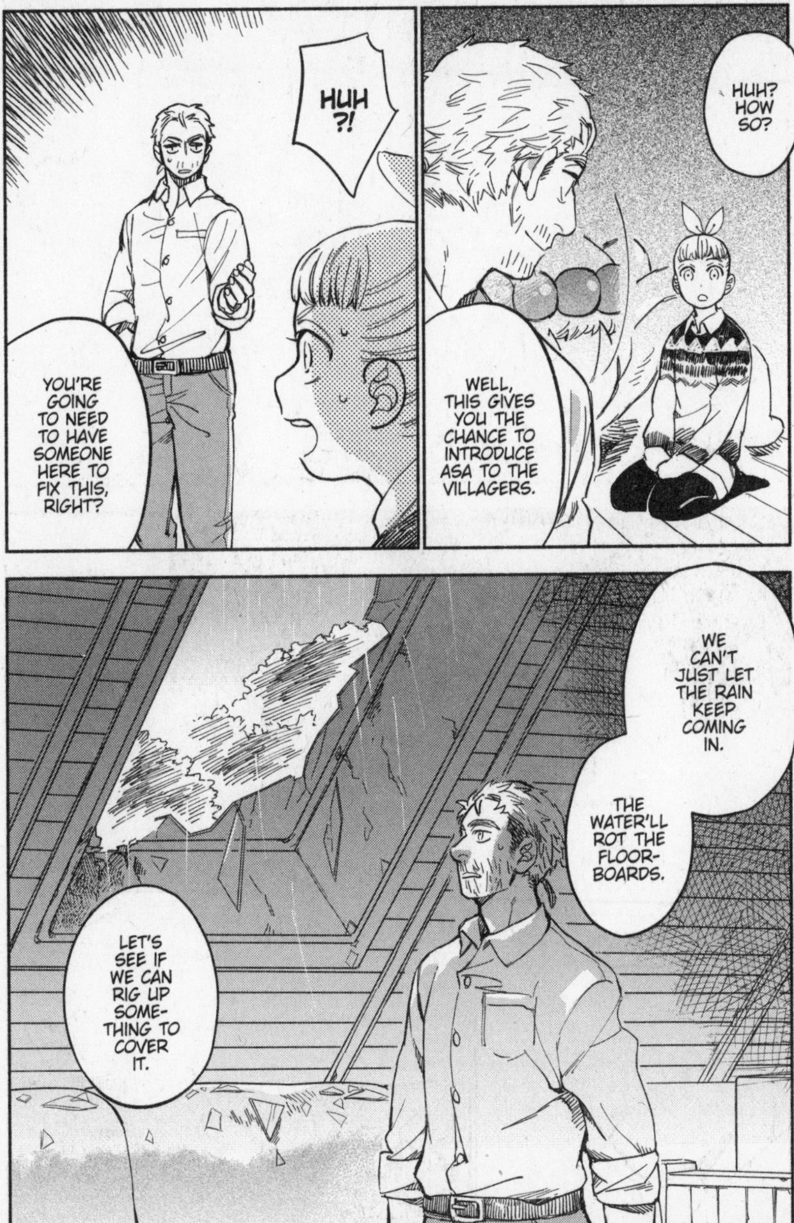
HUH? HOW SO?
WELL, THIS GIVES YOU THE CHANCE TO INTRODUCE ASA TO THE VILLAGERS.
YOU'RE GOING TO NEED TO HAVE SOMEONE HERE TO FIX THIS, RIGHT?
HUH ?!
WE CAN'T JUST LET THE RAIN KEEP COMING IN.
THE WATER'LL ROT THE FLOOR-BOARDS.
LET'S SEE IF WE CAN RIG UP SOME-THING TO COVER IT.

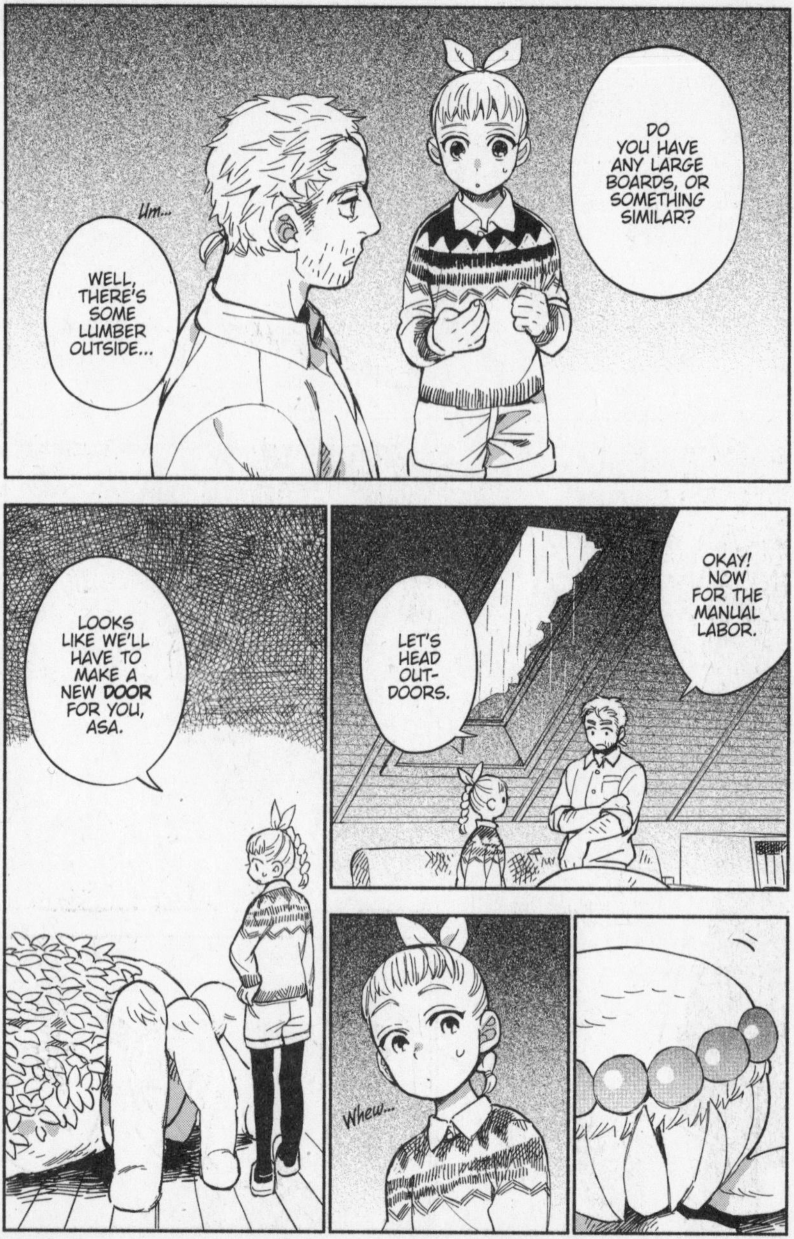
DO YOU HAVE ANY LARGE BOARDS, OR SOMETHING SIMILAR?
Um...
WELL, THERE'S SOME LUMBER OUTSIDE...
OKAY! NOW FOR THE MANUAL LABOR.
LET'S HEAD OUT-DOORS.
Whew...
LOOKS LIKE WE'LL HAVE TO MAKE A NEW **DOOR** FOR YOU, ASA.

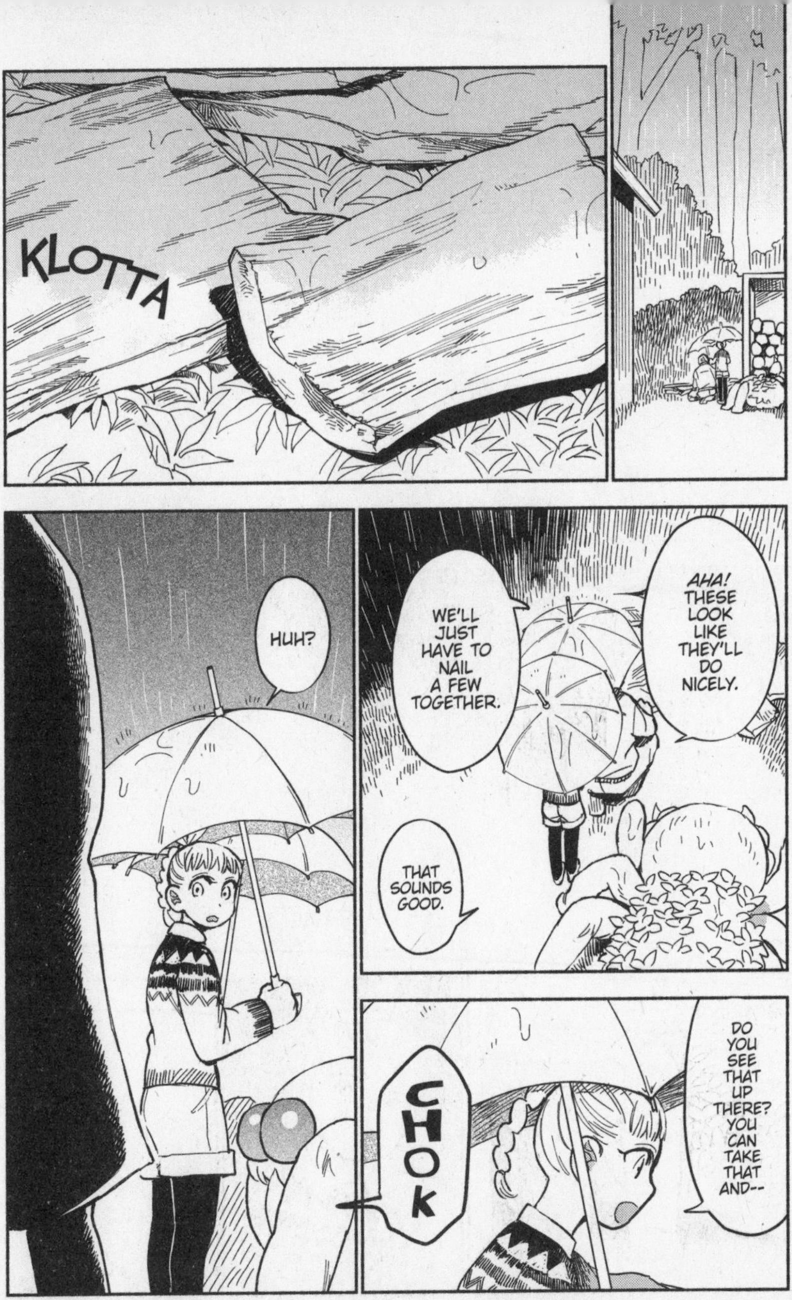
KLOTTA
AHA! THESE LOOK LIKE THEY'LL DO NICELY.
WE'LL JUST HAVE TO NAIL A FEW TOGETHER.
THAT SOUNDS GOOD.
DO YOU SEE THAT UP THERE? YOU CAN TAKE THAT AND--
CHOK
HUH?

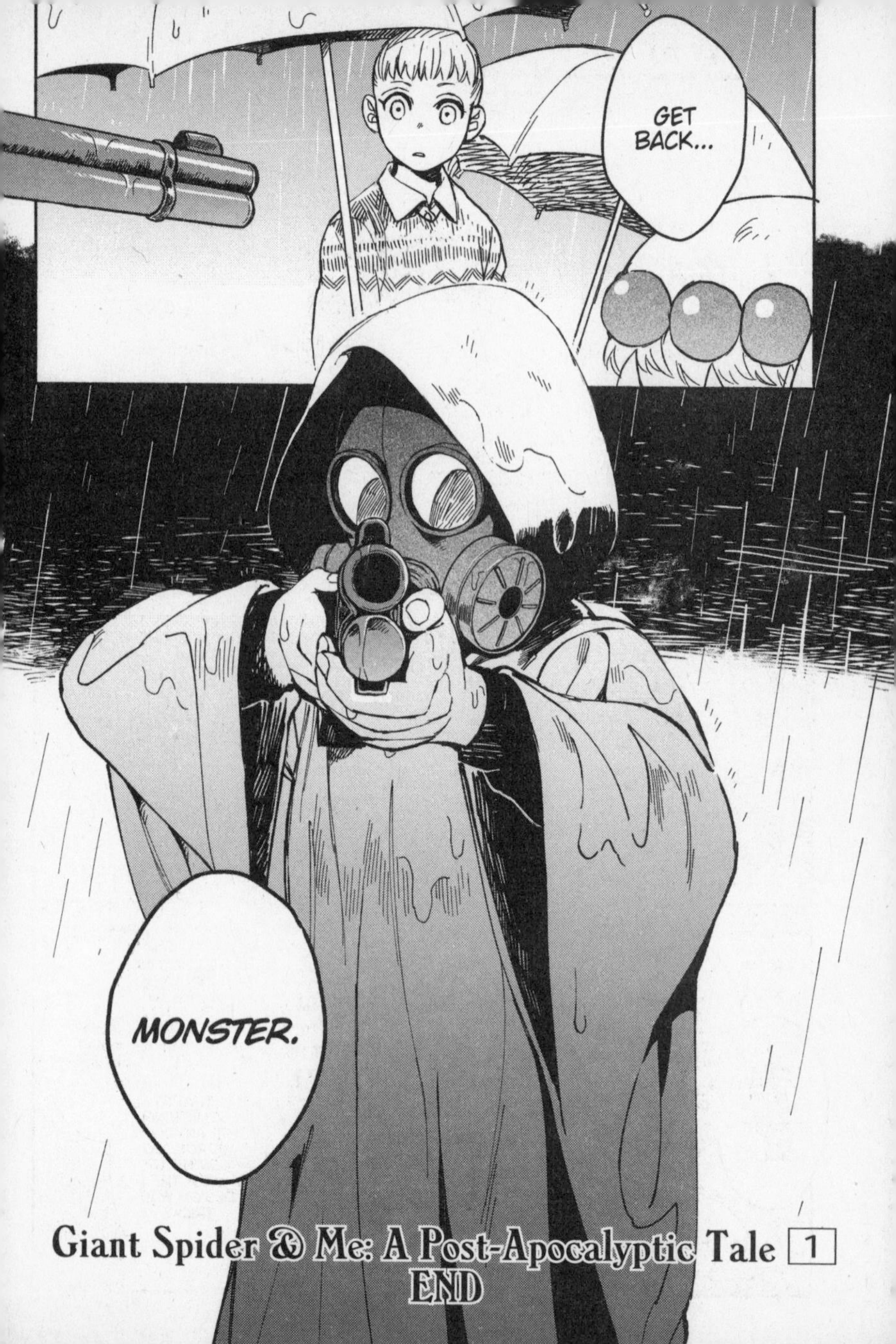
GET BACK...
MONSTER.
Giant Spider & Me: A Post-Apocalyptic Tale 1
END

Afterword

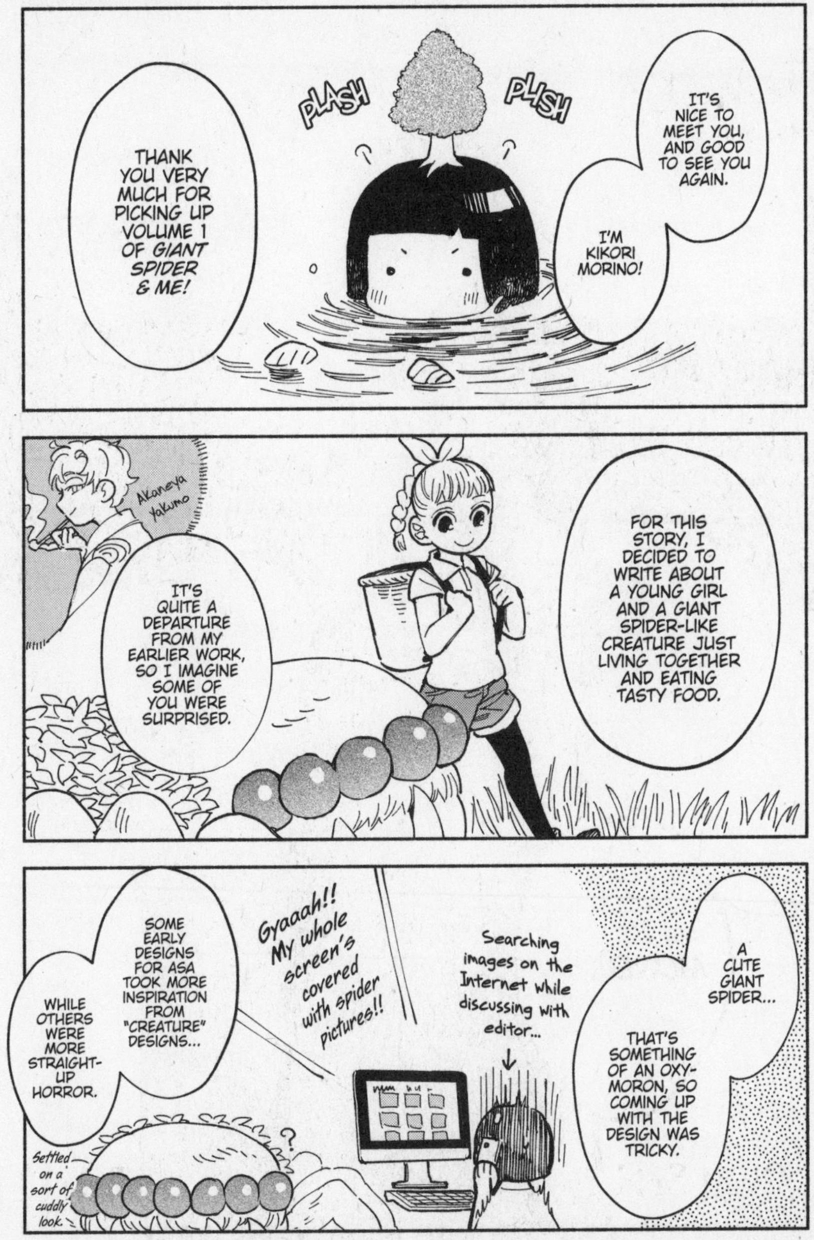
IT'S NICE TO MEET YOU, AND GOOD TO SEE YOU AGAIN.
I'M KIKORI MORINO!
PLUSH
PLASH
THANK YOU VERY MUCH FOR PICKING UP VOLUME 1 OF *GIANT SPIDER & ME!*
FOR THIS STORY, I DECIDED TO WRITE ABOUT A YOUNG GIRL AND A GIANT SPIDER-LIKE CREATURE JUST LIVING TOGETHER AND EATING TASTY FOOD.
Akaneya Yakumo
IT'S QUITE A DEPARTURE FROM MY EARLIER WORK, SO I IMAGINE SOME OF YOU WERE SURPRISED.
A CUTE GIANT SPIDER...
THAT'S SOMETHING OF AN OXY-MORON, SO COMING UP WITH THE DESIGN WAS TRICKY.
Searching images on the Internet while discussing with editor...
Gyaaah!! My whole screen's covered with spider pictures!!
SOME EARLY DESIGNS FOR ASA TOOK MORE INSPIRATION FROM "CREATURE" DESIGNS...
WHILE OTHERS WERE MORE STRAIGHT-UP HORROR.
Settled on a sort of cuddly look.

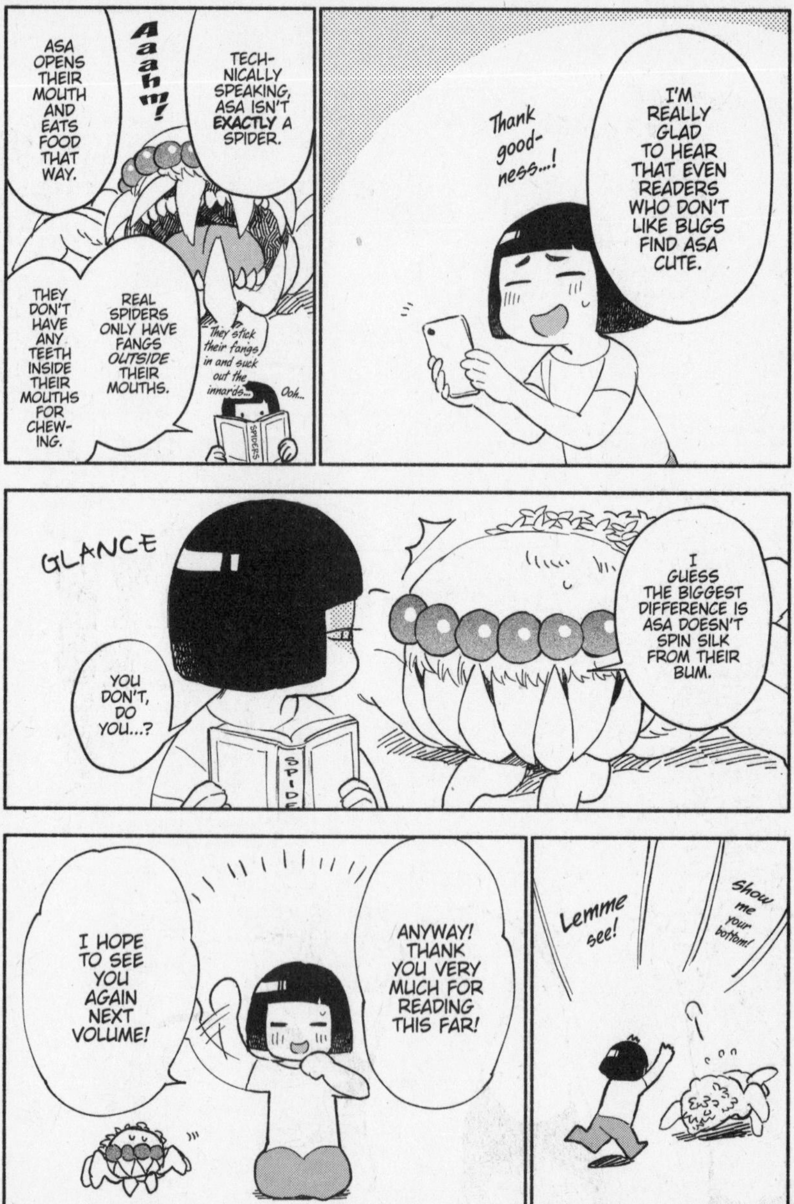
I'M REALLY GLAD TO HEAR THAT EVEN READERS WHO DON'T LIKE BUGS FIND ASA CUTE.
Thank good-ness...!
TECH-NICALLY SPEAKING, ASA ISN'T **EXACTLY** A SPIDER.
Aaahm!
ASA OPENS THEIR MOUTH AND EATS FOOD THAT WAY.
REAL SPIDERS ONLY HAVE FANGS *OUTSIDE* THEIR MOUTHS.
THEY DON'T HAVE ANY TEETH INSIDE THEIR MOUTHS FOR CHEW-ING.
They stick their fangs in and suck out the innards...
Ooh...
SPIDERS
I GUESS THE BIGGEST DIFFERENCE IS ASA DOESN'T SPIN SILK FROM THEIR BUM.
GLANCE
YOU DON'T, DO YOU...?
SPIDE
Show me your bottom!
Lemme see!
ANYWAY! THANK YOU VERY MUCH FOR READING THIS FAR!
I HOPE TO SEE YOU AGAIN NEXT VOLUME!

SPECIAL THANKS

All my readers
My editor, Arafuku-sama
Yuki Amagiri-sama
rice-sama
My designer

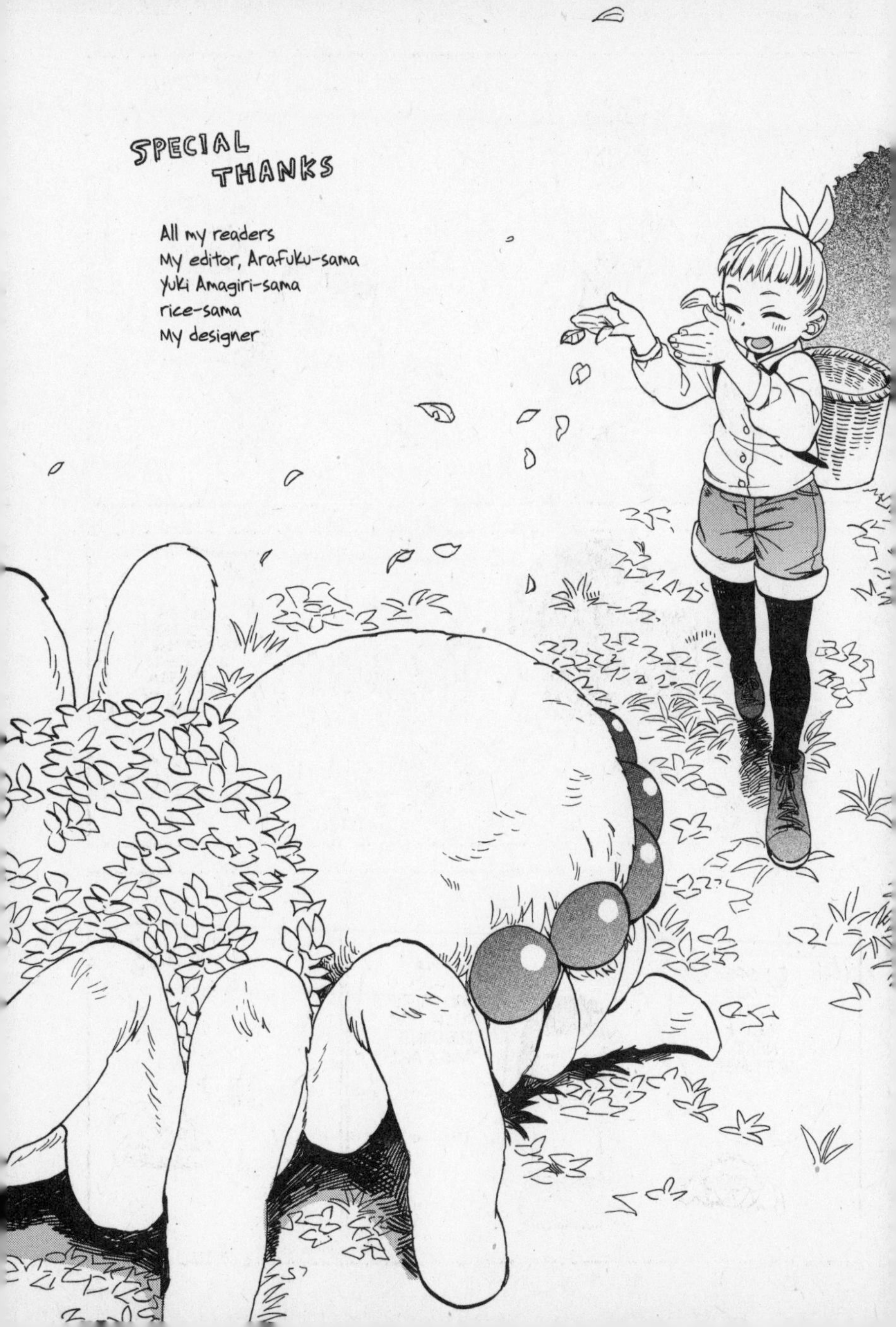

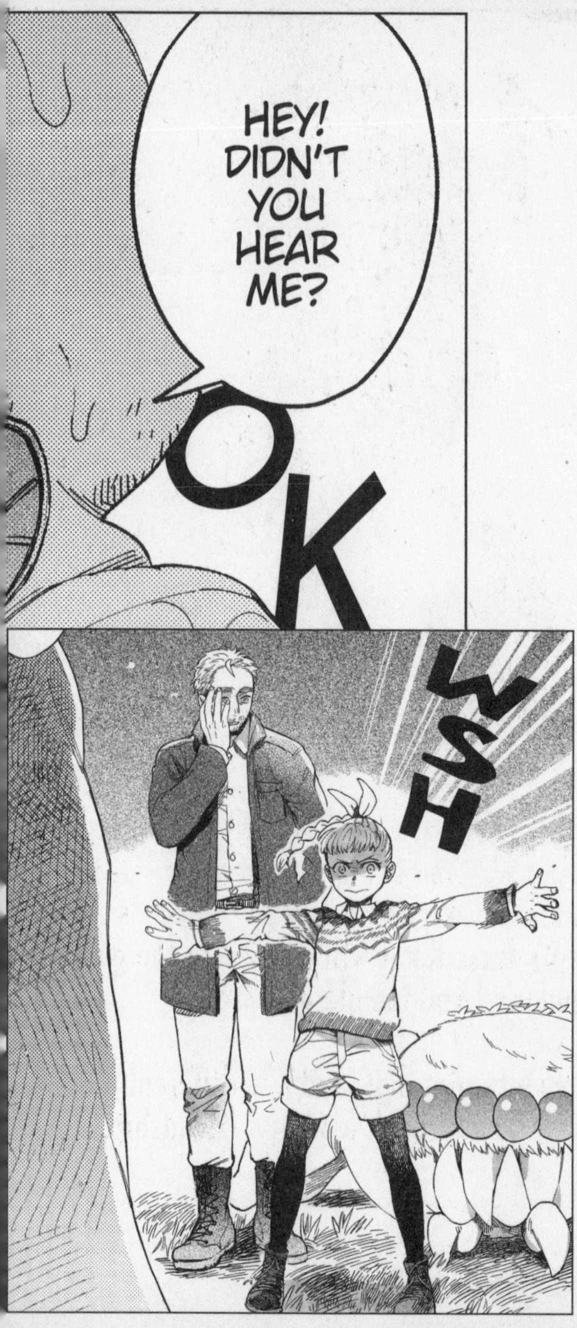
HEY! DIDN'T YOU HEAR ME?
OK
WSH

An uninvited guest arrives...

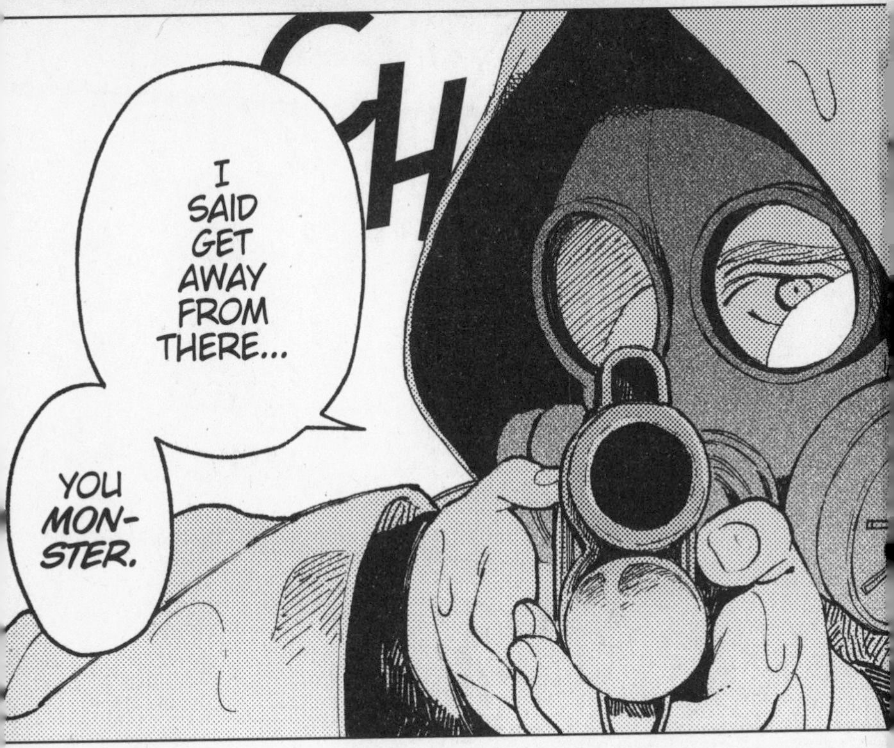
CH
I SAID GET AWAY FROM THERE...
YOU MON-STER.

As she gets used to having Asa around, Nagi begins to think seriously about how the two of them can coexist. But suddenly an unwelcome guest arrives and shoves a hunting rifle in Nagi's face. What will happen to the girl and the spider?! (And the old guy, too?)

A gentle story about quiet days and two different species coming together through food and friendship.

Volume 2
COMING SOON!

SEVEN SEAS ENTERTAINMENT PRESENTS

GIANT SPIDER & ME: A Post-Apocalyptic Tale VOL. 1

story and art by **KIKORI MORINO**

TRANSLATION
Adrienne Beck

ADAPTATION
Ysabet Reinhardt MacFarlane

LETTERING AND RETOUCH
Jennifer Skarupa

COVER DESIGN
Nicky Lim

PROOFREADER
Danielle King
Brett Hallahan

ASSISTANT EDITOR
Jenn Grunigen

PRODUCTION ASSISTANT
CK Russell

PRODUCTION MANAGER
Lissa Pattillo

EDITOR-IN-CHIEF
Adam Arnold

PUBLISHER
Jason DeAngelis

OWARI NOCHI, ASANAGI KURASHI VOL. 1

Originally published in Japan in 2016 by MAG Garden Corporation, Tokyo.
English translation rights arranged through TOHAN CORPORATION, Tokyo.

ISBN: 978-1-626927-54-4

Printed in Canada

First Printing: February 2018

10 9 8 7 6 5 4 3 2 1

FOLLOW US ONLINE: ***www.sevenseasentertainment.com***

READING DIRECTIONS

This book reads from ***right to left***, Japanese style. If this is your first time reading manga, you start reading from the top right panel on each page and take it from there. If you get lost, just follow the numbered diagram here. It may seem backwards at first, but you'll get the hang of it! Have fun!!

1
2
3
4
5
6
7
8
9

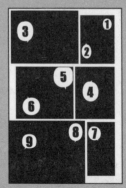

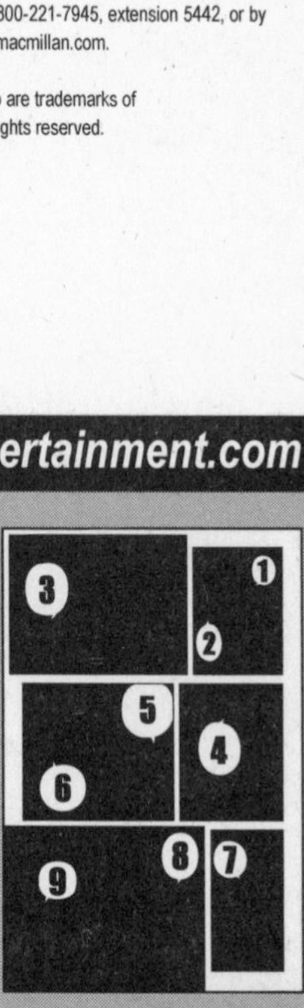